How I Made a Huge Mess of My Life

(or Couples Therapy with a Dead Man)

A Memoir
By Billie Best

W
Widowspeak
Publishing

Widowspeak Publishing

Copyright © 2020 by Billie Best

First paperback edition March 2020

ISBN: 978-1-7345964-0-3 (paperback)
ISBN: 978-1-7345964-1-0 (ebook)

Cover design by Brenda Rose

Widowspeak Publishing
3003 W. 11th Avenue, PMB 193
Eugene, OR 97402
www.widowspeakpublishing.com
books@widowspeakpublishing.com

Also by Billie Best

*I Could Be Wrong: 50+ Blog Posts, Short Reads,
Big Laughs, Wit & Wisdom*

How I Made a Huge Mess of My Life

(or Couples Therapy with a Dead Man)

A Memoir
By Billie Best

TABLE OF CONTENTS

Life is a river, not a grid
You can't keep a river in a hatbox
A river does not fit neatly in a row of cubicles
A river does not hold its shape
A river is not tidy

1. The Juicer

It was high summer 2008. My parents had stayed with us on the farm for a month longer than they planned. Since the day they arrived it had been one emergency after another. They could see my challenges and my pain. My dad drove the tractor and reminisced about his youth working on a farm in Iowa. He was enamored with the chickens, fed them from his hand, and they followed him around the barnyard. My stepmom, Peggy, washed and packed eggs, and took care of our bullmastiff, Henry, her constant companion. The animals focused our minds on the present and gave us purpose. When Chet's health was out of control, the farm kept us on a schedule, distracted us from our fears, and reminded us of the natural order of things, the inevitability of the seasons, the necessity of rain, and the bond of people to the land.

Chet's hair started falling out and my dad offered to give him a haircut outside on the long porch. We took lots of pictures, drank white wine and relaxed in the shade. Cancer had become routine. The chemo was respite from the attack of the tumors. Chet was able to go back to work at the college a few days a week. But when he came home, he went straight to bed. Work took all his energy.

A large package addressed to him arrived at the college mailroom and I went to pick it up because it was too heavy for him to lift.

"It's a juicer," I said after I opened the box. He was in bed, half asleep. "Who would send you that?"

"I don't know," he said with his eyes closed.

"Well, they must know you," I said. "I looked it up online. It costs about $400. That's an expensive gift. Where did it come from?"

"It just showed up in the mail." He rolled over on his side and put his back to me.

"Maybe it's a mistake. Maybe it belongs to someone else. If you don't know who it's from, how do you know it's yours?"

"It's mine," he said.

I went through all the packaging again and searched the shipping labels until I found a name in microscopic text that seemed to correspond to the sender. There she was in black and white, the groupie with the lavender lace bra, a trophy that once hung on his bedroom doorknob when she was his girlfriend in 1984.

"How did she find out you were sick?" I asked, standing over him while he laid there with his eyes closed. "Have you been in touch with her?"

"She must have heard about me through the Boston grapevine," he said

"That's a pretty expensive gift to give someone you haven't been in touch with for 25 years."

"She comes from a wealthy family."

"How did she get your address at the college? Why did she send it there and not here to the house?"

"I don't know."

"She must have been in touch with you. Why are you hiding it? I don't care if you're in touch with an old girlfriend. You never cared if I was in touch with old boyfriends. Why didn't you just come out and tell me it was from her? Why keep it a secret?"

"Bill!" he snapped. "It's just a juicer."

~ : ~

Most of our friends understood the fear and uncertainty of cancer. Ways of coping had become traditions, especially the ritual of giving food. I couldn't keep up with preparing the kind of meals that would entice Chet to eat. He wasn't hungry and he was losing too much weight. So our Food Fairies took over menu planning and delivered a fabulous meal to our house every few days. Men and women who loved Chet and me prepared extraordinary recipes for us — roast pork with prunes, mushroom lasagna, sweet potato ancho soup, baked chicken and olives, turkey meat loaf, poached salmon, vichyssoise and homemade bread. It was a feast of love.

As chemo reduced the size of the tumor in his lung he felt better. He didn't need his oxygen tank anymore and he started spending longer hours at the college. Each day after work I chauffeured him home and went through his backpack to collect the plastic containers from snacks I had prepared for him that morning. Mixed in with all the other get-well cards, I found a card from the Juicer. It included two photos, one of her sitting in a restaurant in a red suit with red lipstick, and another that looked like a high school photo from about 25 years ago. The inscription on the card said, "Luv ya, miss ya. Really wanna squish ya."

Chet's musician friends, both doctors, stopped by the house to check in on him and one of them mentioned that this woman had called him at his clinic to inquire about Chet's status and discuss treatment options.

After they left, I cornered Chet. "Why are you having her call him to ask about your condition? Why don't you have her call here?"

"She can be really intense," he said. "You're so busy. I didn't want her to bother you."

"So, you have her call a doctor at work?"

"I was just trying to make it easier on you."

"He said she wants him to check out a treatment protocol they've developed at Johns Hopkins. I didn't realize she was so up to date on your illness. You must be pretty good friends with her to be talking about your chemo."

"She's a busybody," he said. "I can't control her. Just let it go."

"If she has some ideas about treatment, I'd like to hear them. Have her call me."

A few days later there was another card from her in his bag.

"Chet, it's obvious you're in touch with her. I want to hear about it."

"Do we really have to talk about this?"

"Yes, we do."

"I got in touch with her in 2006 when I started therapy. She's been in therapy her whole life. I wanted to know what she thought about it."

"How did you know how to get in touch with her after all these years?"

"She's in the same place she's always been."

"So, you started up your friendship again talking about your mental health?"

"She's the queen of therapy."

"And you've kept it a secret all this time?"

"There's nothing to talk about."

"Then don't act like you're hiding something. I can see why she would want to reach out to you now. I would want to reach out to you now, too."

~ : ~

He was at the college when a customer service rep from Verizon called us on our land line at home to say that if we were going to use our cell phones to text so much, we should switch payment plans. I said we didn't text. In 2008, I didn't even know how to text. The rep said there were more than 100 text messages received and 65 sent from Chet's cell phone in the last billing period.

"I didn't know you knew how to text," I said to Chet. "You've never texted me. Who are you texting?"

"People at work," he said.

"If you have to text that much, wouldn't it make more sense to have a conversation?"

"Bil, it's just texting," he said. "What's the big deal?"

Next time I was in his backpack, I found a package of expensive vitamin supplements sent to his office by the Juicer, along with a couple more cards, each affectionately inscribed with luv.

"Why is she still mailing stuff to your office?" I asked. "Why doesn't she mail it here? I would feel a lot better if your relationship with her was out in the open."

"What do you want me to do?"

"If you are going to be in relationship with her, do it in front of me. Don't make it a secret. It's been more than 25 years since your affair with her, and you were fully entitled to have that affair. There's nothing to hide. I can handle your friendship. It's okay."

Without saying another word to me, he took the telephone out onto the long porch and sat down in his chair. Then I heard the voice that had been missing in my life for the past two years. The voice of the man absent for so long I had forgotten what he sounded like until I heard him on the phone with her, light as the morning breeze, the flirtatious voice of pleasure, speaking effortlessly for two hours. *Two hours*. I couldn't remember the last time he and I had talked for that long.

When he came back in the kitchen he said, "I invited her to come for the last weekend in September."

"She's going to spend the weekend with us?"

"Yes," he said. "That's what you wanted isn't it?"

"Sure, of course," I said. "She's welcome to come here."

~ : ~

September is a busy month on any farm as the harvest peaks and the change of seasons begins. After several chemo treatments, the trauma of Chet's fragile condition subsided, and things were going well enough for my dad and Peggy to go home to Florida. They had come for a week in June, stayed for three months, and missed their house and their friends. When they pulled out of the driveway a wave of fear swept over me, but I choked it down and put my mind on my chores.

I needed a plan to get ready for winter, a winter I expected to farm alone. If Chet couldn't help running the farm in summer, he certainly wouldn't be able to help in the cold and snow, if he was even alive. I could have shut down the farm, sold the animals and stopped farming. I had a choice. But livestock farming had been my passion for the last five years. I was breeding cows and I had plans for the next five years. Cancer was taking Chet. But I wasn't going to let it take the farm. So, while Chet was still alive, I made a plan to farm alone.

To get the money to buy a barn full of hay, it was time to harvest my cow, Lisa. Selling her meat would bring enough cash to pay for winter hay for my small herd of ruminants. Lisa had flunked out of my breeding program when she tried to kill her newborn calf. I knew then she had to go. The harvest date was set for mid-September.

From the very beginning of our interest in livestock farming Chet and I discussed the best way to kill animals. We saw that every living thing eats and is eaten. We knew we were animals in a hierarchy of predators and prey. We took responsibility for the deaths on our farm. We agreed the process should be done without fear and pain. We believed the energy of the animals we ate became our energy. We thought killing should be a sacred act and the death of our animals should be a beautiful experience.

We knew stories of hunters killing game, but we had never seen a large animal killed with a bullet. We had euthanized our pets in the past and we saw how quickly death came with drugs. We knew death with a knife from our experience killing our chickens. The two of us had toured a small slaughterhouse where the owners felt a bullet to the head was the most humane end for a cow, and for our cows we thought that was the way it should be.

To learn how to do a home slaughter I volunteered to help a friend with one of his cows. He was an experienced cattle farmer, so I assumed he was experienced at home slaughter. I expected to be one of a group of people doing the chore, but when I showed up it was just the three of us, the farmer, his wife and me, and she went into the house as soon as the rifle came out. One bullet in the center of the imaginary X between the ears and the eyes, and the cow shut down like a machine unplugged from its power source; a straight down fall, knees buckled, belly hit the ground. I watched for signs of pain and struggle, but there weren't any. *What a perfect way to go*, I thought. *Lights on, lights off.*

The rest of the process was not as well executed. My tutor's knives were not sharp, and he had no knife sharpener, so it took a very long time to remove the cowhide. Our shade evaporated, sunlight hit us, and after an hour skinning the cow with dull knives in the hot sun the belly swelled and expanded with gas. Finally, we hooked the rear legs and used the forklift on his tractor to raise the carcass off the ground so we could relocate to shade. But first, he wanted to drop the offal on his compost pile, so he drove the thousand-pound swinging meat balloon across the barnyard.

At the compost pile he got off the tractor and I sat in the driver's seat with the carcass raised high in front of me. Then he climbed the bumper onto the engine block and stood with his back to me so he could reach up and stab the swollen belly to slice it open with his knife. His stab released a spray of sour gas with an audible whoosh, sending bits of fermented yellow mush 20 feet in the air. Flecks of slime splattered his face, his hair and his shirt, and the tractor and me. The odor of partially digested cow food gave me new insight into rumination, and I vowed to buy a knife sharpener before we killed Lisa.

~ : ~

Chet wanted to hear the whole story, every detail. He always had a morbid curiosity, but now it was obvious he was thinking through his own options. We had a glass of wine on the long porch and I told him how it went.

"How did farmers kill cows before guns?" he asked.

"Knives, I guess."

"That must hurt."

"I assume so. Fortunately, we have guns."

"You really think the bullet didn't hurt?"

"That's how it looked," I said. "Lights on, lights off. No sign of fear or pain. No noise. No flinching. No reaction whatsoever."

"But what was she thinking?"

"That's a good question."

"Do you think she felt betrayed?" he asked. "Was she lying there thinking, What the fuck, I should have killed that guy when I had the chance.?"

We laughed. "I don't think so," I said. "But who knows…"

"I've read there can be brain activity for 24 hours after the body is pronounced dead."

"If the brain is still attached," I said. "The first thing you do is cut the cow's head off. If there's any brain activity, I'm not sure what it would be processing when it's completely disconnected from the body."

He looked up at the sky and followed a cloud with his eyes. "I don't think I want my head cut off," he said.

"Good," I said, watching him think. "I'm not sure how I would handle that."

"I feel like I need a plan."

"What do you want?"

"Cows have thoughts. I've seen their faces. They know what's going on. Where do our thoughts go when we die?"

"I think thoughts are biochemistry," I said. "Energy. They go wherever energy goes."

"Are my thoughts going to mingle with Lisa's?"

"And your dad's, and Wink's, and Gandhi's."

"You think I'm going to meet Gandhi?"

"Become. Become Gandhi. I think it's all one thing," I said. "Your thoughts, Gandhi's thoughts, Jesus, Jimi Hendrix. You'll all be one thing flowing around — energy."

"I hope you're right."

"I think you start as energy and you end as energy."

"So, Heaven is God's force field?"

"Heaven is bullshit," I laughed.

"But every religion has one."

"Religion is political."

"I like the idea of heaven," he said, looking up at the clouds again. "It's a place I can understand."

"You like the idea of knowing where you're going."

"Doesn't everybody? Everybody believes there's a better place out there. What did Gandhi believe?"

"He probably believed in reincarnation. It's more of a process than a place. You should believe what you want to believe."

"I don't want to be stupid."

"It's not stupid," I said. "It's a choice. You choose what to believe. You tell yourself the story that makes sense of the world in your own mind."

"I think I'll just stick with what I know."

"What's that?"

"This. The farm. Nature."

~ : ~

The butcher I hired to help me harvest Lisa was a marksman, and an artist with a knife, a third-generation dairy farmer who knew cow anatomy. He had learned the craft harvesting cows with his father and his grandfather, 100 years of knowledge in one man. He brought a few guns and looked at the situation — the cow, the distance, the surroundings. Then he chose the right firearm. Chet and I watched as one bullet in Lisa's forehead dropped her straight down. I put my hands on her until her heart stopped beating and thanked her for her gift to us. Then the butcher and I commenced cutting her up into four quarters, and Chet went back to bed.

Later we compared notes. "That's how I'd like to go," he said. "She wasn't scared. One second she was here and the next second she was gone."

"I don't think cancer is that quick," I said. "You have to find a way to handle the fear."

"I'm not afraid," he said. "I'm just trying to understand it. There isn't anything about your energy theory in any religion I could find online."

"It's not religion. It's science."

"Oh," he chuckled. "No wonder it's not popular."

"We go back where we came from. It's a circle."

"Well, it may be unnatural," he said. "But I think a bullet to the head is the perfect death."

"No bullets, Chet."

"I'm not going to die like my father did. Writhing in the fetal position, begging."

"That was your mother's fault," I said. "It doesn't have to be like that. I promise I won't let you be in pain. We'll get the right drugs. You won't need a bullet."

~ : ~

The Juicer arrived on a Friday afternoon. Chet walked out to meet her in the driveway and kissed her on the lips as I watched from the window. It was the first time I had ever seen her other than the photos she had sent with the get-well cards. She and I may have crossed paths in rock clubs in our distant past, but I didn't remember her face. Groupies were wallpaper in those days.

Now seeing her stand in my driveway, I was surprised she was tall and thin, inches taller than Chet and me, and years younger. She had long straight brown hair and she wore high heels with tight jeans. He led her inside and introduced us. Then he steered her away from me to give her a tour of the house and show her to her room.

I made Italian food for dinner because he asked me to. It was her favorite. Afterward they retired to the living room so he could stretch out on the couch. By the time I was done cleaning the kitchen, I was exhausted and excused myself and went to bed. The two of them stayed up talking on the screen porch in the bungalow until one o'clock in the morning while I stared up at the bedroom ceiling in the dark, listening to their voices waft between happy chatter and hushed whispers.

I felt angry, but I couldn't figure out why. I told myself he was dying. He couldn't be held to account for his emotions at a time like this. He deserved the freedom to be himself as he said goodbye to an old girlfriend. I didn't want to seem like a nagging wife. He was being so brave about everything. I needed to be brave, too. Now was no time for jealousy. I was a big person. Jealousy wasn't my style. When he finally came to bed, I was wide awake, but I pretended to be asleep.

The next morning, I took the trash to the dump and went into town to get chicken feed. When I returned Chet was stretched out on the couch again, smiling up at her sitting barefoot beside him in a spaghetti-strap teddy. The sight of that was like a shitty postcard from a foreign country. I couldn't get it out of my head. Where was I? Who were these people in my house? It was disorienting.

As I carried the recycling bins from the car to the pantry, they continued to talk to each other without even looking at me. It was as though I didn't exist. Maybe jealousy wasn't my style, but good manners were very much my style, and they were being rude to me. I grabbed my car keys and slammed the front door as I left.

Chet bolted after me with startling athleticism. "Bil, what's the matter?" he shouted from the front porch.

"You're having an affair with her!" I shouted back before I could even think about what I was saying. *Fuck,* I thought. *What just came out of my mouth?*

"No, I'm not," he said, walking over to the car. "We're just talking."

"You know her too well."

"You're over-reacting."

"I'm going to the market. I'll be back in an hour." My tires spit up a rooster tail of gravel as I peeled out of the driveway in a blind rage.

When I came home, they were dressed and ready to go out on an excursion into town. He was wearing the new blue shirt I had given him for his birthday. It was the first time he'd worn it. Seeing him look good for her was like eating glass. I had never been so humiliated. The shock of it was immobilizing. I didn't know what to do. So I did nothing. I said nothing.

"I'm going to show her around Great Barrington," he said. "Tonight, we'll cook for you."

And with that, they left in her car, while I watched from the window.

This was the day my brain began to separate from itself, cleaved into sections like a melon split with an axe. I couldn't process all of it at once. It was too much. I couldn't integrate my new reality with my history. I couldn't believe that my dying husband had betrayed me, was betraying me right in front of my eyes. I couldn't accept that he preferred to be with her when we had so little time left, and every day was precious. I couldn't reconcile my self-image with all of this. So I separated myself into pieces, and after September 27th, 2008, wherever I was, part of me was always locked in a box someplace else.

2. Orchestra Luna

Chet met both the Juicer and me in the music business when he was a celebrated bass player in a popular rock band. Music was our common ground. As a girl growing up in the 1960s on a gravel road between cornfields, music was the thing that interested me. My parents were music lovers who both played and sang at the baby grand piano in our living room. I studied music in school, took piano lessons and voice lessons, and performed in choirs and musicals. I wanted to go to college to study music. But my college funds were lost in my parents' divorce. Then my mother sold our house and I was on my own.

In 1973, I moved into an apartment in Chicago with Karla, my best friend from high school, and her friend Annette. I had a series of jobs, scooping ice cream at Denny's, serving pizza, shop girl at a boutique, manicurist at a barbershop, waitress at the lunch counter of Walgreens on Michigan Avenue. There I was discovered by the regional managers who moved me across town to be an underage cocktail waitress in one of their upscale chain restaurants. It was an education in the male ego, and I learned to work my personality like a cash machine.

By the summer of 1976, Annette had gone off to grad school, I was waitressing in New York City, and Karla sang in a band from Boston called Orchestra Luna who occasionally came to New York to play a club called CBGB's. That dingy music emporium was a far cry from my white tablecloth world, but the band put a halo over it, and after one show, I was hooked on their sound.

To help out with their accommodations in the city, I invited them to use my apartment in Brooklyn Heights. Sitting around my living room, their arguments were my introduction to the music business and a flashback to the disintegration of my family. I instinctively tried to fix things for them and asked my boyfriend for $500 to pay for their equipment repairs. Then they hired me to be their new road manager. The vote was five in favor and three against. I took the job and moved to Boston to live with them in the Luna House.

Chet was one of the three who had voted against hiring me. He liked the previous road manager better. He thought I was a blow hard. His words. He was skeptical of my prettiness. He didn't like the idea of me using my good looks to weasel my way into a job I wasn't qualified to hold. I didn't like the idea of him equating my looks with my intelligence, and I've always been loud. My nickname in fourth grade was Mouth. My mouth comes with the outfit.

~ : ~

One of the first things I did as road manager was cut costs by reducing the number of motel rooms we rented on the road. There was a lot of grumbling. It meant I shared a bed with Karla, and Chet shared a bed with the keyboard player. The four of us crammed into a tiny motel room with stained carpeting, two queen-size beds, one tiny bathroom, and a tube TV. By the time we got there it was three o'clock in the morning. Chet flipped through the television channels until he landed on an old black-and-white movie.

"Cool," he said. "*The Day the Earth Stood Still.*"

"*Klaatu barada nikto,*" I replied.

His chin jerked in my direction and he raised his eyebrows. "Seriously?" he asked.

"Seriously," I said. "Gort is my dream date."

"Holy shit."

Suddenly, I was cool, and he didn't seem so grumpy anymore. We bonded over vintage sci-fi sitting cross-legged on the floor and watching the movie, snarking at the cheesy sets and goofy music. He had a TV in his bedroom at the Luna House with an antenna covered in tinfoil, gaffer taped to his windowsill. Between gigs, the two of us spent hours together watching old time TV shows, sharing stories about our childhood.

The Luna House was an eight-bedroom Victorian in a typical Boston neighborhood. We — the band and the crew and I — lived communally, using income from gigs to pay our shared living expenses. Each of us got $35 a week pocket money and had our own shelf in one of the four refrigerators in the kitchen. We had a communal meal every day paid for by the band with a planned menu and rotating cooks. There were charts on the kitchen walls assigning housekeeping chores, displaying weekly menus and the latest shopping list. This elaborate arrangement was in place when I arrived. It reminded me of Girl Scout camp. I fit right in.

The band's rehearsal space was in the basement. Living and working together every day, male and female, gay and straight, with only two bathrooms in the house, we saw each other in our underwear, we heard each other on the toilet, we smelled each other. The intimacy was inescapable. For the love of music, eleven young people cohered into one bizarre family, and I became the de facto matriarch in charge of it all, booking the gigs, collecting the money, paying the bills, repairing the equipment, renting the truck, managing the debts, and soothing the dramas. My bedroom became the band's office. I bought an electric typewriter and organizing became my superpower.

Chet's bedroom was my sanctuary. It was where I could sit and listen to music. He had gone to Berklee College of Music to study jazz. He was a more talented musician than I was, and he had a huge collection of albums neatly arranged on shelves with his stereo system. I wanted to hear all of it. Music fed our relationship. It was a shared language that put us in sync with each other. We always had something to talk about.

When I looked at his face, I saw a handsome man, tightly curled hair, full lips and a strong jaw. He was a good kisser, and I liked the way his hands felt on me. His fingers were muscular from playing his bass guitar, strong and shapely. He spoke through his hands. I thought he was sexy. I wanted to be his instrument. I wanted him to play me with those hands. I loved watching him perform with the band. His

14

sense of melody struck a chord in me. He charmed me with his smoky croon. His bass solos intrigued me. I followed them note for note, hanging on his choices as he slipped into his stage trance and set his fingers free. We were in psychic harmony. And we shared a deep belief in the work we were doing. Orchestra Luna was our love child.

~ : ~

It was challenging to be a couple living and working together. Other couples in the group provided awkward examples of how a live/work/love arrangement could go sour. At band rehearsals, at the dinner table, passing in the hall, there was no escape from the fetid tension of estranged lovers, slammed doors, tears and yelling, loud make-up sex, then more slammed doors, tears and yelling. Chet and I were determined not to let our union deteriorate into such a display of disaffection. So, weeks after we started sleeping together, we made a plan to go to a salad bar in Harvard Square to hash out our discontents.

"My parents were the storm troopers of table manners," I said, dabbing my lips with my napkin. "Meals were military rituals with rules about what you could touch and how to hold a fork."

"Really?" He spit an ice cube at me and hit me square in the forehead. "What's your point?"

"I think table manners are important." I spit an ice cube back at him and missed.

"You think too much." He spit an ice cube and hit me in the face again.

I spit another ice cube at him and missed.

"You need to up your game, Bil," he said. "Don't talk to me about how to hold a fork when you can't aim an ice cube."

"Didn't your parents care about table manners?"

"We ate on TV trays in the living room. My mother's idea of cooking was an electric can opener."

"On Sundays after church, my mom made pot roast, and we ate dinner with a tablecloth on the good dishes."

"Church fucked you up," he said. "We never went to church. No church. No pot roast."

"By my family's standards, you should be some sort of criminal."

15

He laughed and spit another ice cube at me, a direct hit, right on my cheek. I broke into giggles. Then he leaned over the table and said, "Let's get serious about this. I won't hold my fork in my fist and eat like I'm shoveling coal. But you have to stop hiding my shoes. I hate it when I can't find my shoes."

"They're in the closet."

"That's another one of your bourgeois ideas? Keeping shoes in the closet?"

I spit an ice cube at him and hit him in the nose. "I like things neat," I said.

He spit an ice cube back at me and missed. "Don't tell me where to keep my shoes."

"Really, that's your line in the sand?"

"No, my line in the sand is keeping my albums in order. Miles Davis under M, not D. Talking Heads under H. Rolling Stones under S."

"That's ridiculous," I said.

"Maybe so. But it's my line in the sand."

"Really. That's what this whole thing comes down to?"

"Yes."

"How long have you been holding this in?"

"Since I went crazy looking for *Kind of Blue* and I found it in the D section."

"That must have been very traumatic for you."

He spit a rainbow arc of water into the air and landed it on my blouse. "I'm serious, Bil. Don't fuck with my albums."

"I had no idea you were so fragile," I said, wiping down my boobs.

"Well, there you have it. That's what I need."

"I need to make the bed every day. I don't want to feel like I'm sleeping in a used bed."

"Fine," he said. "Make the bed."

"That's it? That's all you've got?"

"That's all for now."

"Another 30 days then?" I reached across the table and offered him my hand.

"Another 30 days," he said, shaking hands with me. "Deal."

"Deal," I said. "Until next month."

~ : ~

Not long after I joined the band, the guitar player's boyfriend, a psychic who foretold the future, said he wanted to give me a reading. He thought it was important to tell me what he saw. Sitting across from each other in the guitar player's bedroom, he closed his eyes and breathed deeply. Then he said, "I see you on your hands and knees in a dark cave with a bucket and a scrub brush cleaning the floor."

"What does that mean?" I asked.

"I don't know what it means," he said. "But it seems like an impossible task."

Chet was not impressed. "It doesn't mean anything," he said. "Don't listen to him. The future takes care of itself. Focus on what's in front of you."

"A bucket and a scrub brush," I said. "It's not very glamorous."

"He doesn't know everything. Maybe you were wearing a sequin dress."

"On my knees in a sequin dress? That's comforting."

"I'm always here for you, babe."

~ : ~

In 1977, a year after I moved to Boston, Orchestra Luna disintegrated when Karla quit the band to join Meat Loaf. The collapse of our beloved performance art project was emotional upheaval for all of us, but instead of pulling Chet and me apart, it pushed us together. We rented a loft apartment in the Piano Factory in Boston's South End and set up housekeeping with some trash-picked furniture, a futon and a pair of kittens.

Chet and some of the other musicians morphed into a new band called Luna, all guys, no back-up singers. Spandex dawned and they were flamboyant, loud and guitar heavy. Audiences grew, the clubs got bigger, and they got gigs on concert stages in music halls. My work with them evolved from logistics to producing demos, getting radio airplay, and soliciting record companies for a distribution deal. Things were going quite well until our first potential deal was killed by the producer of one of our demos, a cocaine addict who was deep in debt and made demands for cash that spooked the record company. When our record deal collapsed, our lawyer suggested we stop performing until the terms of our contract with the junkie expired. That meant no gigs for Luna for a year. Then Chet got sick.

"You don't have to stay with me," he said. "I don't want to drag you through this."

"You're not dragging me through anything," I said. "I make my own choices."

"I could go back to Columbus and live with my parents."

"What about me? I don't have a home to go back to. This is my home. You are my home. We can do this."

Living with Chet in our first apartment was the first time I had a happy home since I was a child, before my parents started warring on each other. He was my best friend, and our loft was our new art project, the thing we created together, a joint expression of our history and our aesthetics. That filled me, and I wasn't letting go of it just because Chet had an ominous diagnosis. I was ready to fight.

When the lump along his jaw was small his doctor said it was a swollen gland. Then the lump got so big it hurt when he chewed. Surgery to remove it was a one night stay in the hospital in 1979. The biopsy of the swollen lymph gland showed he had Hodgkin's disease, a type of lymphoma. Next his doctors wanted to remove his spleen to prevent the spread of the disease, and biopsy his liver and bone marrow.

That surgery kept him in the hospital for several days. When he came home, he had an eight-inch incision stapled down the middle of his torso. The next day his fever spiked, and he was listless. Back at the hospital they opened him up and discovered infection. To prevent it from returning, the doctors wanted him to heal from the inside out, so they left a narrow hole in him that looked like a wall of hamburger around something else that looked like a skinless chicken breast. These were my boyfriend's guts.

Nurses taught me how to do a sterile procedure at home, pack the hole with gauze, and change the gauze twice a day until the hole closed by itself. I didn't get that Girl Scout First Aid Badge for nothing. As I peered inside him and cleaned his wound, I had a sense of stewardship. His body became my body, my responsibility. He was mine. My love for him was a convergence of my emotions and my intelligence. I was going to save him. I took up reading books about health and nutrition, and I changed our lifestyle to be focused on our overall wellbeing. We started going to the gym and exercising, we cut back on eating meat, and we committed to eating organic, if at all possible.

The good news was the biopsy showed his liver was clean. He was in Stage 1 of the disease and the surgeries had effectively cured him. Still, he had radiation treatment as a preventative measure. Then he had radiation sickness, no energy, his hair fell out, and his skin burned brown.

"If I live through this," he said. "I think I want to get my ear pierced."

"Cool. I'll do that."

"By a doctor."

"No way," I said.

"Yes, by a doctor."

"Doctors don't pierce ears."

"Well, whoever does it, I'm going to have a professional do it."

"I want to do it," I said. "I pierced my own ears. I can definitely pierce yours."

"How did you do it?"

"I put a rifle up to the side of my head and fired it right through my earlobe. I'm a very good shot."

"I think I should have it done by a professional."

"Oh, right," I said. "Like the professionals who gave you an infection during surgery? That kind of professional? Or like the professional who cleaned up your guts every day after you came home from the hospital?"

"You're brutal, Bil."

"Thank you, darling."

~ : ~

On Chet's 26th birthday in June of 1980 we went shopping for a gold earring and I pierced his ear with a sewing needle and a potato. He was well again, and we put Hodgkin's disease behind us. Some of the musicians from Luna started a new band called Berlin Airlift, and

Chet and I signed on to the project. For the past year I had been doing advertising for a chain of record stores. That job gave me connections with the regional record company sales guys. Finally, I had a network of business relationships that aligned with my career goals.

Berlin Airlift had a pop rock sound and the disc jockeys on Boston radio were tuning into the local music scene. Cocaine still greased the wheels, but we were older and wiser. It took a year of performing showcases and making demos to land a national distribution deal with a major record company. At last we would have access to audiences from coast to coast because we would have product, a record company to sell it, and promoters to get us airplay on the radio. All the pieces were in place.

We had barely digested our steaks after the contract signing dinner when our record company went bankrupt. No record company, no vinyl. No vinyl, no distribution. No distribution, no sales. No sales, no money. It was a slow painful death. Audiences dwindled. Chet and I left the group, and the others went their way.

That was it for me. It was 1983 and I became a calloused unbeliever. No more music dreams. I had been to the shining glass and mahogany offices of record company executives, lawyers and agents. I saw how easily they picked up their corporate paychecks and padded their wallets with their expense accounts. I knew instinctively I was smarter than most of them. But it didn't matter how smart I was if I was working in smelly rock clubs, nursing egos, trying to make a living selling something that cost $8.99 and had to get airplay on the radio during rush hour before people would buy it. I wasn't high on Orchestra Luna anymore. I wanted money.

3. Cancer Boy

When Chet and the Juicer returned to the farm after their day together in Great Barrington, he found me lying on our bed, staring at the ceiling. Again. For the past couple hours, I had been planning my suicide. It wasn't the first time I had contemplated killing myself. There were two other times before.

In 1970, when I was in high school, my life was falling apart, and it was so painful that the only remedy I could think of was suicide. I knew my situation couldn't be fixed. My father was leaving my mother to be with his girlfriend. My mother was having a nervous breakdown and sleeping with a gun under her pillow. My brothers were running wild, falling into the wrong crowd, detaching from our family.

My boyfriend's father got a job in another state and he was moving a thousand miles away from me. We were 15. He was my first love, my most profound emotional connection, and he was going to disappear. In the midst of this turmoil, I had decided my religious faith was a lie. I had been an ardent Christian until it all fell apart for me. God was dead. There was nothing left to live for. I wrote poems about my need for death, and it was writing poetry that brought me out of the darkness.

The second time I contemplated suicide was in 1975, when I was 21. I had an evil genius boyfriend, a handsome bartender I met waitressing in New York City. He conned me into living with him until one night he disappeared with the $2,000 in tip money I had hidden in the closet. I was broke and he was gone. I couldn't pay the rent and had to move back into an apartment with friends in Brooklyn Heights. Then a few months later my gynecologist, who had been looking for a cyst on my ovaries, told me I was pregnant, something neither of us thought was possible. After my abortion, my doctor gave me a ride home from Harlem to Brooklyn Heights and raped me. That was a very bad day. My spirit withered and the idea of death was my constant companion until I connected with Orchestra Luna. Their music helped me find my way back into the light. And then I found Chet.

On my bed at the farm, more than 30 years later, reviewing my history and comparing past thoughts of suicide, the present I was living in seemed worse than those two previous episodes. Losing Chet's love was the worst thing that had ever happened to me. It was worse than being raped by a man I didn't know. That was circumstantial. The shitty luck of the draw. It could have happened to anyone. But love is carefully crafted, an organism of shared experience, a fire you build together and feed. Chet was the love of my life and he was going to die soon. Cancer was also the shitty luck of the draw. But his affair with the Juicer was carefully crafted. I could hear it in their voices. I could see it in their eyes. They were intimate. And so, for the third time in my life I mused about the efficacy of suicide as a pain reliever.

"What's the matter with you?" Chet asked when he saw me dressed for farm chores, on our bed, laying on top of the sheets.

"My dying husband is having an affair with another woman," I said.

"I'm not having an affair with her. We're just friends."

"You're more than just friends."

"Look we connected at a time when I was really low," he said. "She helped me out. But that was a couple years ago."

"The two of you are completely self-absorbed. It's like I'm not even here."

"Bil, don't do this. Don't overreact. Come out and be with us. I want you to be friends with her."

"Then why didn't you invite me to go into town with you today? Why didn't the three of us spend the day together?"

"I invited you," he said.

"No, you didn't."

"Bil, don't do this to me now. Come out in the kitchen and be with us."

My eyes were puffy from crying and I looked awful. But I took a seat at the kitchen counter and poured myself a glass of wine. She seemed pleased with herself, unpacking bags of wine and cheese, paté and French bread, fresh pasta and mushrooms.

"She paid for the groceries," Chet said. "So we got the expensive stuff."

He cheerfully recounted how the two of them went window shopping and wine shopping and had lunch in an outdoor café before he gave her a tour of the Berkshires. He was chatty, almost giddy, as I sat watching them cook together, standing close, touching, familiar, comfortable with themselves, a couple.

After dinner he excused himself and went to bed. *Coward*, I thought, sitting in a chair across the room from her. She sat on the couch, drawn into herself, looking out the window into the night.

"It's obvious you and Chet have a very warm personal relationship," I said. "Tell me about it."

"There isn't much to tell," she said. "We connected in 2006 when he was thinking about going into therapy and we've stayed in touch since."

"How long have you been in therapy?"

"About 20 years."

"How often have you seen each other?"

"Just back then. But not since."

"Back then?"

"2006. I was in Boston on a business trip."

"Really? You seem to know each other so well," I said. "You seem so comfortable together shopping and cooking. It looks to me like you've spent a lot of time together."

"We haven't," she said.

"I've seen the cards you send him, and the gifts. You're in love with him."

"But he's not in love with me. That's why he's still here with you."

"How do you know that?"

"I've lost him to you twice," she said. "Once in 1984 and once now."

That was too much for me. I couldn't wrap my head around it. I didn't know how to respond. All of my emotions were in check, and I froze. If one tiny leak of anger escaped, I would boil over. So I locked up. "I'm going to bed," I said, and left the room.

~ : ~

The next morning the three of us had coffee together. I made breakfast, but she didn't eat. He announced he was giving her a tour of the farm before she left, and he took Henry with them. After a couple hours they returned, and she rushed upstairs to pull her things together. Chet seemed anxious looking out the window as he waited for her to go.

"Goodbye," she said to me, standing at the front door with her suitcase. Then she handed me a scented candle. "Thank you for being such a good hostess," she said.

"Goodbye," I said and walked away, mentally shoving the candle up her ass. *A fucking candle? Are you fucking kidding me?*

Chet walked her to her car, and I watched through the window as the two of them embraced and kissed. Then she drove off leaving him standing in the driveway waving goodbye. When she was out of sight, he was a dying man again. He stumbled into our bedroom and collapsed on our bed, crying in deep sobs I had never seen before, like a teenage girl jilted at the prom.

"Where did you take her?" I asked as I unlaced his boots and pulled them off his feet.

"We went for a walk up the road and came back down through the woods," he said, unzipping his jeans.

"How far up the road?" I pulled his jeans off and threw them on the chair.

"To the horse farm," he said, crawling under the bed covers.

"Chet, that's a two-mile hike. I'm surprised you made it. I'm surprised Henry made it."

"We had to stop and rest a couple times."

"Do you have any idea how that fucks me up?" I asked as I gathered his dirty clothes and threw them in the laundry basket. "How long has it been since you and I went into town and had lunch together? You took her for a walk in the woods, our woods, the place where you and I used to walk. You walked our dog with her."

"Bil, I'm never going to see her again." He closed his eyes. "So what difference does it make?"

"Do you know how much I would love to do all those things with you? Do you know how much I miss you? You had the energy to do all those things with her, but you don't even have the energy to have a conversation with me."

"My back really hurts," he said, wincing with his eyes closed. "Would you please hand me my pills."

"Of course, your back hurts," I said, picking his socks off the floor. "You went for a two-mile hike in the woods. You went for almost five hours without medication."

"Could you please get my pills for me?"

"Call her and ask her to get your fucking pills for you." I slammed drawers open and shut as I put his clothes away. "Look at how exhausted you are. Look how she left you."

"Please," he moaned.

"She used you up and spit you out. You were a fucking concierge! She had no idea she was exhausting you. She was completely oblivious. It was all about her. She had fun with you until there was nothing left, and now I'm stuck with Cancer Boy."

"Please get my pills for me."

"Let her take care of you!" I yelled. "Let her cook and clean and manage your fucking healthcare and sit with you while you die. You don't even have to divorce me. Just fucking go. Let her be your wet nurse. See what a great job she does taking care of you."

"She's a broken doll," he groaned. "Forget about her. I don't want her to take care of me. I want you to take care of me."

"Of course, you want me to take care of you! I'm really good at it. She's a fucking narcissistic asshole. You probably shaved a few months off your life being with her this weekend."

"Yes, she's a narcissist." His jaw bones flexed as he ground his teeth. "Please."

I gave him his pills and he sank into a two-day comatose sleep.

~ : ~

On the way home from his last chemo treatment we stopped for lunch at Joe's Diner, a place where we'd eaten many times before, back in the day when Orchestra Luna played at the Music Inn in the Berkshires, and the band went skinny-dipping in the Stockbridge quarry. We sat on vinyl stools at the lunch counter and had meatloaf and mac-and-cheese and drank cherry colas. His mind was hazy. Mine was ablaze.

"She told me she lost you twice," I said. "Once in 1984 and once now. I didn't know she was so in love with you in 1984. I thought your thing was just sex."

"It was more than sex for her," he said. "She wanted me to move in with her. But I couldn't do it. I was in love with you and we got married. It messed her up."

"Why didn't I know that before?"

"Back then it was all about you. You were all I could handle. She got dumped."

"But she never disappeared."

"She let it dangle."

"For 25 years?"

"She's damaged goods, Bil. She's never been in a stable long-term relationship with an available man. That's why she's been in therapy for two decades."

"So, you just slipped back into her life."

"She made it easy."

"You had both of us."

"I chose you."

"After you had both of us."

"Bil, I chose you. I chose you in 1984, and I choose you now."

4. Adam & Eve

In 1984, after his band Berlin Airlift died, Chet worked for a friend as a plumber's assistant. Then he started skipping dinner with me, coming home late, buzzed from a few beers with the boys, and I started sleeping with my boss.

"You didn't leave me when I had Hodgkin's disease," he said. "You're leaving me now because I'm a plumber?"

"I'm leaving because this is not the life I want. Obviously, it's not the life you want either."

"I'm trying to figure it out. I don't understand. I love you."

"I love you, too," I said. "But for now, I'm going to love you from a different address. I can't live like this."

"Live like what?"

"You've given up, Chet. I'm not giving up. I'm moving on."

"To Beacon Street?"

"Yes."

"So, you'd rather live with roaches than with me?"

"Yes. I guess so. If you need to put it that way."

"I'm just looking for clarity," he said. "Arm candy is an interesting career choice."

"Arm candy is not a career," I said. "It's a carnival ride. I want to have some fun for fuck sake. I've been dragged through the mud by all this and I'm tired of it."

"I'm tired of it, too. But I can't find some rich guy to fuck."

"Up your game, man. The world is out there waiting for you."

"Can we still have sex?"

"Seriously?" I asked.

"Seriously," he said. "I don't think we should stop having sex just because you have a new boyfriend."

"It's good to know your priorities."

"Just answer the question."

"Yes," I said. "We can still have sex."

"Cool."

~ : ~

He had invested ten years in bands he thought would achieve commercial success and none of them made it. A bass player is part of a rhythm section. He needed other musicians to accompany. He was not a one man show. And he was not ready to dedicate himself to a new band. He was orphaned. I shared his loss, but I had my own anxiety to cope with as I cleaned up the band's trail of debt, which was in my name and hit my credit rating. The band never had enough money to pay for new equipment. We were selling our sound as much as the personalities on stage and without the newest, most technically advanced equipment, the sound was handicapped. In the days of Orchestra Luna, solving the debt problem made me feel heroic. By the end of Berlin Airlift, I was resentful.

I took a job with a music magazine that put me and my organizing skills in the spotlight. Then the publisher purchased a Kaypro desktop computer for the office. It was the first computer I had ever seen. The idea of information traveling over wires was familiar to me because I understood the band's sound system. I was comfortable with the technology, and soon I was leading the process of going digital at the office.

After we broke up, Chet and I both dated other people, but we never stopped seeing each other. I explored life with a music business mogul and Chet dated one of Berlin Airlift's groupies. He didn't have to tell me about her. She left her bra hanging on the doorknob of his bedroom where anyone could see it.

"Whose bra is this?" I asked, fingering the lavender lace, holding it up to my chest. I had stopped by his apartment to get a frying pan I left behind. "She's pretty flat," I said. "I thought you were more of a breast man."

"Beggars can't be choosers," he said.

"How sad for you."

"It's not that sad. She likes anal sex."

"I did not need to know that."

"Then put her bra back where you found it and get out of here."

My own promiscuity was a sandcastle. Wading in money was fun, but I didn't want to be an old guy's sixth wife. I didn't want diamonds. I didn't want to have his children. I was 30, old enough to see how I could age out of being arm candy. Still, to prove to myself I could do it, I kept a busy schedule of anxious men, sometimes two dates in one day. Then my body made some decisions for me.

I landed in the hospital with a cyst on my ovary and Chet was the first person I called. My mogul said, "Just tell me where to send the check, kid." Chet sat with me for three days in the hospital. I went home with him to recover in his bed, the bed that used to be our bed before I got busy sowing wild oats. He made me tea and gave me my medicine, cooked for me, and asked me how I felt. I wasn't a fast car he was driving to impress his friends. He cherished me.

It was a maturing experience to witness these two men side-by-side, my mogul committed to his business, glad to throw money at me whenever I needed it, and my musician, committed to me, and glad to share everything he had because he loved me. I saw that I could be rich, or I could be loved, but probably not both.

~ : ~

A month after my surgery Chet took me to a charming old hotel in Montreal for the weekend. We walked around the city holding hands, browsing shops, kissing on a park bench, and capped off the day with cocktails, listening to a singer in the hotel piano bar.

"That guy probably makes more money than I do," Chet whispered. "But I'm never doing that again."

"You're not the tuxedo type," I said.

"I think I can get gigs doing audio."

"In the music business?"

"Soundtracks, jingles, voice overs. And maybe bands, too. I'll never be rich, but I think I can make a living."

"Rich is overrated," I said.

"Wasn't money the whole point of all this?" he asked.

"I'll figure out how to make my own money."

"Why are you here, Bil?"

"Because I love you," I said.

"So what?"

"I want a partner. I want a partner that I love."

He finished his martini, set his glass on the table, and turned to look me in the eye. "My parents are just getting used to us split up. Our friends have finally stopped trying to get us back together. How are we supposed to take you seriously?"

"What do you want?" I asked.

"I want to get married," he said.

"Really?" I was taken aback. "I thought marriage was bullshit."

"I want a public record of our choice."

"Wedding rings and all?"

"Yes."

"Really? Wedding rings?"

"Yes."

"The whole 'til death do us part thing?"

"Yes."

"I never thought we would do that," I said. I slugged down the last swallow of my martini.

"I'm not going to drift back into this. Either it's a permanent commitment or it's over."

"Is that a proposal?"

"It's a choice. You need to make a choice."

"I really don't like the word wife."

"It's your choice."

"Husband and wife? ... Really?"

"Yes," he said. "Husband and wife. Really."

"I need to be kissed while I think about this."

He kissed me, and we kissed again, and the pianist segued into "Moon River" and we knew he was singing to us.

~ : ~

On February 14th, 1985, we were married in the Adam & Eve Wedding Chapel, a place we found in the phone book. The chapel was the home office of a justice of the peace who was also a psychotherapist, an older gentleman with gold rimmed glasses and suede elbow patches on his tweed jacket. In the spirit of the occasion he took a vase of plastic flowers out of his desk drawer and put them on the mantle with a pair of candles. His wife came out of the kitchen to be a witness, taking off her apron and draping it over the back of an armchair, smiling at us as though we were family.

The next morning, we drove to a resort in Maine and spent a few days there. At breakfast in the dining room overlooking the golf course and the ocean, the hotel manager offered us a $200 gift certificate for their four-star restaurant if we participated in a brief sales presentation for the resort's new timeshare condominiums. That was an offer we couldn't refuse. Restaurants were our favorite thing, and the timeshare condo turned out to be our wedding present to ourselves.

Holding hands, we walked along the breakwater on Penobscot Bay, and Chet asked, "What's your worst fear?"

I knew the answer to that question. It had first occurred to me months earlier as I ate breakfast in the mogul's hotel room, contemplating a life of limitless abundance. "Boredom," I said. "My worst fear is being bored with my life."

"You're dangerous when you're bored."

"I need to be creative. I want to be an artist, but I don't know how."

"A lot of people who look like artists aren't," he said. "Some of the best musicians I know are the least creative because they're too technical. Creativity is freedom."

"I feel like I'm chasing it."

"Don't chase. Practice. To be your best at anything, you have to practice. No matter how good you are, you still have to practice."

"But look at how our lives are organized," I said. "We're grown-ups now. We just got married. When are we ever going to have the freedom to be creative if we're busy having careers and making money?"

"You just bought a one-week vacation for the rest of your life, right here on this beach."

"I don't feel it. That was just a lot of words on paper. It doesn't feel like anything."

"Bil, it's a week one year from now," he said. "One year from now you'll be standing here looking out at this ocean again. You'll be free to do whatever you want."

"What about you?"

"It's my present to myself, too."

"I don't see how we come out here for a week and suddenly turn on the creativity. Besides, I need to be alone to write."

"So, come by yourself."

"What about you?" I asked.

"I'll be by myself, too."

"That's our wedding present to ourselves? Separate vacations?"

"Don't think of it as separate. Think of it as a solo. Focus on developing your voice."

"That's an interesting idea," I said. "Who gets the first solo?"

"We'll flip a coin."

"You're a genius."

"No, I'm not," he said. "I just know how you think."

5. The Boss Cow & The Concierge

For more than 20 years after we got married in February 1985, we alternated years at our timeshare condo in Maine just as we had planned on our honeymoon, each of us solo for a week, going deep into an art project, reading, relaxing and exploring our individual selves. I tried painting and wrote a novel. Chet took his musical instruments and spent his time composing and arranging. In 2007, I wrote a collection of essays with the hope of publishing my thoughts on the politics of farming. In February 2008, it was Chet's turn again.

"What are you going to work on?" I asked, watching him pull clothes out of his drawers and put them in his suitcase.

"I don't know," he said. "I may not work at all."

"What music are you taking?"

"I'm not taking any music."

"What are you going to do?"

"I don't know. I'll figure it out when I get there."

"But you're not taking any music?"

"Bil, it's my week."

"You're a musician. How can you go on an art sabbatical without music?"

He rolled his eyes at me.

Usually when one of us was on the road we called home at night to check in. It was our long distance buddy system, a way of knowing the other person was safe. That night I was looking forward to his call from the resort, but it never came. When I called him, it was quite late. I wanted to be sure he was okay. He seemed drunk, but I was pleased to hear the lilt in his voice. All he could talk about was the Italian restaurant he'd discovered.

That phone call was our only communication for the week. By the time he got home the lilt in his voice was gone. He was withdrawn and he kept his eyes from me.

"Nice bathrobe," I said, hovering over his suitcase as he unpacked. "It looks expensive. Where did you get it?"

"I did some shopping," he said, keeping his eyes down.

"You went clothes shopping in Maine?" The words came out too fast. I couldn't hide my surprise. He hated shopping. I tried to conjure a mental map of the luxury brand stores near the resort, because that bathrobe was luxurious, conspicuously luxurious, not like something he would ordinarily buy for himself.

"I needed some stuff," he said. "So I went shopping."

"How much was it?" I reached out to touch the bathrobe and he pushed my hand away.

"I don't remember."

"You always remember how much things cost. How could you buy a bathrobe like that and not remember how much it cost?" He didn't respond, all my thoughts collided, and I had to leave the room.

~ : ~

In April, when the snow melted, the farm was soggy and the chickens were delighted to be free ranging again, looking for bugs and grubs in the wet lawn. Frogs woke from hibernation peeping and croaking, and foxes and coyotes encircled us, hunting for chickens to feed their new litters.

Late one night Henry sensed a predator and ran from window to window through the house growling. Chet bounded out of bed, ran out the front door, and gave chase with his dog across the barnyard and into the woods, a manly man and his trusty hound. The next morning his back was hurting, and we assumed he pulled a muscle running.

A week later his asparagus roots arrived, but his back hurt too much to plant them. Asparagus was his favorite vegetable and he intended to grow it in his new vegetable garden in the field across the road from the barn. The asparagus and the seedlings he bought sat on the porch until I finally planted them myself.

To solve our predator problem, we bought a $99 rifle at Walmart and signed up for a gun safety class to get our gun permits. Chet's back hurt sitting through the six-hour course in the plastic folding chairs. At home with the rifle, he found he couldn't stand comfortably for long enough to shoot a sneaky fox. That meant the fox was left to Henry, and Chet scheduled a series of massages to see if deep muscle relaxation would release the pain between his shoulders. When that didn't work, he saw a chiropractor.

~ : ~

On the evening of May 5th, I was already in my pajamas and Chet was making dinner when we heard an unearthly scream. I jammed my feet into my muck boots and ran out to the west pasture in the twilight. Our cow Lisa was hysterical, shrieking at a little mound of brown mush, her newborn daughter, soon to be named Cinco de Mayo.

Lisa's mother, Ruby, was a very good mother, and we expected her daughter to have those same traits. It's hard to know why she didn't. As I stood watching in my pajamas, Lisa lowered her head, put her ears back, tucked in her chin, and head butted her new calf six feet across the grass. I spoke softly to her, cooing and encouraging her to sniff her baby, but she gave Cinco one lick and hit her again. A couple more head butts and I drove Lisa away, kneeling beside the soggy little creature, peeling off the placenta as her mother should have done.

It was a quick decision that Cinco would be a bottle baby and we would raise her without her mother's participation in the process. Chet brought the car out to the pasture. But when he tried to lift Cinco onto the tailgate, he gasped and dropped her. The pain in his back was so sharp he froze and his face darkened. I manage to hoist Cinco into the back of our SUV and crawled in after. We got some milk from a neighboring farm and that night I slept with my new calf in the barn.

A few days later, Chet saw pregnant Ayla lying on her side in the pasture for what seemed too long, so he tromped out to check on her. A pair of tiny hooves peeked from under her tail and she pushed without progress. Just as he'd seen online, he slid his hand inside her along the length of the calf's legs and checked to be sure the infant was positioned correctly. Then he pulled on the tiny legs in sync with Ayla's breathing until out slipped Rouge.

"It was amazing," he said. "You should have seen it."

"I'm so jealous," I said. "Three births on our farm — Lisa, Cinco, and now Rouge — and I haven't seen any of them."

"She's bigger than Cinco."

"How is your back?"

"I didn't even feel it," he said. "I was so into Ayla that I didn't even think about it."

That night at his jazz gig, he passed out cigars and bragged about being a new father. I was glad to see him enjoying himself and hoped he was starting to heal from whatever it was that was hurting him. But the respite from the pain didn't last long. A couple weeks later, he was supposed to be doing tractor work, but he was in bed, flat on his back.

We were discussing the failure of his chiropractor to solve his discomfort when the phone rang. It was the animal hospital calling about our recently adopted Cairn terrier, Burt. He had a lump on his hip and that morning I had taken him for surgery to remove it.

On the telephone, the veterinarian said, "I'm sorry to have to tell you this. The lump on Burt's hip is a tumor that has wrapped around his spine. I can remove some of it, but I can't get all of it. He went to sleep a happy little dog. If he wakes up, he's going to be in pain for the rest of his life, which won't be more than a few months. If he were my dog, I would let him go happy. But he's not my dog."

Chet and I shared a long look and knew we agreed. "Don't wake him up," I said to the vet. Then I laid down on the bed beside Chet and we both cried.

After a long time staring off at nothing, Chet said "I feel a disturbance in the Force."

The next day I brought flash frozen Burt home in a white cremation box and put him on a shelf in the meat freezer in the barn. Chet planned to dig a hole and bury him in the pasture beside the apple tree. But his pain stopped him from digging with a shovel. Then the tips of his fingers were numb, and he didn't have the dexterity to hook up the backhoe to the tractor. As a result, Burt remained in the freezer.

~ : ~

For all of spring 2008 Chet was incapacitated by pain, and I was scattered across too many tasks, hauling five gallons of cow's milk a day to bottle feed Cinco, wrangling cows, sheep and goats, feeding chickens, packing and selling eggs, taking care of Henry, cooking, shopping, trash hauling, and housekeeping. Then Chet insisted I learn to drive the tractor because the pasture had to be mowed before the weeds went to seed.

"This thing makes no sense to me," I said, sitting on the tractor seat. "One stick shift is labeled with a Z and the other is labeled with an H."

"Each stick is for a different set of moves," he said.

"What's the cinnamon bun for?" I pointed to the peeling symbols on the dashboard.

"That's not a cinnamon bun, it's a snail. A rabbit and a snail. Get it? They're speed settings. You can do this, Bil. Just think about it."

He sat down in his Adirondack chair on the long porch and instructed me as I sat on his machine on the lawn. I was supposed to be thinking about the tractor, but I was thinking about my husband being disabled by chronic pain. The rattle of the engine sounded like my mind felt. I was shaken, parts of me were crumbling and falling, there was a chance I was broken, but I had to roll on.

"Lower the throttle before you shut down the engine," he said. "And always, always, use the emergency brake."

"It's too much to remember." I wanted to cry. "I don't do this often enough to remember all of it."

"It's not too much to remember," he said. "If you had to have a high IQ to drive a tractor there wouldn't be any farms. Just slow down and think about what you're doing."

"I hate tools."

"Well, you're going to have to get over your tool phobia if you want the pastures mowed, because I just can't do it."

~ : ~

My family reunion at the farm was approaching. It took a year of phone calls and emails to organize events for a weekend in June. We planned to celebrate Father's Day, my dad's 75th birthday, and my youngest brother's 50th. My dad and my stepmom, Peggy, arrived from Florida in their RV a few days before the others. After we got them parked in our driveway, and hooked up to electricity and water, Chet and I went to his doctor appointment.

The voice mail from the nurse had said, "We have the results from Chet's CT scan. Come in any time before eight o'clock tonight, the doctor will see you as soon as you get here. Just come as soon as you can."

In the car on the way there Chet said, "There's something I have to tell you because you're going to find out anyway — I've been coughing up blood."

"When did that happen?" I was alarmed.

"A couple weeks ago."

"You've been coughing up blood for a couple weeks and you didn't tell me?" That was all I said. But in my head, I said, *How am I supposed to take care of you if you don't tell me what's going on?*

"I didn't want to worry you."

The doctor was a plump Indian man with a thick accent. He held a single sheet of paper that said URGENT across the top in all capital letters. I didn't understand most of the terminology, but I understood the list: bronchus, lungs, lymph, liver, adrenal. It was cancer. I had the sensation of being dropped naked into the ocean, alone in a new reality, so cold, condensing, disappearing. In my head I screamed. *WAIT! WAIT! I'm not ready for this. Stop the clock. I'm unprepared. We are unprepared. Take back that sentence. Don't say that. Those are just words on a page. Words! Not my words, your words. Take them back. We don't want them. Don't give us cancer.*

The doctor said additional tests were required to confirm the results of the scan and provide an official diagnosis. He wanted an oncology report as soon as possible. Biopsy surgery would be required. A cancer diagnosis had stages. We needed to know what stage Chet was in so a plan for treatment could be formulated. The voice in my head practiced saying, *My husband has cancer. My husband has cancer. We have cancer.*

Chet was silent in the car on the way home. "What are you thinking?" I asked as I drove.

"I don't want to die the way my father did," he said, turning his face toward the window. "I don't want to be humiliated by this process. If I'm going to be the first to go, and everyone is going to be watching me, I want to be a role model."

"Chet, I don't even know what that means."

"Neither do I," he said.

But he had been thinking about it. He had clearly been thinking about his own death. He had thought about it enough to compare his death to his father's. I could see how he would. His father had died seven years earlier, in March 2001, in a soap opera of bad family behavior and conflicting ideas about how a person should die. All while the dying man himself curled in the fetal position in his bed and begged for someone to help him. The imprint of that was left on both of us forever. I could understand how it was the first place Chet would go in thinking about his own death, imagining himself on that bed, begging. He was way ahead of me there. He was thinking about how to die. I was thinking about how I could stop death.

"What do you want to tell Dad and Peg?" I asked, as we pulled into our driveway beside their RV. "My brothers will be here this weekend. What are we going to tell them? How are we going to keep this a secret? I don't think I can fake it with my parents."

"We aren't going to fake it," he said. "It is what it is. Keep it real."

Keep it real? My husband has cancer. My husband has cancer. Keep it real.

When we got inside the house, I helped him to bed and gave him his pain pills. Then I went to visit my parents in their RV in the driveway. Sitting at their table I told them the news. They were stunned and poured me a shot of bourbon. It was just a string of words but saying them aloud for the first time made it real for me. I felt my chest quake with a deep ache, and I sobbed with my face in my hands.

A few days later, after my brothers had come and gone, Chet's pain was so extreme that his pain pills gave him no relief, so I drove him to the hospital emergency room. There they gave him another CT scan and we waited for the results while pain medication dripped into his body through an IV. In the wee hours of the morning someone somewhere interpreted the scans and the report was emailed to the ER doctor.

"Hello, Mr. Cahill," the doctor said, holding a printed copy of the email, as the two of us sat beside Chet's bed in the ER cubicle. "The scan shows you have a very large mass at the top of your spine, and it appears to be creating pressure, which is where your pain comes from. I would like to admit you to the hospital and have our neurologist see you as soon as possible."

"Let's do it," Chet said.

"Is this part of the cancer?" I asked.

"Most likely," the doctor said. "I'm sorry."

By the time I got Chet settled into his hospital room, the sun was coming up. I went home to do chores and get some things for him. When I tried to tell my dad and Peggy what the doctor said, I fell to my knees in anguish. They made me a cup of coffee and calmed me down. Chet's situation was too much to comprehend, but the needs of the farm were obvious. After living in their RV in our driveway for a couple weeks, they were familiar with the routine. They had planned to leave the next day, but they decided to stay on and help me. I gave them a farm tour, talking through each animal group — the cows, the goats, the sheep, and the chickens — handed them my farmsitter notebook, and they took over the farm for me, while I managed Chet's healthcare.

6. Stuff

Chet's dad, Maurice, which the family pronounced Morris, was an antique dealer expert in the glorious inventions of the 19th century. He read books about the history of American glass and collected slag glass figurines. He repaired old clocks and converted oil lamps to electricity. As an auctioneer for estate sales he knew how things were made and sleuthed for signs of authenticity, hoarding rarities and broken relics to harvest replacement parts for his restoration projects.

On stage at auctions, wearing his cowboy hat and snakeskin boots, Maurice was known for calling out his amusing colloquialisms: fine as frog hair, slick as snot, useless as teats on a boar hog. He was a very funny man and he loved the spotlight. At his antique shop in Westerville, Ohio, he held court behind the glass display counter, and when folks stopped by to browse, he always had a few jokes ready to entertain them.

"How are you today, Maurice?" they would say.

"I'm just fine," he would answer. "Fine as frog hair."

In his basement workshop a thin layer of oil and dust coated stacks of tobacco cans and cigar boxes. Broken Lionel trains were parked along narrow shelves, green and blue medicine bottles clustered around rusty wind-up toys, and a collection of pocketknives whittled history. Dozens of antique clocks in various states of disrepair chimed, cuckooed, clanged, dinged and donged, calling on Maurice to fix them with his drippy eyes looking through filthy glasses, a cigarette dangling from his lips. Here among his bits and bobs, overflowing ashtrays and nail jars, using tiny tools and magnifying glasses, he was a wizard, magically fixing things that had been broken for a hundred years.

Chet's mom was named Mary Evelyn, but everyone called her Mick. She was a sassy card player who collected the Heisey Lariat pattern of clear glass dishes in three curved-glass oak china cabinets stacked with serving platters, relish trays and bowls. She collected these things, but she didn't use them, and they rarely made the journey from display case to human hands because, although she was fastidious, she didn't like to clean. Her kitchen had bright red linoleum countertops, a big enamel sink, and a 1950's stove with rounded corners and plastic knobs, all in pristine condition because she refused to cook. She grew up in the 1930s and 40s when a woman was expected to slog over a hot stove. Then she discovered canned soup and the microwave.

Mick's stuff was her savings account and she kept everything that didn't rot. Plastic laundry baskets filled with neatly folded old clothes, towels, bedding and throw rugs lined the walls of the attic, the bedroom closets, the pantry and the basement storeroom, approximately one laundry basket for each year of Chet's life. Anyone who cared to could travel back in time to find his Mickey Mouse bed sheets, or his sister's turquoise pedal pushers, or the Hawaiian shirt Maurice burned the time he fell asleep with a cigarette in his mouth.

Her dining room hutch was jammed with bags of incense, scented votive candles, tea candles and tapers, although she rarely burned candles because the melted wax was a chore to clean. Her bingo accessories were lined up in ziplock freezer bags beside rows of aerosol spray air fresheners, one in each scent, and a dozen little boxes of potpourri she got on sale at the dollar store. Tall nests of bowls and plastic containers clustered in her cupboards, some bought at Tupperware parties and never used.

Mick and Maurice were both smokers and Chet grew up in a cloud of burning tobacco. Maurice smoked whatever was easy. Mick smoked Pall Mall filterless cigarettes because they were a tidy cigarette she could let fall to the ground or the rug, and erase with the toe of her shoe. Her ashtray, like her house, was immaculate but for the white nits of ash that clung to the glass and dotted the brown vinyl hassock where she kept her stack of newspapers. As she rocked on her loveseat reading, occasionally something would annoy her, and twin tornados of smoke would swirl out of her nostrils onto the pages of the *Columbus Dispatch*.

Rocking was Mick's thing. It soothed her anxiety. Summer mornings she sat on the porch swing chain smoking and rocking in her nightgown. If she was feeling ambitious, she might get a bottle of weed killer out of the garage. Then barefoot, with a cigarette in one hand and the squirt bottle in the other, she'd walk up and down the driveway and the sidewalk, squirting poison on anything green that dared poke up from cracks in the cement.

If Maurice happened to see her through the kitchen window, while he made his morning Sanka with hot tap water and drank it over the sink, he would yell at her through the window screen.

"Mick get in here and put some damn clothes on. You look like a damn hillbilly out there in your damn nightgown."

And she would yell back at him, "Oh, Maurice, shut up. You'll wake the neighbors."

Mick was solidly middle class and intentionally uneducated. She didn't want to learn anything new. Her main interests were sports and shopping for things on sale. In the basement her shelves were lined with incredible deals she got on baked beans and tuna fish, paper towels and plastic cups. She stockpiled rows and rows of canned food in case there was another Depression or a war shortage.

Her whole family tried to change her, but her ways were set, and trying to talk to her about her unhealthy diet, or the expiration date on the cans in the basement, could get a person's eardrums blown out by a sudden increase in volume on the TV. Mick didn't want to change. It was just that simple. She got married, had kids, kept a nice house, and made sure there was always plenty of lunch meat in the fridge. After that, she was entitled to do whatever she pleased.

~ : ~

We bought our first house in Boston in 1987, and then my career took off in the 1990s, and we started looking for a vacation house in the Berkshire hills of Western Massachusetts. The real estate agent's photo of the farm intrigued us with its long porch under tall trees, rocking chairs overlooking a gracious lawn, and a stand of lush ferns in the shade. The first time we visited the place, on a hot day in May 1998, our car overheated. There was no one else around and we had an hour to wait while the engine cooled. Chet went off exploring and I stepped into the trees to relieve myself.

"Where did you go?" he asked. "You disappeared."

"I was right there under those trees. I thought I had to pee, but I took a massive dump. It just came out of me. It was amazing."

"God, Bil. We've been on vacation for a week and you didn't shit the whole time. You just took a crap on some farmer's lawn? That's pretty symbolic."

"I know. It just came out of me. Subconsciously, I think I was marking my territory."

"Well, okay then," he said. "Oz has spoken."

A couple months later we purchased the farm from the estate of the woman whose family had bought the place in 1907, from a guy who bought it in 1889, from another guy who bought it in 1847. At the closing, the two elderly ladies who were the heirs to the estate brought us the chain of deeds passed on to them, large pieces of paper scrawled with a fountain pen in ornate cursive. Town records traced the history of the land back to the 1700s.

All those previous owners built a house, a barn, an icehouse, an outhouse, a chicken coop, a corncrib, a duck shed, a bungalow and a garage. And they didn't leave those buildings broom clean when they sold. Centuries of farm stuff decayed in every corner. That's what we liked about the place.

"I can't wait to go through all this junk," Chet said.

"I know," I said. "I have to show you these medicine bottles I found in the barn."

~ : ~

Before we made the purchase, Maurice came to the Berkshires to have a look at the place. Picking through the musty barn he was gleeful with memories of his childhood during the Depression when his mother sent him to live in the neighbor's barn where he could trade doing farm chores for food. Sleeping in the hay, living with the animals and milking the cow, Maurice knew farming as a way of life. He was enchanted by every pile of rust and dust on the property. In particular, the house was still furnished with the family's stuff, and he had seen a pair of Wedgewood lamps in the bedroom he wanted us to keep. So, he urged us to buy the entire contents of the estate as part of the deal.

In the car on the way to the closing, Chet said, "We need to be flexible about buying their stuff. There are some things they might want to keep for themselves."

"Those lamps may be Wedgewood," I said. "But I don't like how they look."

"Dad says they're worth a lot."

"I don't care what they're worth. I really like the teapot. I've never seen one like it."

"Bil, it's a teapot."

"It's got good juju. I can feel it. You can't say that about the lamps."

"No, you can't say the lamps have juju. But you could say they're worth some dough."

"We're buying a house from dead people. I think we want the good juju."

On the phone the next day, Maurice said. "You did what!? You traded those lamps for a teapot? Those lamps were worth ten times as much as that teapot!"

"I know," I said. "Sorry, Maurice. I really liked the teapot."

"Jesus Christ, girl. You are useless as teats on a boar hog."

~ : ~

For a while we had two big houses and eight outbuildings filled with stuff, and our lives were split between a city street in Boston and a dead-end gravel road 125 miles west in the Berkshires. We hired an architect to remodel the farmhouse and commenced a gut renovation to replace the heating and electrical systems, insulate the walls, and put on an addition big enough for Chet's pool table and a chef's kitchen. We were building our dream house.

"Bil, can we afford this?" Chet asked.

"Yes, we can afford this," I said.

"I feel like I'm out of my league."

"Just take your shoes off and let's see how it feels."

In a bathroom fixture showroom in Boston, under bright lights, with salesmen all around watching and other shoppers passing by, Chet and I took off our shoes and our coats and sat down in the giant bathtub facing each other.

"Feels good to me," I said. "Does it hit your back in the right place?"

"I don't know if I can tell with my clothes on."

"It has lumbar support. You should be able to lean back and feel it."

"I need a martini," he said.

"It's definitely deep enough to drown in."

Chet snapped his fingers in the air. "Waiter! Waiter!"

"Stretch your legs out all the way," I said.

A salesman walked across the room toward us. Chet waved at him and smiled. "We'll have two vodka martinis, dry, with olives," he said. The man laughed and we climbed out of the bathtub and bought it.

"You're sure we can afford this," Chet said.

"Yes," I said. "I'm sure."

~ : ~

On weekends we drove from Boston to the Berkshires and lived on the construction site so Chet could wire the house for audio and install a sound system, while I made plans to convert the tiny dining room into a big deluxe bathroom with a giant bathtub. As soon as the new plumbing was working, we started inviting friends and family to visit.

Mick hated the farm as much as Maurice loved it. He would have happily moved in with us, but she couldn't sleep in a place without streetlights. She grew up on a farm in Summit Station, Ohio, where her mother baked bread and killed chickens, then walked a mile along a dirt path into town with her four young children in tow to trade the bread and meat for cotton to sew their clothes. Mick preferred city sidewalks, canned ham, and clothes made in China.

The first time she came to visit the farm she got sick. Folded up in the car seat on the thirteen-hour ride from Columbus, her diet of saltines and lunchmeat hardened into cement, trapping gas in her abdomen. In the middle of the night she let out a plaster chipping scream that woke all of us, and Chet drove her to the emergency room. Twenty-four hours later she was short one colon and consigned to a life of catching her feces in a plastic bag glued to her stomach. The story of her necrotic intestines sold a lot of salad that day in the hospital cafeteria.

~ : ~

Maurice had health problems of his own. He had had two open heart surgeries, but he never took an interest in the mechanics of his anatomy. His morning ritual was a teaspoon of decaf Sanka in a cup of hot tap water with a cigarette over the kitchen sink. The earthworm scar on his sunken chest showed above the neckline of his undershirt, and the little wire that held his bones together poked up from beneath his yellow skin. He was dying. He didn't know why, but he could feel it, and it unnerved him.

He had been a young soldier in the Army during World War II and fought on Omaha Beach during the invasion of Normandy. He had seen his friends get blown apart. Although he rarely talked about it, we knew the experience left a tableau in his mind of death as a horrific event. When Chet and I tried to talk to him about those memories he would shut down. The same thing happened when we tried to talk to him about his health.

Maurice had an overriding sense of command structure, and in his mind his doctor was his superior officer. He never questioned the doctor's advice, even when he didn't understand a word of it. The doctor was in charge. He didn't need to understand. He just needed to follow orders. His illness was his battle, and he was dutiful, willing to die without question.

In spring of 2001, there was nothing more that could be done to keep his heart pumping blood and his lungs pumping air. He was too weak to walk and sat in his hospice bed with his family gathered round, not eating his favorite food, a big thick juicy steak the nurse had put on a plate in front of him. After years of telling him to eat less meat, everyone knew the significance of that. His eyes brimmed and he sobbed, but he wouldn't talk about his prognosis or his feelings. He had always been a chatty guy, but he refused to discuss what came next, even when death was knocking loudly at the door and all of us could hear it.

Chet and I had long conversations about Maurice as we sat in the hospice waiting room. We read the brochures, and we were curious about what to expect. Maurice's death was our first experience with watching a person die.

"He seems so scared," Chet said. "I wish I could talk to him about it. He never cried my whole life. Now he can't stop crying. I don't get it."

"I think most people are afraid to die," I said.

"Everybody is born, and everybody dies. Was I afraid to be born? I don't think so. What is he so afraid of?"

"Death is the boogey man. It's mysterious and scary."

"He's not a child. And I don't think it's mysterious and scary. It's reality. How could he watch guys get blown up in the war and then be afraid to die in bed? I don't get it."

"War is a fast way to go," I said. "This is really slow. Who knows what he's thinking about? People are afraid of what they don't understand."

"He's not even trying to understand it. He'll spend days trying to figure out how a fucking clock works, but he has no fucking idea how his own body works. He's given up on himself."

"It's too late now," I said.

"I know," he sighed. "He was my hero my whole life. Now I feel mad at him. I wish he would just say something, anything to acknowledge the obvious. I want to tell him goodbye. I want to tell him so many things. But how can I if he won't let me?"

~ : ~

Shortly after our visit to the hospice ward, they moved Maurice home and put him on an electric bed in the dining room where he was expected to die. I stayed with him while Chet, his sister, Cathy, and his mom went to meetings at the funeral home. There Mick's anxiety peaked in a disagreement with Cathy over details of the flower arrangements, triggering a temper tantrum that left permanent scars on both her children.

While Chet was refereeing his mother and his sister, I answered the door for the oxygen tanks to be delivered, and I was the one to get the lessons on how to hook them up, keep the tubes clean, and stop the smokers from burning down the house. "Righty tighty, lefty loosey," the technician said. Those words are chiseled in my memory banks right beside the image of Maurice moaning in the fetal position on an electric bed, beside the three curved-glass china cabinets in the sunny dining room where no one ate.

The power struggle for control of Maurice's death continued to the very end of his life.

"Mom," Chet said. "You have to give Dad his morphine on a regular schedule so he's not in pain."

As Chet spoke, just a few feet away, Maurice was writhing in bed, mumbling in a barely audible voice. "Please God, take this pain away. Please God, take this pain away."

Chet squirted an eye dropper of liquid morphine in the corner of his dad's mouth.

"I'm not doing that," Mick said, turning up the volume on the TV.

"You have to," Chet snapped at her. "He's in pain."

"I am not going to be the one to kill my husband," she said, without looking at anyone.

"It's pain medication!" Chet was incredulous. "You have to give it to him. He's in pain. Can't you hear him?"

"It's going to kill him!" She slammed her fist on the arm of her loveseat and set her jaw. "I am not going to be the one to kill my husband. I won't have that on my soul."

"Mom!" Chet yelled at her. "He's in pain. You need to give him his pain medication."

"I'm not going to!" she yelled back at her son. "You're going to kill him."

"Jesus Christ!" Chet hollered. "He's dying. I'm not killing him. Look at him. He's dying right in front of you. You have to help him, Mom. You have to."

"I'm not going to," she said. And she didn't.

After that Chet and Cathy took shifts watching over their father and giving him his pain meds, while their mother sat just a few feet away watching TV.

~ : ~

Eventually, Maurice unwound to a stop like one of his antique clocks. The funeral was tense because Mick was angry with everyone for a long list of reasons no one cared to hear. Afterward family and friends went to a reception at the VFW hall.

"Dad would have loved this," Chet said, watching the boisterous crowd fill their plates with food. "I wish we had done something like this for him while he was alive."

People were laughing and swapping stories about the time Maurice helped them fix something, retelling the jokes he told over the counter in his antique shop. The room was buoyant with the charm of the missing man.

Back at the house Mick had us go through Maurice's bedroom closet, his nightstand and his dresser drawers, to take something personal for ourselves as a remembrance of the day. Chet took his dad's Army dog tags and a ceramic ashtray of a pretty girl in a seashell. I took a stack of soft white undershirts, the kind working men wear on a hot day when they're getting their hands dirty.

After the funeral, the memories of Maurice's last hours didn't comfort us. The thought of him buried in his new suit in a shiny box in a park where people came to cry didn't give us peace. It didn't feel right to leave him in ground he didn't love. He loved the farm. His initials were carved in the cement threshold he helped us pour across the front of the barn door. His ingenuity was in the chestnut posts he pounded upright to reinforce the beams in the milking parlor. His creativity was in the cow collars he soaked in motor oil and softened to use as tiebacks for the icehouse doors. He was alive in those memories on the farm.

Mick missed her husband, but she reveled in her newfound independence. Her whole life she had been lorded over by a man — her father, her brothers, Maurice. Now she was Queen of the Empire, including the basement and the garage, two greasy fiefdoms she had been wanting to control for decades. She missed having a man around the house, but she did not miss the dirty cardboard boxes he brought home from sales. She did not miss the black fingerprints on the hand towels, or the mountains of wadded newspaper left in the basement, or the bits of straw and styrofoam peanuts sprinkled on the carpet. She had no interest in broken clocks, gadgets, tools and toys. She wanted her basement to be as tidy as her china cabinets, and she wanted the garage empty so sparrows wouldn't poop on her stuff.

A few months after the funeral, at her invitation, Chet and I filled a cargo trailer with Maurice's things. It took a week to sort through his legacy, and while we were doing it, we swore we would never leave the same burdensome accumulation of possessions in our wake. But still we came home with a thousand pounds of heavy metal tools, antiques, furniture and gadgets. On our way out the door Mick threw in a plastic laundry basket of brightly colored twin bed sheets and a case of canned tuna from 1992, and the farm absorbed all of these things into the mass of stuff we already owned.

7. Work

Through a series of jobs in the 1990s, I became a marketing consultant expert in computerizing processes for businesses that wanted to make the move from pen and paper to keyboard and screen. Chet worked as an audio engineer for film and television. He was digitizing his sound studio as fast as we could afford to. We were both riding the leading edge of the high tech revolution, we both had desktop computers in home offices, and we both had a keen interest in owning the latest high tech gadgets.

When the Worldwide Web was launched as a business network, I was working for a computer manufacturer in Boston, and my talent for simplifying complicated ideas was a boon to my clients. The IT guys I met reminded me of the nerdy soundmen and recording engineers I had worked with in the music business. They spoke their own language. It was my job to translate their hardware and software inventions into benefits for customers. We were trying to convince big businesses to use email, websites, search engines and big data. To help make the pitch I wrote user guides and sales presentations for the technology. That work got me a gig with a marketing consulting group that helped big businesses figure out how to use the internet to build their brand.

I was in the right place at the right time. Within a few years my income increased substantially, and Chet and I started looking for ways to invest in real estate. That's when we found the farm. We planned to keep it as a second home because we thought we needed to stay in Boston to maintain our work relationships. But within a couple years email and file sharing became ubiquitous, and we realized we didn't need to be based in Boston anymore. We could live on the farm and work anywhere in the world.

In 2000, the year before Maurice died, we sold our three-family house in Boston, moved all our city stuff to the Berkshires, and became fulltime residents in a rural town. I took a job with a dotcom start-up in New York City and commuted weekly between the farm and an apartment in Gramercy Park. Chet built a sound studio for himself in an upstairs bedroom of the farmhouse and worked from home. He spent much more time on the farm than I did, and it conjured his love for restoration projects on a much grander scale than fixing old clocks and refinishing furniture. He set about the process of repairing every outbuilding and it gave him a connection to the land he hadn't experienced before. One night he rolled over in bed and said, "I think I want to farm."

"Really?" I said. "Farmer Chet? If you still feel that way in the morning, let's talk about it."

I wasn't interested in farming. All my mental real estate was occupied by the technology business. The internet was a boomtown and I was prospecting for gold. The farm was a nice place to be on weekends, but I couldn't focus on learning about farming. During the week I had to be extremely competitive. On Saturday and Sunday, I wanted to relax in an Adirondack chair on the long porch, drink wine, paint my nails, catch up on my reading, and hike in the woods.

Dotcoms went boom-and-bust every day in New York and the start-up I worked for was no different. It was a flashy but flawed idea. One day the money dried up and *poof!* it was gone. I gave up my apartment and moved back to the farm. A few months later it was September 11th, 2001, the planes hit the World Trade Center and our lives were forever changed. We got out the American flag we had found in a coat closet when we bought the farm and hung it on our porch as a symbol of solidarity with the nation.

Glued to our television, we worried that there would be another attack. We watched TV channels run black screens expressing sympathy with the victims. For a while most advertising was suspended. Brands went silent and marketing budgets froze as companies reconsidered their public image. With that contraction, many people employed in marketing, advertising and media lost their jobs. My marketing consulting work dried up. Weeks passed and Chet's audio gigs resumed. But I was unemployed.

~ : ~

My work energy spilled out of me in a flurry of tasks, arms and legs wind milling, brooms and rags flying. I swept the spruce needles off the long porch, raked up sticks and pinecones, put a rag on the end of a sapling and snagged the cobwebs over the pool table, scraped the dog goobers off the walls, got a ladder and scrubbed the fireplace soot off the ceiling fans; washed, wiped and put away the dishes, polished my grandmother's silver, and removed the stains from tablecloths and napkins, shirts and underwear. Then I folded the laundry into perfectly symmetrical rectangles and reorganized dresser drawers to fit the stacks on a perfectly symmetrical grid, squeegeed water spots off the mirrors, mopped floors, sorted vases on the shelf in the pantry by style, canning jars by size, light bulbs by watt, and pencils, pens, paper and envelopes by color. Then I unhooked the rubber bands from the paper clips, separated the nails from the screws, and labeled the CD shelves with little pieces of white tape.

"Billie's home again," Chet laughed.

"How can you tell?"

"I can't find my coffee cup."

"It's in the dishwasher."

"I drink coffee all day. Please leave my cup where I put it."

"I'll try. But I can't make any promises."

"Find something else to do."

"I need a new project."

"I could use a hand outside," he said. "You could help me clear that brush by the barn. I'd really like to get it cleared before it snows."

Living on the farm together after 9/11 was a new experience for us, our first time living and working together every day since the Luna House. The open meadows around the farmhouse and the surrounding forest were part of our homestead. After 20 years of neglect the forest was encroaching on the meadows and invasive weeds were climbing the outbuildings. The feeling of abandonment gave the place its own mystique, but we intended to reclaim it. We made lists and started mornings with long conversations about landscaping, architecture and history, sharing ideas with a passion reminiscent of our days with Orchestra Luna.

Chet bought a chain saw and we cut down trees and split firewood together. On hikes with Henry we picked through the rusty junk we found in the woods, excavated ancient barbed wire fences from the forest floor, cut them loose from the trees, and spooled them into wire wreaths. Each hike we went deeper and deeper into the woods and higher up the hill. We followed deer paths and lumberjack trails, and the more we hiked, the better we were at finding our way through the wilderness. The newness of it all rekindled our interest in each other and the clock seemed to roll backwards. In a couple of years, we would be 50, but the farm made us feel young again.

Chet did the sawing and I did the hauling to clear the invasive shrubs that had created a dense thicket on the hill beside the barn. We piled the branches and burned them. Fire tending was child's play for us. We sat in lawn chairs, stirred coals with long sticks, drank beer and told stories. It was a slow smoky party followed by a long luxurious soak in our giant bathtub.

"What happened to your fingernails?" Chet asked as he sank into the bubbles.

"I cut them off," I said, sitting in the water across from him. "I'm going for a new look."

"Farm girls don't wear nail polish?"

"It seems stupid to me now."

"It was always stupid," he said. "Manual labor looks good on you."

"It feels good."

"You smell like a guy."

"I'll take that as a compliment."

"It's not my favorite thing about you."

"I can feel my muscles. See." I flexed for him, he kissed me, and our bodies fit together perfectly.

~ : ~

Cleaning the outbuildings was my 40 days and 40 nights in the wilderness. I stopped reading the *Wall Street Journal*. I checked my email every day, but I was slow to reply. Morning light drew me outdoors. I paid a visit to every plant in every garden. I inspected scat with a twig and got spider bites on my ankles. I found a root cellar under the bungalow. My ears opened to new voices. I watched a pair of male cardinals duel. I heard crows kidnap baby birds. I noticed Henry making mental notes of the deer, bear, foxes, bobcats, coyotes, raccoons, possums, groundhogs, skunks and squirrels that crossed our paths. The farm had my complete attention.

In the absence of daily conversations with clients and colleagues I lost track of trends and buzzwords. Then I started to think of marketing consulting as a game, a series of moves on an imaginary chess board. It didn't exist in the physical world. It was just a bunch of ideas that changed the way people behaved, nothing I could put my hands on. Manual labor on the farm felt real. It felt honest. It wasn't about persuasion. We were changing the lives of every living thing around us just by being there. I started to feel a moral obligation to the farm. As though I had a duty to tend the Earth. I didn't feel that way about the corporations I had worked for. They were faceless global businesses, soulless conglomerations of money. I wasn't there because I cared about them. I was there because I wanted a slice of the pie.

On the outside I was doing chores, but on the inside, I was moving around the furniture, rearranging my beliefs and my vision for myself. On the farm I was part of a community. In the chicken coop a thick layer of hickory nuts covered the floor, collected there by the army of squirrels that moved in once the last hen was gone. The corncrib, built to hold winter feed for the cows and chickens, was emptied of its last kernels by rodents who littered it with seed hulls, chewed up rags and bird feathers. The duck shed was filled with iron scraps, the remains of old coal burners, and piles of asphalt shingles, a virtual mouse palace. Snakeskins crisped in old hay. In my mind these creatures were my responsibility. My farm was the Ark and I was Noah, preserving life for the world to come. Farm work was heroic.

As the season changed the cold weather made laboring outside more comfortable. The insects were gone, and the spider webs were empty. The plants died back, the bones of the farm were exposed, and we could see the naked land. I tied a bandana over my face and used a long sapling to catch cobwebs big as dishtowels in the corners of the barn. Bat guano speckled the wood floor of the hay mow beneath the bat roost in the ceiling. I swept the guano into a dustpan and sprinkled it on my garden.

In the milking parlor crumbling swallows' nests were tucked in the crotches of posts and beams. I poked at them to knock them down and the dust made me sneeze as it settled on the ancient artifacts of the farm, leather cow collars, medicine bottles, enamelware dishes, rusting buckets and wizened locust fence posts. All the while my mind sorting through my options for paying work, wishing I could get paid to do something I loved, knowing I had to go back to earning money.

"This looks great," Chet said, standing in the doorway. "Maybe you could get a job cleaning barns."

"I wouldn't mind that," I said. "If it would let me stay here."

"What do you mean?"

"If I'm going to get back in the consulting game, I have to be in the city."

"You can do that," he said. "But you might have to bathe."

"I don't want to do that," I said. "I don't want to leave this place. I feel like I just got here. Like I just woke up."

"Okay. Stay here. But you still have to bathe." He smiled and turned to walk away. Then he turned back to me and said, "You're amazing, Bil. You'll figure it out."

~ : ~

When the snow melted in spring of 2002, rain filled deep puddles in the fields and on the lawn. Eventually the puddles connected into shallow streams moving across open land. We could see the flow of rainwater from our wetlands to the river across the highway. We didn't appreciate the placement of the outbuildings until we saw the water move. The house and the chicken coop were set on the highest ground. The icehouse was built up on a stone foundation beside the pond, so ice would be near, but high water couldn't touch the wooden walls. The wooden corncrib was built on raised concrete footings very near the house where it could be guarded. In April mating frogs laid masses of tiny black eggs like caviar on the surface of the pond and around the shore we found salamanders in the grass. Our farm was a water system.

Our drinking water came from a shallow well a couple hundred feet away from the pond. Chet and Henry and I traced the water ways from the pond to the springs and swamps around the house, to the intermittent streams across the fields, to the brook coming down the hill, and finally to the Green River. We saw the sky pull up water from the land and we realized that weather was mainly moving water. It made sense to us that our water was not really our water, and our neighbor's water did not belong to them either. There was only one water and it was always on the move. Most important to us, water tests showed our well water was clean and we liked how it tasted.

When we came to the farm, we had an urban mindset and a condescending air toward the low tech rural past. Seeing the farm's resilience season after season gave us more respect for the systems put in place by the people who came before us. The farm had a storied relationship with Nature that was new for us. In the gardens and fields, we saw how the Earth belched up stones every spring, and how stonewalls made sense not just as a line of separation, but as a place to make use of a continuous supply of stone. We saw how the buildings were situated to maximize solar gain and wind resistance.

Our farm was a system of systems, a community of communities, a network of networks. I understood computer networks. For years it had been my job to help businesses exploit the internet. Now I saw that Nature and the internet had similar organizing principles, a universal way of operating that ensures everything is connected. I knew apps that weren't compatible with an operating system would crash. So, if Nature was Earth's operating system, our farm had to be compatible with Nature. That seemed logical to me, but I was a long way from understanding how to accomplish it.

To learn more we started to visit other farms, go on farm tours and attend farming workshops. Then we went to the Northeast Organic Farming Association annual conference for three days in August 2002. Instead of staying in a motel, to save money we slept on a twin bed in a college dorm room.

"This might be the second shittiest bed we've ever slept on," Chet said as we squeezed together on the narrow mattress. "Thanks for bringing these sheets."

"I can't get those oxen out of my head," I said, turning out the lights.

"They're beautiful," he said. "Beautiful, but slow."

"I think going slow makes it a more conscious experience."

"I can be conscious on the seat of a tractor."

"Think of oxen as a pet tractor," I said.

"A pet tractor that goes really slow."

"Speed isn't everything."

"Yes, it is," he said. "Why do you think farmers use greenhouses?"

"I thought they did it to keep the bugs off their tomatoes."

"Speed. Farming is all about the need for speed. Just like everything else."

"But we eat food," I said. "We don't eat everything else."

"Perhaps you've heard of fast food."

"This whole conference is about how bad fast food is."

"Easy to say. It tastes pretty good when you're hungry."

"But slow food is better for the planet."

"If I have to choose between oxen and a tractor, I choose a tractor," he said.

"But isn't that a false choice?"

"It's math, Bil. It's just math."

"There is so much I don't understand about all this," I said. "I wish I could go back to school."

"What's to understand? Grow food. Eat food."

"I think it's more complicated than that. It feels political."

"It's only political if you want it to be."

"This whole organic thing feels very political to me."

"No one in my family ever went to school for farming, and they all farmed — and they all hate organic."

"But they all had other jobs," I said. "They worked on the side."

"They worked jobs," he corrected me. "And farmed on the side."

"And then refrigerators were invented, and they didn't have to milk a cow every day to get fresh milk."

"So now you're against refrigerators?"

"No, I'm not against refrigerators."

"Good," he said. "Because I like my beer really cold." He rolled over on his side. "Now go to sleep."

"I can't," I said. "There's too much to think about."

"Shut it down, Bil."

"Do you think the farm should be organic?"

"Stop," he said.

"Okay. But I'm going to ask you that again tomorrow."

8. Wendell & Berry

Within months of attending the farming conference in 2002 I was accepted by two university food and agriculture programs. The other big outcome of the conference was that Chet and I decided to get a flock of chickens. While he renovated the chicken coop, I read a stack of books about farming.

To buy our first chickens we paged through a mail order catalog with pictures of each breed and characteristics like the size and color of their eggs, and how many eggs they produced. We chose heritage breeds, colorful birds from Europe and South America, popular in the days before factory farms. When I called the hatchery 800 number a friendly woman took my order.

"Your chicks will arrive on May 20th," she said. "Be sure to let your post office know to call you as soon as they arrive."

"May 20th!" I yelped. "It's April."

"Once I put your order in it will be three weeks."

"But I thought they were day-old chicks."

"They are day-old chicks."

"Then why can't we have them tomorrow?"

"Because it takes three weeks for an egg to hatch."

"You have a hatchery and you don't hatch chickens every day?"

"Yes, ma'am, we do hatch chickens every day, but once we place your order the chickens have to lay the eggs and then it will take three weeks for them to hatch."

"So, we aren't getting our chickens tomorrow?"

"No, ma'am. It takes three weeks for your chickens to arrive."

"Is there any way we can get some chickens tomorrow? We're all ready for them."

"Ma'am, if you want 25 broilers, I can send you some tomorrow. But if you want five Rhode Island Reds, five New Hampshires, five Silverlace Wyandottes, five Barred Rocks and five Auracanas, you're going to have to wait until they hatch."

"Oh," I said. "It's not like buying goldfish at the pet store, is it?"

"No, ma'am, it's not."

I had read an encyclopedia about chickens, but I thought buying them from a mail order catalog would be like shopping on Amazon. In my mind there was a vast warehouse of chicken merchandise with pickers on roller skates filling boxes of chicks for their customers. The system I envisioned was retail, not farming. Chickens are not stuff.

~ : ~

Three weeks later our day-old chicks arrived at the post office in the backroom of the general store down the road. Chet and I had set up a pen for them with a heat lamp over their food and water. Like the books said, we took them one at a time out of the box, dipped their beaks in water to give them their first drink, and set them down near their food. When they drank, they blinked, raising their beaks to swallow. Then they began to peck at their grain and eat. It was a simple instinctive process that stirred my sense of cosmic order. They were hardwired to find food and I was hardwired to care for them. My inner Earth Mother fluttered to life and my entire nervous system plugged into the farm. She was my womb. I was her child. These were my children.

We put a pair of chairs beside the little pen and watched our chicks cavort delirious with life.

"Do you think they're really that happy?" Chet asked.

"That's what it looks like to me," I said. "Although I don't think they're capable of complex emotions."

"They're definitely not worried about looking stupid."

Henry came in the room and put his head over the pen to sniff the chicks, exhaling his moist dog breath onto them as they peeped in terror and rushed into a pile in the corner.

"Henry, sit," Chet said. Then he cupped one of the chicks in his hands for Henry to smell. It was a light bulb moment for the big dog. "This is your sister," Chet said. "You have to protect her." He put the baby bird back in the pen, and he and Henry sat together and watched the birds for a half hour, until the chicks calmed in Henry's presence and fell asleep.

~ : ~

In their first week the downy chicks grew wing feathers and, in a month, their whole bodies were covered with feathers the color of their breed. Finally, it was time to open the door of the chicken coop to the wide, wide world of the barnyard. Following a trail of cracked corn, 25 chickens gradually made their way onto the grass, pecking and scratching the dirt, rushing back and forth across the lawn, hunting for food and hiding in shadows, navigating life without an instruction manual. Chickens do not read an encyclopedia to learn how to be a chicken.

Books are my key to the Universe. I read and do, read and do, read and do, until finally I'm certain I know, and I don't need to learn anymore. I just do. Often that's when I make my biggest mistakes. I'm so certain of what I know that I don't allow for the possibility of learning something new. My knowledge becomes a series of switches, on/off, yes/no, right/left, open/closed, a grid of pre-existing ideas that becomes a filter for everything that enters my mind.

The grid extrudes new information so it looks a lot like the old information and my thoughts become a pattern that repeats itself in my behavior until parts of the grid are so worn from overuse that they become deep ruts, and I bury myself in certainty until my grid is shattered by my own humiliating ignorance.

Chickens do not have this problem. They repeat an endless pattern of searching for food, eating and procreating, until the pattern is interrupted by fear, which they will soon forget whether they survive their fear or not. A chicken is never certain. Therefore, a chicken is never humiliated. There's always something to learn from animals.

~ : ~

Chet's family warned us not to get serious about farming. "There's no money in it," they said. They couldn't understand why we would want to do so much unnecessary work and pour our money down a hole with no hope of retrieving it. Collapsing barns dotted the countryside from coast to coast because farming was dying. It was a bad investment. We were fools. They shook their heads and worried about us over pie and coffee.

Everyone called Chet's grandfather Wink, but his real name was Charles Wellington Starr, a fancy name for a plain man who worked hard and drank hard and saw the land as a way to make money. Chet remembered bouncing on the front seat of Wink's clattering jalopy as they drove along dirt roads and the old man yacked, pointing out the window with the stub of his cigar.

"If I had me a cow, I'd put her over there," Wink said. He once bought four heifers to raise and sell to local dairy farmers, and his grandchildren named them John, Paul, George and Ringo.

Chet's mom, Mick, and her sister, Mamie Lou, were Wink's daughters. Mamie Lou and her husband raised Charolais, a creamy white beef cow that glowed against the green hillsides of their farm in southern Ohio. One of Chet's most vivid childhood memories was that Mamie Lou had a pig named Millie, a very big pig, which was housebroken and knew where to go when Mamie Lou yelled, "Millie, get back in the kitchen!" Mamie Lou was tearful as she recalled the day Millie had to be picked up with the tractor and put onto a truck bound for slaughter because she had lived the good life of a pet pig for so long, she was too fat to walk. Even selling her farmland for house lots and getting rich and moving to Florida couldn't wipe away Mamie Lou's sadness for saying goodbye to Millie. But farming is a life of hard choices and when farm animals become pets, hearts get broken. It's a rule.

~ : ~

Pretty much everything Chet's family thought about food and farming was explained away in the required reading for my agriculture classes. The curriculum included analysis of academic research papers and government documents, farm and food business tours, case studies, lectures, and lots of writing. It was a good fit for me. I enjoyed my classmates and I began to develop a network of colleagues in agriculture.

The more I studied, the more I became convinced that small farms and "sustainable agriculture" were the cure for all that ailed the world. The idea of sustainability was a revelation for me. Until then, I had not considered whether the Earth was big enough for everyone who lives here. I had never thought of myself as being a member of a species. I didn't see Earth as a food system.

I gave to charity and I volunteered to help the poor. But realistically, I thought life was every man for himself, survival of the fittest. Somebody somewhere had to die. As a businessperson I saw natural selection as economic selection, and it seemed like a good system to me. After all, it had been working for thousands of years and life on Earth was getting better and better. Human civilization was building on itself, continuously growing, reaching for the stars.

It never occurred to me that you can't have infinite growth on a finite planet. Earth is finite. We have only one Earth. Continuous growth is not possible. We are nearing the end of our supply of natural resources. It's simple math. Divide the amount of resources on the planet by the number of people who live here, and watch those numbers get spookier and spookier as the population goes up. If we divide up Earth equally, everyone's slice of the pie is getting smaller and smaller. Without shared resources, economic survival of the fittest starts to look a lot like slavery.

Sustainable agriculture felt to me like the Girl Scout ethic I had learned when I was eight: Leave things better than you found them. Sharing was the Girl Scout way. We were taught to share tasks, responsibilities and food. We were taught that sharing kept us safe. In my mind the rules for sustainability were like the rules for sharing. I started to think of being wealthy as hoarding.

~ : ~

On class fieldtrips across the Northeast we visited many different types of farms. I saw people living minimalist lives, devoting themselves to producing healthy food, and it changed my idea of what was cool. I felt like Chet and I had to live differently. I wanted to grow our own food and I wanted our farm to be a model for regenerating Nature.

"Organic is sharing the wealth," I said.

"Farmers don't have enough wealth to share," Chet countered. "That's why no one farms anymore."

"People don't farm because big corporations made farming a game that small farmers can't win."

"Blah, blah, blah," he said. "What's for dinner? That's what people care about."

"Wendell Berry said, 'Eating is an agricultural act.'"

"That's very sweet. Please pass the money."

"It's not about money," I said.

"You've lost your mind, Bil."

"I know. But I think it would be really cool."

"It is cool! It is totally cool to look at and to read about. But you don't really want to live like that."

"How can you say that?" I asked. "Look at our chickens. I think we do want to live like that."

"Our farm is an art project. Having chickens is like having goldfish."

"You don't eat goldfish."

"You may end up eating goldfish," he said. "Our savings account is down to nothing."

"I can make money with the farm," I said. "I just need more time."

"Farmers are poor, Bil."

"I can live on less money."

"Ha!" he laughed.

~ : ~

As homework for one of my classes I did a case study of a local livestock farm. The farmer walked me through her breeding operation and explained how she and her daughters managed the sheep and the goats. I was wide eyed and envious of her herd. Lambs and kids were bleating, and back in a corner there were two white baby goats nursing on a brown nanny, twin boys, the result of her daughter's 4H project to crossbreed a LaMancha doe and an Angora buck. The kids were handsome and healthy, but they weren't the right genetics for her herd. She told me I could have them for $15 each.

Chet was in the midst of planning a new fence for the chickens when I announced I wanted to buy two baby goats.

"They're beautiful," I said. "You should see them. They're like puppies."

"Bil, I can't think about goats."

"She'll sell us the pair for $30."

"Let me get this fence figured out before we start on something new."

"Their breath smells like goat cheese."

"I feel like we're still learning how to deal with the chickens," he said. "Can't we just do one thing at a time?"

"How can you achieve synergies if you only do one thing at a time? Now that we have chickens, we just integrate the goats into the chicken processes."

"I'd like to think about it for a while," he said.

"They're babies now. I think we want to get them as soon as possible."

"The chicken grain is so expensive. How can we afford to feed goats, too?"

"Goats don't need grain. They eat the leaves on bushes. We can use them to clear the barberry."

"So, they're going to be working goats, not pets, right?"

"Of course," I said. "Working farm, working goats."

When we visited the goats, Chet was as smitten as I was. They were petite and mischievous with fine bones and delicate hooves, prancing and playful as puppies. We named them Wendell and Berry in homage to Wendell Berry, the renowned Kentucky farmer who had inspired us to farm from the heart.

Wendell and Berry had their mother's tiny ears and their father's pink nose and curly white coat. We took their mother on loan so they could continue their diet of mother's milk and she could teach them to forage. We named her Linda — Linda LaMancha.

Sitting in the hay with Wendell and Berry, holding them in my arms, smelling their breath and touching noses, they imprinted on me. I felt love for them and the land that held us together. Now that I had chickens and goats, I needed the land. Chet and I had owned land in Boston, but I can't say I loved it. That tiny patch of turf was barren and perfunctory, a separation of houses and a place to park cars. I didn't see it as an ecosystem, or Nature, or a community of living things. Living with farm animals changed my worldview.

~ : ~

When we needed a farm name to write on our egg cartons, I made a list of my ideas to show Chet: Salamander Song Farm, Dancing Goat Farm, Singing Swamp Farm, Rocky Frog Farm, Stone Goat Farm, Green Rock Farm.

"You take all of this too seriously," he said.

"You can't feed your brain bumper stickers and expect to have encyclopedic thoughts."

"People remember bumper stickers, not encyclopedias."

"So, what do you want to name it?"

"Something funny," he said. "Something that doesn't sound like every other farm name."

"I want a name that celebrates Nature," I said. "That's what we're doing here."

"Thoreau is a snooze, Bil."

"Okay. You name the farm. If it's a funny name, you can name it whatever you want. But the domain name has to be available. We need a website."

"I think we should call it Crazy Wife Farm," he said.

"Seriously?" I asked, thinking *Well, that just rolled off the tip of his tongue.*

"Seriously." He didn't flinch.

"Okay." I called his bluff.

"Let's do it." He pointed to my computer.

We registered the domain and the farm was named.

~ : ~

The goats' horns were starting to grow, so I read up on horns in my goat book. Even though removing them was highly recommended, it seemed unnatural. Horns can be dangerous, but plenty of children in third world countries herd goats with horns. Why couldn't I? Horns are a goat's cooling system. Blood circulates through them. They are warm to the touch. I wanted my goats to have the full expression of their goatness, so I let them keep their horns. Weeks later, Chet was reading the fine print in his fencing catalog as he shopped for a solar battery.

"According to the catalog, electric poultry netting isn't suitable for animals with horns," he said.

Evidently horns snag on the plastic mesh fence and the tugging to escape can wreck the fence, or if they don't escape, critters can get wrapped up in the pulsing electric mesh and twitch to death. My goats' horns were already a few inches long. I could have had a vet cut them out. Lots of farmers do it. I didn't.

"Bil, this is not a third world farm," Chet said. "Children in third world countries are not penning their goats in electric mesh."

"I know. I'm really sorry," I said. "But their horns are beautiful. Look at them. They're like these curved white bones coming out of their heads. And they're warm. They're warm when you touch them. It's not like trimming your nails."

We did some more research on fencing and decided to build a permanent electric fence around the barnyard. It was a big commitment of money and time, but we were all in for farming. So Chet commenced the project.

By then I was on the board of directors of a regional nonprofit that produced farmer education programs, and I worked as a grant writer making the case for community-based food systems. Writing essays and opinion pieces, and speaking at events, I was an outspoken voice for change, willing to go out on a limb with criticism of the industrial food system.

For the first time since the band, my work and my passion aligned to become my mission. The farm gave me purpose beyond a paycheck the way Orchestra Luna had. But this time around I was the one making the music. The farm was my orchestra and I was conducting a symphony in harmony with Nature. All of my skills for logistics and communications were put in service to my future as a farmer, and I had the feeling that nothing could stop me, because it was the right thing to do.

By the time I realized Chet had purchased chemically treated wood fence posts, he already had a few of them in the ground.

"We can't use chemicals because they're cheaper," I said. "That's the fallacy of cheap. We'll end up paying for those chemicals with our health and polluted water."

"I don't want to use them because they're cheap," he said. "They'll last longer. My time has value, too. You'll need two cedar posts over the life of a pressure treated post. In ten years, I'll be doing this all over again."

"We have to walk the talk, Chet. I can't tell people to farm one way and then break the rules on my own farm."

He was aghast. "What about me, Bil? Where do I fit into your rules?"

Still, he made the switch to cedar posts and wired them with the perfect symmetry of sheet music. It was a beautiful line drawing around the heart of the farm. When he hooked the fence to electricity at the barn, after a couple painful pops in the nose, the goats were safely contained. But the chickens walked right through the fence without getting a shock, as though they were stepping over dead wood. After all our planning and Chet's hard work, the fence did not contain our chickens.

"I can't fucking believe it," he said. "All that for nothing."

"It's not nothing," I said. "It's fabulous. You did a great job."

"Who gives a fuck." His jaws clenched in fury.

"I do. It's amazing. Having a fence like this opens up so many possibilities for the farm. This is huge."

"It's overkill. We're fools!"

"It may not keep the chickens in, but it will keep the predators out."

"Fuck me!" he yelled as he stomped off to the house. "Fuck!"

"It is a work of art, Chet," I called after him. "I love it!"

It took some research for us to learn what the chickens seemed to know instinctively. Feathers do not conduct electricity. Now we were farming with the wild in a way we never intended. I hung a clipboard on the wall of the chicken coop and every night we counted our chickens and wrote down the number. Our flock was slowly disappearing in the mouths of the predators that lived in the forest all around us.

~ : ~

"I'm going to take that job at the college," Chet said, putting his coffee mug in the sink. He had applied for a job as events manager at a liberal arts college in the Berkshires.

"Really?" I said, gathering up our dirty plates. We had just finished breakfast. "You like them?"

"They seem like pretty cool people and it pays really well. It's a fulltime gig and I get benefits. I've never had a job with benefits before."

"That's great," I said, loading the dishwasher.

"They have a marketing department. Maybe you could get a marketing gig with them."

"I'll check it out," I said. "But I think I have enough work going on right now with all this grant writing." I didn't want to work at the college. I wanted to work in agriculture. But I didn't say that.

"When I told the dean I lived on a farm he was impressed. I guess the students are interested in farming."

"Students get it," I said. "We've created a world where it's easier to get insulin than salad."

"You can't get rich making salad, Bil." He rolled his eyes.

"As Judy Garland said, 'You can't eat glamour for breakfast.'"

"You can't have it both ways." He put on his coat to take Henry out. "Either food is cheap enough for all of us to have some, or it's something to get rich on. But you can't feed the world and make money farming. My parents shit their pants when I told them we were selling eggs for $5 a dozen."

"We should be measuring our wealth in the cleanliness of our air and water."

"Who cares how much clean air you have if you don't have bling?"

"I care," I said, wiping off the countertop. "If the Chinese consume as much as we do, they'll need a planet of their own."

"You're not going to stop a global food fight."

"I'm not so sure about that." I looked out the window at the chickens running across the lawn. "When a butterfly flaps its wings here on the farm, the motion of the air ripples and amplifies around the world until it becomes a typhoon in China. That's the Butterfly Effect."

"Ha! Right," he laughed. "Maybe you could flap your wallet here on the farm and amplify the amount of money in our bank account."

"That's exactly what I'm trying to do," I said, throwing the sponge in the sink. "We need to find the balance between consumption and production."

"Great," he said, petting Henry's ears and hooking him to his leash. "I'm looking forward to it. Maybe you can find the balance between consuming and producing money."

"You mean the way the band did?" I strangled a dishtowel. "Because this is just like that. This farm is just as ridiculous as the band was."

"Yeah, I know." He opened the door to take Henry out, then he turned around and gave me a sharp look. "That's what scares me."

~ : ~

As a present to himself after he took the job at the college, Chet bought a rusty red 1986 Massey Ferguson tractor. It was a big toy and right away farm tasks were more fun. Riding around on the high seat behind the roar and rattle of the engine gave him dominion over the land. He channeled his dad and Wink and made sure he had all the right tools and knew how to change the attachments. The barn became his garage and he took a fresh interest in pasture management. He loved to use the brush mower. The meditative rhythm of mowing acre after acre relaxed him, and our weed infested pastures began to get grassy again.

We planned to get beef cows for a year before we wandered through a friend's herd and chose pregnant Ruby and her daughter, Ayla. It was July 2005. A month later we woke up to find Ruby had given birth during the night to a female calf we named Lisa. Chet and I came upon the two of them standing in the morning sun on the hill above the pond. Ayla meandered over to investigate her new sister. Then the goats joined us, nibbling at our clothes. Soon there were chickens scattered at our feet, scratching in the grass.

"Pretty cosmic," Chet said, sitting on a tree stump, watching Lisa take her first awkward steps.

"It's so beautiful," I whispered. "I feel like I'm living in a dream."

Sitting beside my husband on that tree stump, I felt a deep inner peace. The birth of the calf was the christening of our farm, our confirmation into a religious order. Cue the choir of angels. I could feel myself ascending into Heaven, riding a beam of golden light in biblical ecstasy. I believed in the idea of farming and our essential connection to Nature. In that moment I could feel the farm swelling inside of me. I felt complete. Our farm was a living being, an organism created by our shared experience. We were regenerating life. Everything I did on the farm had a larger significance. I gave myself to these ideas the way a nun marries the cross.

~ : ~

I bought Tea and Pinto, a pair of six-month-old black lambs, soon after Lisa was born. The two sheep were more difficult to manage because they were small and wild, but they seemed content to graze with the cows and they were unfazed by the bullying of the goats. As their wool coats darkened and filled out, their horns grew long and black, and our landscape was quite picturesque with three red cows, two white goats, two black sheep, and many multicolored chickens. Sometimes people stopped by the farm just to watch our animals graze.

Our first winter with a small herd of livestock brought a new set of chores on a more tightly wound clock. It was our first experience buying bales of hay and feeding hay to animals. Beginning in October

2005, each morning and each evening we carried bales of hay to the fence and threw them into the paddock by the barn. The ruminants gathered, tore at the bales with their teeth and filled their mouths with crunchy dry plants, scattering loose hay across the ground.

"I have a rehearsal tonight," Chet said as he threw a bale over the fence. He had met some local jazz musicians and begun to play music again.

"How are they?" I asked.

"It almost doesn't matter how well we play. It's just nice to hang out with guys my own age who like the music I like."

"Are you going to play clubs?"

"Probably."

"I hope so. It would be great to hear you play on stage."

"Yeah. I need to hear myself play on stage," he said. "I'm getting lost here."

"You're doing amazing things here, Chet. I love doing this with you."

"I love it, too. But it takes a lot of time."

"It would be a lot easier to feed the cows if we got a hay feeder and put it in front of the barn so we could just drop hay into the feeder. They wouldn't waste as much. I feel like I'm watching them waste money."

"They'll make it too muddy in front of the barn," he said. "I just got grass started there."

"Who cares about mud?"

"The tractor will get stuck. And — I don't want to look at it."

"You don't want to look at mud?"

"Yes," he said. "I don't want to look out the window at mud. Our barn is beautiful. I don't want mud in front of it."

"Well, I know what you mean about time," I said. "I need to start blowing through chores in the morning because I'm going to be working in Troy full time."

"That's great, Bil."

"It could be a regular paycheck for a while. Maybe a year."

"That's good news because both of our cars are going to need work, and I really don't want to put it on a credit card."

"I'm sorry this is so much financial pressure."

"I am, too," he said.

"Chet, I don't want to make a game of my life. I don't want to take the fastest, easiest route. I don't want to feel like I am always trying to get something."

"That sounds really good, Bil. I'm with you on that. But we have to live in the real world," he said. "You know, I get vacation time. I've been a freelancer my entire life. I'm 51 and this is the first job I've ever had in my life that pays vacation time. We haven't been on a real vacation since we went to Italy in 1997, before we bought the farm."

"Wow…" I said. "I can't even think about a vacation right now. I'm deep into this. I don't want to leave. Not now. Not when there are so many new things going on. I don't want to miss anything. I couldn't relax on a vacation right now."

"I could," he said. "I would love a vacation."

9. Pig Fever

During those first years of learning to care for animals on the farm, I was also learning to care for my mother again. Rosemary was a pretty gal who had few friends because she wore them out with her endless schemes, and few family members were willing to come near, because she always needed saving. About once a year we would get the call, her car broke down, her bank account was empty, her credit cards were cancelled, she was fired from her job, she had a mysterious illness, and she needed help. Of course, on some level I felt sorry for her. She was my mother. But her problems exhausted my goodwill, and when she visited the farm for the first time, I was wary because I knew she would have a plan for how it fit into her future. And she did.

"I could take the upstairs and you could have the downstairs," she said. "That way I could have my own bathroom."

"We need the upstairs for Chet's studio and the guest room," I said.

"I could move out of the guest room when you have guests."

"Mom, you can't live here. You need to have your own place."

When I was young, she was a good mother. Her skills, her sense of style and her imagination made her stand out from the other small town moms. She was a Girl Scout troop leader, president of the PTA, committee chair in the Women's Club, costume maker for the theater, Sunday school teacher, singer in the choir, and a card-carrying member of the Republican Party. Everyone knew her, so when my parents split, it was a public affair. Divorce was shameful in 1971 and she was publicly humiliated. My dad disappeared with his girlfriend into a deluxe apartment in Chicago, and my mom disintegrated. She sold our house and most everything in it, and before long she was broke, looking for handouts from her family.

The thing about Rosemary that was both her strength and her weakness was that she loved being the boss. Anyone in her company was her minion, and her three children were her army. There was no end to the list of tasks she planned for us. As soon as I was old enough to hold a spoon and stir, she taught me how to prepare food. By the time I was ten it was my job to cook dinner every Wednesday night. Twice a month she drove to the supermarket a half-hour away because she thought the grocery store in our town center was too expensive and didn't have a good selection. She planned 14 menus for breakfast, lunch and dinner, and how leftovers would be used from meal to meal. In the 1960s, two weeks of groceries for a family of five cost about $100 and filled the back of our station wagon. I was expected to learn this routine and know how to prepare the meals on the list.

In summers we had a large vegetable garden, and in fall Mom and I canned the harvest of tomatoes, corn, cucumbers, beets and beans. We put up sauces, soups, relishes, jams and jellies. Our basement shelves were lined with dozens of Ball jars, named and dated, some of them years old cherished family delicacies.

Because our vegetable garden was so important to our food supply my brothers and I were required to tend the plants. Weeding and watering were chores that had to be done before we could go out and play. She tried to make it interesting. She taught us how to tie off gourds with string to give them funny shapes, and to encourage us to grow our own pumpkins and melons, she gave us prizes for the ones that weighed the most.

My dad, my grandfathers and my uncles hunted for food, and brought home the carcasses of deer, pheasant, ducks, geese and rabbits. Mom taught me how to pack and wrap game meat, labeled and dated for our freezer.

Cheese was orange, butter was oleomargarine, bread was white and spongy, Jell-O was considered a salad, and we cooked with lard until we discovered Crisco. To get fresh milk twice a week, the local milkman delivered milk to our house. He was a dairy farmer and the name on the milk bottle was the same as the name on the silo of his farm. We put a handwritten sign in our front window at night saying how much milk we wanted, and we put our empty bottles in a crate on the front porch. When we got up in the morning the empties were gone, and our fresh milk was there.

There was no question that many of the skills I brought to our farm in the Berkshires I had learned from my mother. But I did not want to live near her. She had already declared bankruptcy twice. The first time was a joint effort with her second husband, a widowed veteran with one leg and seven children. She thought he was rich because he had been in the military, he wore velour suits and drove a Cadillac. He thought she was rich because she acted like it, she had gone to college and she had a closet full of evening gowns. They met at a Parents Without Partners fundraiser and discovered they both loved to dance. Our family begged her not to marry him, but she was lonely, and she really wanted to have a party.

After they were married, he left the house every morning to go to work as an insurance man "salaried" on 100% commission. She thought 100% was a lot of money. "It's the most you can get," she said. One day she discovered him having afternoon coffee at the local diner and heard a waitress call him the king. The waitress was annoyed because he spent all day there, five days a week, and never bought more than a cup of coffee. A few years into their marriage, when the repo guys showed up to take the king's new TV from the living room and the king had them take my mom's new refrigerator instead, she finally decided to divorce him and declare bankruptcy.

The second time she declared bankruptcy it was her own achievement. With the help of the credit card offers that arrived in the mail daily after her first bankruptcy, she hit her maximum debt load in just a few years. Once again, all her credit cards were full, all her payments past due, and she was without a steady job, forced into bankruptcy court again.

It's not that she was lazy. She worked hard at odd jobs here and there, as a cashier, a hostess, a receptionist, a janitor. But she wasn't able to earn a paycheck for very long before her difficult personality got in the way, and she was fired. I had been willing to mail her money for most of my adult life, but I had kept a thousand miles between us. Then right around the time Chet's dad, Maurice, was dying in 2001, she showed up at the farm.

I think Maurice's death made me more susceptible to my mother's plea to be included in my life. I couldn't shun her so easily with the memory of human mortality so fresh in my mind. She was 71 years old. I helped her find an apartment an hour from the farm, and while I was learning to manage livestock, I was also learning how to handle living near my mother for the first time since I was a teenager.

~ : ~

My brothers drove a rented truck full of my mom's stuff from Waukesha, Wisconsin to Pittsfield, Massachusetts. Along with her furniture, she brought 183 boxes itemized on a list she wrote in pencil on a yellow legal pad and carried with her on a clipboard. She also brought rolls of used chicken wire from her garden, broken lawn chairs, dirty camping equipment, a set of four tires she trash-picked because they looked like they would fit her car, a bicycle with a bent wheel, and an extra bed frame, even though she was moving into a one bedroom apartment on the second floor. The landlord provided pallets for her boxes in the basement and the stacks went from floor to ceiling.

Her boxes were no surprise. We knew she kept them. They were her obsession. But we had never seen them all in one place. Over the years when she didn't have space for all of them, her parents and her sisters kept her boxes in their basements. Friends and landlords had held them for her when she moved again. At times her boxes were spread out across the countryside of Illinois and Wisconsin, but she always knew where all of them were, and she had gathered them all for the trek to Massachusetts, where she intended to keep them with her.

On the day she arrived in Pittsfield, my brothers and Chet and I dutifully unloaded the truck and stacked her boxes in her landlord's basement. At her request, someone pounded a nail into a wooden post, and she hung the clipboard. We rolled our eyes, but it wasn't even worth discussing. This was Rosemary. We knew her. We didn't expect anything different.

~ : ~

For the first couple years, I enjoyed visiting her apartment and taking her to see the sights in the Berkshires. She had her own car, found her way around, joined a church, and grew vegetables in a community garden. Then she decided to have a new vegetable garden on the lawn around her landlord's house. That's when her deterioration began to show. She was a very experienced vegetable gardener, but she planted her new garden in the shade of the maple tree at the end of the driveway on a barren patch of dirt dense with tree roots. Not long after that, our bank called me. She had bounced 23 consecutive checks.

"Mom, this is junk mail," I said, standing in the living room of her apartment going through her mail. "These are not bills. Stop sending these people checks."

"I have to pay them," she said. "I owe them money. If I don't owe them money, why did they give me an envelope?"

"It's a trick. They're trying to trick you."

"I owe them $10 a month. It says so right here."

"This is advertising!" I yelled. "This is not a bill!"

She got tears in her eyes and I felt really shitty for yelling, so I took her out to lunch. And so it went. We made her checking account a joint account so I could manage her finances. She got food stamps and had a benefits card in addition to her Social Security payments. I gave her cash and made sure her bills were paid, and the situation was manageable for another year. She even had Chet and me over for a candlelight dinner.

"Rosemary, this is delicious," Chet said. "What's in the sauce?"

"It's water," she said. "I ran out of cream."

We were supposed to be eating creamed asparagus on toast, one of her favorite meals when I was a child.

In the car on the way home, Chet said, "I hope we don't ever have to do that again."

I laughed. "Pretty gross, huh."

"Oh, my god, Bill!" He was laughing, too. "That's the grossest thing I've ever eaten!"

"You didn't have to eat it."

"Right."

"Come on, Chet. You didn't have to eat it."

"It's your mom, Bil. It's your mom."

"I know. I know."

"It was easier to smile and eat boiled water on toast than to say anything."

"It was hideous." I laughed. "I'm so sorry."

"Well, consider it payback for my mother's instant potatoes and powdered gravy."

~ : ~

Within weeks of her arrival in the Berkshires, Chet became the representative man in her life, and the magnet for her strategic helplessness. "Chet, would you carry this upstairs for me?" "Chet, would you take this out to my car?" "Chet, next time you go to the store would you please buy me some AA batteries?" "Chet, would you please fix this for me?" He did what she asked, he never complained, and he took every opportunity to avoid her. But he was always kind.

On a visit to the farm when he and I were debating how to stack firewood, she whispered loudly to me, "Don't use that tone of voice with him. You're too bossy. You have to make him feel like a man."

"Yeah, Bil," Chet snickered. "Don't use that tone of voice with me."

"Really, Mom," I said. "You're giving me advice about men?"

"I know how to make a man feel needed," she said. "You don't."

Then it happened. One day she was driving around the Berkshires and couldn't remember where home was. A kind man rescued her and delivered her to her apartment. He found my phone number on my business card in her purse and he called to tell me what had happened.

He was a car salesman, and when he closed up the dealership showroom for the night, she was sitting in a chair looking out the window. She didn't know where she lived. He got her address from her car license plate, left her car at the dealership, and drove her home. That made it convenient for me to sell her car. Afterward it became my responsibility to visit her apartment a couple times a week to see how she was doing. Between visits she left me voice mail.

"Billie, this is your mom, Rosemary. I want you to bring me five yards of white cotton. Polished, not coarse. Not the cheap stuff. I need a dust ruffle for my bed. Bring it Tuesday when you come. And don't forget my 7-Up and prunes. I haven't had a good bowel movement in a week. Thank you, sweetheart. See you Tuesday."

Some days she left several voice mail messages in a row.

"Billie, this is your mom, Rosemary. Don't forget I want my encyclopedias when you come."

"Billie, this is your mom, Rosemary. I don't have any money. Can you bring me $5? I need deodorant."

"Billie, this is your mom, Rosemary. When you and Chet come, tell him to bring his electric drill. I have some pictures I want to hang."

"Billie, this is your mom, Rosemary. I can't find my American flag. I need a flag I can wave. Maybe you can buy me one. I'd like it here by Saturday morning."

~ : ~

We bumped along for a few more months, until it seemed dangerous. Her housekeeping skills were disappearing along with her logic.

"What's that smell?" I asked, looking around her kitchen.

"I don't want the meat to get moldy," she said.

"Where's the meat?"

She pointed to the cupboard above the countertop. The white paper wrapper said she had purchased five pounds of pork chops a few days earlier. There were nine left, nine pork chops stored at room temperature, gently culturing other life forms in my mother's kitchen cupboard.

"I didn't want the meat to get moldy," she repeated, looking at the refrigerator.

When I opened the refrigerator door the stench of cabbagey gas filled the room. Inside blue green filaments stretched from a pot of wooly soup to slimy vegetables. A wedge of orange cheese was coated with grey fur and a loaf of bread was blotched with blue. It had not occurred to me to check her refrigerator every time I visited, and I had missed a significant warning sign.

She had unplugged the refrigerator and pulled it away from the wall so she could sprinkle powdered insecticide on the floor where ants were eating spilled sugar. The canister of insecticide sat on the kitchen counter labeled "for outdoor use only." Mice left a trail of tiny turds through the sugar into a hole chewed in the side of the cabinet where they had made a nest in an empty box of Grape Nuts. When I threw the cereal box into the wastebasket a mouse fell out and ran away.

"I have to eat that to keep my bowels moving," she said, fishing the box out of the wastebasket.

"I'll buy you some more," I said, putting the box back in the trash.

~ : ~

Three years after she moved to the Berkshires, in the summer of 2004, I found my mother a room in an assisted living facility where she would not have a kitchen, and she would have 24-hour supervision. To get the facility to accept her, I had to apply for government assistance on her behalf. A social worker helped me complete the forms that qualified her to receive supplemental income from the government as long as she followed certain rules. Chet and I moved her into her new room, but she was resistant, and shortly after she arrived, I got called to the social worker's office for a meeting about my mom's behavior.

The social worker said, "This is an assisted living facility. We keep track of the kinds of assistance our clients require in order to get reimbursed by the government. If your mother doesn't accept assistance, I can't fill out the monthly assistance form for her, and they won't give us money for her care, and she won't be able to stay here."

"Is something wrong?" I asked.

"She refused to let the aid wash her hair," the social worker said.

I turned to my mother. "Please, Mom, let them wash your hair."

"It doesn't matter how my hair looks," she said. "No one here looks at me."

"Of course, it matters how you look," I said. "How we look is a reflection of how we feel."

"Well, I feel better when I don't have someone watching me in the shower."

"Mom, just let them help you zip your dress or wash your back."

"If I wash my back it itches and then I have to put cream on it, and cream costs money," she said. "You're always telling me I don't have any money. So why do you want them to wash my back?"

The social worker pursed her lips and frowned.

"Mom, this is the nicest place you're ever going to live. If you screw this up, I don't know what will happen to you."

"I'll be just fine," she said. "God will take care of me. I don't want to shower three times a week. I wash up at the sink."

The social worker said, "Your mother told me she lifts her feet up into the bathroom sink to wash them."

"I do," my mom said smugly. "The sink is too high, but I do it anyway."

The look of skepticism on the social worker's face scared me. "Please," I said. "Please let her stay here. Before she came here, she sprinkled insecticide on the kitchen floor to kill the ants that were crawling all over because she spilled sugar and never cleaned it up. She burned stuff on the stove and then burned up the countertops. She wasn't safe." I turned and looked at my mother. "Mom, you have to accept some kind of assistance. What's it going to be?"

"I'd like to have my hair done before church on Sunday."

"Fine," said the social worker. "I'll have the assistant come to your apartment at 7:30 on Sunday morning."

"I don't want them telling me when to wash my face."

"They are there to be sure you don't fall," I said.

"I'm not going to fall," she said. "And if I do, I'll get up."

I smiled at the social worker. "I think it'll be easier to assist her if we don't try to make such specific plans." Then I hustled my mother back to her apartment where she plopped down into her armchair in a huff.

"Okay," she said, in a tone I knew too well. "How incompetent do I have to appear to be, and how are we going to make it believable?"

"You don't have to pretend anything, Mom. Just let them assist you. This is an assisted living facility. If you don't require assistance the government won't pay for you to stay here."

"I don't need assistance."

"You don't need physical assistance. But you do need the supervision of the staff here."

"This morning when I took a shower the girl just stood there and handed me my towel."

"That's fine," I said. "That's all they have to do."

"That's asinine."

"I know it's asinine, but that's how the government works."

"I can't believe you told her I have memory problems. What have I been forgetting?"

"When we were at the doctor's office you said I was your sister."

"That's because I was intimidated by the doctor. Sometimes I'm so frightened by authority it's hard for me to speak. I don't even know what I said in that doctor's office. I was terrified."

"Mom, I have to go now. I have to get back to the farm." I headed toward the door.

"Okay, sweetheart," she said, pointing at her waste basket. "Don't forget to take my garbage with you when you go."

~ : ~

The yellow legal pad still hung from that nail in the basement, and most of the 183 boxes were right where we had stacked them on the day she moved in. She had a box for each year from 1948, when she graduated from high school, to 2001 when she arrived in the Berkshires. That 50 years was itemized in a box per year, each containing a record of the seminal events of her life, the greeting cards and letters, her college graduation, her wedding, her children's school report cards and homework, invitations and thank you notes, calendars and cancelled checks, tax records and invoices, newspaper clippings and postcards, thousands of pages, the data points in her accounting of herself.

I started out opening each box and looking at each piece of paper, but after a few hours I went numb. It was the history of our whole family she had saved, but I was there in that basement by myself. There was no whole family. There hadn't been a whole family for 30 years. No one was interested in this detritus. We all had lives of our own. The things she had saved didn't represent us anymore. Those boxes represented her. She was in those boxes.

There were a couple dozen boxes of Christmas decorations and Easter baskets. She had saved our children's toys and some ratty dolls I didn't recognize. There were boxes of board games and dominoes. Her wedding dress was crumpled into itself with some dried flowers and a lot of mouse poo. She had enough camping gear for a Girl Scout troop. One box held dozens of pairs of pantyhose, each worn once or twice then bunched into twin nylon rosettes and stashed in the box. Evidently, she had subscribed to a service that mailed her ten pairs of pantyhose every month and automatically charged her credit card.

Another box was filled with bars of used soap, smooth pastel chips that had lost their scent and split into waxy shards, used eye shadow and face powder in decorative compacts, used tubes of lipstick in all the fashionable shades, and many, many empty perfume bottles. There was a box of broken jewelry and another filled with buttons, and another filled with zippers and sewing trimmings, and another filled with cake decorations and plastic flowers. And she had four complete sets of encyclopedias in brand new condition, each one purchased by a subscription that was automatically charged to her credit card.

Several boxes were filled with Amway products. She was an Amway distributor and believed she was going to get rich selling their catalog of products to people in her community. But most of all she liked going to Amway conventions where top sellers were awarded big prizes on a ballroom stage before an audience of men and women in eveningwear. Rosemary loved a fancy night out in a long dress with a tiny purse and matching gloves. Her association with Amway promised a bright future even though she was her own biggest customer. She bought inventory she couldn't sell to maintain the sales volume required for her distributor's discount, until her credit cards were cancelled, and Amway bid her a fond farewell.

For the first time in my life I saw my mother as mentally ill, clutching the artifacts of her identity, desperate for belonging, prone to dishonesty, unable to calibrate her behavior to her surroundings. She had a princess wedding with a lace gown and men in white dinner jackets. She had graduated from college and lived in a three-bedroom house with beautiful gardens, a husband, and her children playing in the yard. She was a leader in her community, and a mother active in the school system. And she had lost all of it in a catastrophe of rejection. Looking at the trail of evidence, I couldn't be angry with her anymore.

~ : ~

Eventually, she got kicked out of the assisted living facility for wandering. First, she wandered into other people's apartments and couldn't find her own. Then she wandered around the parking lot looking for her car. Then they put her on half-hour watch, locating her every 30 minutes and writing her location in a logbook. Regardless, sometime after 5:30 in the morning she managed to escape and walked two miles down the highway to a landscaping nursery where the employees found her shopping for plants when they arrived for work at 7:00 am.

The state police brought her back to the assisted living facility and the director gave me one week to find a new place to put her. He said it was for her safety. The truth was that she was no longer in compliance with their insurance policy, and she took too much of the staff's time. The staff was watching out for her when they should have been taking care of someone else. They were covering for her incompetence, hiding it from their supervisors because they thought she was cute, and because they knew what I didn't know. They knew what came next.

I picked the nursing home closest to the farm, and they put her in the memory care unit, a locked hospital ward with a nurses' station in the center circled by a wide corridor. Each room had two beds with plastic covered mattresses and bedside tables on wheels. Every surface was made to be sanitized. Glass, scissors and other sharp objects were not allowed. Residents were asleep in chairs in the hallways or roamed about aimlessly and jabbered in doorways.

My mother would never again be allowed to leave home without a chaperone. She would never again be allowed to have china teacups or a crystal vase. Her name would be written on all her clothes and all her clothes would have to be machine washable. She would share a room with someone who was unable to converse, and she would share meals with people who wore bibs and drooled. Her food would be tasteless mush and her toiletries would be dispensed by a nurse's aide.

"Why am I here? I don't live here."

"I know," I said. "Let's just see what the doctor has to say."

"There's nothing wrong with me," she said. "I don't live here."

"The doctor says you need to be here for a little while."

"Someone told me I live here now."

"I guess we'll have to wait and see what the doctor says."

"Why am I here? I don't live here. I want to go home."

"It's just for a little while," I said. "You can go home when the doctor says so."

"I don't live here."

"No, you don't live here. We're waiting to see the doctor."

"What doctor? I haven't seen any doctors. The doctor told me I'm just fine and I should go home now."

"You can go home in a little while."

"I can't believe you're doing this to me."

~ : ~

I cried and flogged myself for betraying my mother's trust, but I didn't know what else to do. I was stretched for time between my consulting gigs, farm chores, selling eggs and keeping house. Chet was busy managing events at the college, doing farm chores, painting the house, going to band rehearsals and playing the occasional jazz gig.

My mother was a danger to herself and her neighbors. She no longer qualified for assisted living. She could not remember how to take care of herself and I could not care for her at my house and work full time and manage the farm. And I didn't want to. I had to admit I did not want to devote my life to caring for my mother.

"Stop blaming yourself," Chet said. "When you're feeling guilty about her, just remember the gun."

"That was anomalous," I said.

"Don't bullshit yourself," he said. "Our lives could be a lot different now."

Long before she went to the nursing home, when she was still in her one-room apartment in the assisted living facility, I was planning to bring her to the farm for the weekend, so she had packed a suitcase. When I picked her up, before we left her apartment, I wanted to be sure she had packed warm socks, so I opened the suitcase. There on top of her pastel undies was a .38 caliber handgun.

"It's not loaded," she said.

I popped open the revolver. It was loaded with five bullets.

"I lost the other one," she said, referring to the empty sixth chamber.

This handgun had been hidden in one place or another for most of my childhood. Our house had been robbed in the 1960s while we were away visiting my grandparents for the weekend. After that my dad bought the handgun for protection. Each of us knew how to use it and usually we knew where it was hidden. I had not seen it since high school when my mother was feeling anxious and slept with it under her pillow.

I unloaded the gun and put the bullets in my pocket and the gun in my purse.

"That's mine," she said with stubborn authority.

A chill ran through me one tingle at a time and the hair on my neck stood up so high I could feel it in my ears.

"Yes, I know," I said. "I'll carry it."

"It's mine," she said. "Give it to me."

"Let's go get some ice cream." I smiled and took her hand, and we drove to Friendly's.

As I licked my chocolate fudge swirl, my brain was zooming from room to room in my recent past trying to figure out where my mother could have hidden the revolver. When we moved her from Wisconsin to the apartment in the Berkshires, I thought I went through all her stuff. Then when we moved her to the one-room apartment in assisted living, I thought I went through all of it again. I sorted each item we packed for her, and Chet and I moved her ourselves. I thought I touched all her stuff again when we unpacked her clothes and arranged her furniture in her new room — a bed, a chair, a table, a dresser and a nightstand. The gun was obviously very well hidden. But where? How did I miss it? What made her remember it now? Why was she bringing it to the farm? When did she load it?

89

"We're never going to know," Chet said. "But I don't see how it could have been a good thing."

"Maybe she was bringing it to me for safe keeping," I said.

"If she was giving it to you for safe keeping, it would not have been loaded."

"We don't know that. She may have had good intentions."

"But we don't know that."

"It's my mom, Chet. I want to think the best of her."

"Think what you want," he said. "But never forget what might have happened."

~ : ~

After my mom was admitted to the nursing home memory care unit, I had another meeting with another social worker.

"Physically she's completely healthy," I said. "She isn't on any medication. She eats well. She can bend over and tie her shoes. When she ran away, she walked two miles. I know she can be difficult, but I don't want the staff here managing her moods with drugs. I've heard that happens in nursing homes, and frankly, everyone here looks over-medicated."

"I'll make a note on her file and tell the nurses," the social worker said.

"I don't want her doped up just so you can manage her more easily."

The woman raised an eyebrow at me. "Do you ever have a glass of wine when you come home from work?" she asked.

"Sure. Of course, I do," I said.

"And why do you do that?"

"To chill out and relax. Obviously."

"Well, we can't give your mother a glass of wine. But we can give her some medication that will take the edge off her mood. Do you object to that?"

"I want to be kept informed of her condition. I don't want her being given any medication without my permission. And I especially don't want you tinkering with her memory now that she's here. The last thing

I want is for her memory to wake up and for her to realize she is trapped here."

Months earlier I had taken my mom to see a neurologist, a young doctor with a new private practice. After we looked at her brain scans on the computer, the doctor suggested we give her drugs to improve her memory. She opened a closet behind her desk and perused a stash of pharmaceutical samples. I imagined the pharmaceutical salesman hosting a free lunch for the local healthcare professionals while he presented a promotional video of the company's research and a slideshow of all the benefits of their magic pills.

The neurologist said, "Let's experiment with—" I don't remember what drug she named, but it was in colorful packaging like the medicine on TV commercials. She read the label out loud as if to remind herself what it was.

"What will it do?" I asked.

"It will improve her memory… Marginally," she said. "Memory drugs typically work for limited lengths of time and then you have to change them. The effects of this one could help your mother for several months. But it will be about a month before we see any results. If it works."

"What are the side effects?"

"It will upset her stomach, so she'll have to take it with meals. Nausea is a common side effect of most of the drugs that would help her. In extreme cases, it could cause kidney failure."

"But she's completely healthy except for her memory. Why would I give her a pill that would make her sick?"

"To improve her memory for a few more months."

"If it works."

"We aren't going to know unless we try."

"So, we are experimenting on her."

"To a certain extent."

"If I were her, I wouldn't want it. I wouldn't want to be nauseous every day for months on the chance that my memory could be temporarily improved. Being nauseated is miserable. What's worth remembering about that? It will just make her feel sick and right now she believes she's healthy. Besides she can live without her memory, but she can't live without her kidneys."

"Kidney failure is unlikely in your mother's case."

"Using the pills isn't going to create good memories," I said. "It's just making her sick for a few months before she continues forgetting. I think she would rather be as healthy as she can be. At least her body feels good. And frankly, since she doesn't remember what she's forgetting, she's perfectly happy with how things are."

"It could make her more manageable," the doctor said. "It could allow you to keep her in assisted living for a few more months. I'll write you a prescription and you can decide if you want to fill it."

I never filled that prescription.

In the nursing home, when I told the social worker that story, she said, "You're doing the right thing."

"Am I?" I asked. "It doesn't feel like it. It feels like putting my mother in prison. I don't know whether to help her remember or help her forget."

"She's safe here."

"She's physically safe. Is she mentally safe? She seems to be functioning at a much higher level than everyone here. Isn't being with these people all day just going to hasten her demise?"

"She will get a lot of attention here because she is high functioning."

"Why isn't there a better place? Why does she have to go from assisted living to this, this snake pit? Why isn't there a nice place where people will watch her and just make sure she doesn't disappear?"

"You might find a place like that if you lived near a big city where there are more options. In the Berkshires these are the only options we have."

"But she doesn't need the medical staff, or the therapists, or the nurses. She isn't on any medication. She can dress herself and feed herself. She just needs someone to keep track of her and cook and clean for her."

"We have what government programs fund."

"But this must be really expensive. She doesn't need all this infrastructure and overhead. She could live in a place that doesn't cost this much to operate."

"I know what you're saying. You could write your congressman. But that's about it. This is the system."

~ : ~

I made a point of being visible at the nursing home and learning the names of the employees, but there was a very high turnover among the staff, and it was hard to keep track of who was in charge. Sometimes when I visited, no one seemed to be in charge. Sometimes there were no nurses on the floor. And there never seemed to be a doctor anywhere. The memory care unit was more like a warehouse than healthcare.

I went through my mom's closet and drawers to be sure her stuff was all there. When things were missing, I complained at the nurse-less nurses' desk. The women were nice, but they shrugged me off. At first, I was angry. But after a few visits I understood. My mother was becoming one of the animals in the zoo. I brought her pictures of me and my brothers and hung them on her walls, and I brought her fresh flowers. I did her nails and styled her hair and took her out for ice cream, and for a while every time I brought her back to the nursing home, we had the same discussion.

"Where are we?"

"We're just going in for a minute."

"I don't live here. I want to go home."

"You can go home as soon as the doctor says it's okay."

"The food here stinks."

"I know. It's just for a little while."

And it was just for a while. Soon her ladyhood disappeared, she forgot she was a mother, and the clothes she wore were not her own. She slept in the nearest bed and wore the nearest pair of shoes. She read magazines out loud in the TV room, while the TV blared, and no one seemed to notice. Occasionally she wet her pants, but no one really knew why. Maybe she couldn't find the bathroom. Maybe she kept forgetting she had to go until she went. It didn't matter. They tried to keep a diaper on her, but she refused to wear it. Once I tried to help her use the bathroom and after she washed her hands, she wiped them dry on a dirty diaper someone had left sitting beside the sink. This was the hell hole that gives us nightmares about getting old. But it was the best place I could find that would accept my mother.

~ : ~

To distract myself I dreamed about the future of our farm. It was part of my job at a nonprofit to produce education programs for farmers. Pastured pork was a hot topic and I went on a few farm tours that showed how different pig farms operated. That got me fantasizing about how I could have my own pigs, and I began making plans for a piggery on our farm. I thought I would buy a heritage breed sow and sell her offspring. Then one night Chet caught me sitting at my desk looking at pig porn online — pictures of Tamworths, a very old breed known for its bacon.

"What are you doing?" he asked. "We can't have pigs. Do you know what they'll do to the grass?"

"I've heard they really like orchards."

"We don't have an orchard."

"There's that apple tree across the road. We could put them over there."

"That apple tree isn't on our land."

"We could keep them in the woods behind the barn. Then we could connect their fence to the paddock."

"Fence!" he snapped. "I can't believe you even said that."

"They have to be fenced," I said.

His eyes bulged at me and his face blushed fire. "We are not getting pigs."

"You can make a lot of money selling pork."

"What the fuck!" he yelled, sending sparks of saliva into my desk light. "Pork is not pigs! Buy some pork chops if you want pork."

"I was thinking we could grow our own. You can get a really good price for organic bacon."

"Jesus Christ, Bil." He had tears in his eyes. "It's like you have Pig Fever. You're insane."

"I know," I said. "If you had told me when I was 13 that I was going to be a pig farmer, I would have slit my wrists."

"Pig farmer? You are not going to be a pig farmer!" he yelled again. "Get real! This is fucked up. It's like you've become your mother. You seem to have a genetic disability to manage money."

"Shit."

I shut down my computer and never mentioned pigs again. Sometime after that Chet started psychotherapy.

10. Band Reunion

By 2006 we were different people than the Boston couple who had bought a country house on an abandoned farm in 1998. Maurice had died, my mother had moved to the Berkshires, I had studied agriculture and begun to work for nonprofits, Chet had taken the job at the college, and we had become livestock farmers. Since her return to my life, my mother's health had deteriorated from independence in an apartment to assisted living to confinement in a nursing home. And I was the matriarch in charge of it all, organizing, planning, dreaming and scheming.

Those were the years I came into my power as a woman. I wasn't striving, climbing, or looking to be somewhere else. I had finally arrived in the place I wanted to be, driving the magnificent she machine inside myself, fully confident in my accomplishments and my abilities, independent and self-directed. I wasn't measuring myself by money anymore. I was having impact. I could see it on the land, I could see it in my animals, I could sense it in the eyes of others, I could hear it in my voice. It was a very good feeling. I was 52 years old and for the first time in my life I had everything I wanted — the house, the man, the work, the mission.

Running the farm took a few hours every day, if nothing went wrong — if the cows didn't get out of the fence, if the hose didn't freeze, if the coyotes didn't kill the chickens, if the tractor started, if we had enough hay. I was writing grants and research reports for agriculture programs and circulating my own opinion pieces. One long diatribe of mine entitled "Return to Slavery: Will you be eating China's dust for breakfast?" opened doors for me as a speaker on college campuses. My schedule was full, but my income was about a quarter of what I had earned as a marketing consultant before I started farming. To finance my operations, I was spending Chet's paycheck.

He was busy at the college managing their events, swimming at the pool every morning, eating lunch in the cafeteria, going to weekly appointments with his therapist, and playing jazz on weekends. His early enthusiasm for a salary was dampened by the bureaucratic experience of academia. He had discovered that his job wasn't really about show business. It was just business. He was behind the scenes, doing the work to make someone else's show possible. When the flurry of emails about a band reunion landed in his inbox, he was energized. His band mates from the 1970s and 80s, the musicians who had been members of Orchestra Luna, Luna and Berlin Airlift, were planning a band reunion at a club in Boston for the last weekend in January 2006.

"I'm looking forward to turning up the volume," he said.

"I think it's going to be a lot of fun," I said. "I wish I could go."

"You have to go, Bil." He seemed shocked. "It's the band. You have to go."

"I don't think I can leave here. Not now. Who would take care of everything?"

"Bil, it's the band. You are as much a part of it as everyone else. You have to go."

We had several long conversations about it. He seemed to really want me to go. Then just when I had figured out how to manage the trip, he changed his mind and agreed that I should stay. I stayed on the farm and Chet went to the band reunion alone. Or so I thought. Years later I would learn that he changed his mind about me going because he had arranged to spend the weekend with the Juicer.

~ : ~

After the band reunion, he began to put in very long hours at the college. I went to bed before he did. He got up in the morning after me. I did farm chores by myself. He stopped eating our eggs for breakfast and ate most of his meals in the college cafeteria. My car died and I didn't replace it. That meant I was trapped at home when he was away. I couldn't drive to meet him somewhere or show up unexpectedly at his office or a gig. I rode with him to his jazz gigs and fell asleep in the car on the way home. Sometimes I fell asleep in my chair in the audience.

"You need your own car," he said. "This is embarrassing to have only one car. I don't want to share a car with you."

"I don't want to spend money on a car," I said. "If I'm going to blow $20,000, I'm going to blow it on the farm."

"That's crazy!"

"It's not crazy. There are a lot of things I want to do around here, and they all cost money. Besides we're doing the planet a favor. We'll drive less."

"I don't want to drive less."

"Okay, I'll drive less. You do what you want. You take the car and I'll stay here. If I need to go somewhere, I'll figure it out."

"Bil, you can't stay here without a car."

"Yes, I can."

It wasn't easy. I had to be super organized with my time and I had to ask his permission to use the car. I asked friends for rides, and now and then, I had to rent a car to get to an appointment for work. But for the most part I didn't mind not having my own car. I liked staying on the farm night and day. The farm was my research project. Nature was my subject, and I intended to become a master of the systems I was managing. Animal behavior was all around me and I wanted to be absorbed into it, to fully experience it, to be tied to the sun and live like an animal on the land. I didn't need a car to do that.

~ : ~

Our cell phones didn't always work in the Berkshire hills and Chet was often not at his desk to answer email or the phone. I usually spent all day outside on the farm. Long stretches of time passed without us speaking. Then he announced he was working on a new documentary with colleagues from Boston and he left on Saturday mornings for a series of weekend film shoots. For a while, I was by myself seven days a week without a car.

I thought I was handling the chill in our marriage until he refused to have sex with me. That had never happened before. It was complicated. I was embarrassed. I knew being aggressive was the wrong response. He hid his face and mumbled something about being depressed. I told myself erectile dysfunction was a normal occurrence. But I had never been pushed away by a man.

To get us back in sync with each other I planned a summer road trip. Driving long distance, listening to music and talking was something we had always enjoyed doing together. Finally, I had enough confidence in my farming skills to leave the farm for a week. In the summer of 2006 friends from Boston stayed in our house and took care of the animals while Chet and I toured the Adirondacks and Lake Champlain. I made hotel reservations and researched restaurants. But on the drive, he wanted to listen to music in silence. He had no interest in talking to me.

In our motel room we sat in bed together and watched movies, but we didn't chat. We didn't kiss. We didn't touch. He didn't look at me and I didn't want to provoke him. We stood on mountaintops and pondered the horizon together, but he wasn't there with me. The vacation I thought would bring us together instead only confirmed the distance between us.

On the drive home anxiety was welling in me. "I feel like you've fallen out of love with me," I said. "I'm an old shoe."

He tightened his lips and kept his eyes on the road while I cried.

"Please talk to me," I begged. "Please tell me what you're thinking. Please tell me what's happening to us. I don't understand. I didn't think this was possible."

He didn't answer.

~ : ~

For a year, the year 2007 — a year I don't remember very well because I worked so hard at hiding myself — I was as humble, cheerful and subservient as I could manage to be. I avoided talking about the farm, made his favorite foods, and played his favorite music in the house. I minimized my need for the car and tried to do all the farm work by myself so he would hardly notice we lived on a farm. I took every gig I could get to make as much money as I could. I tried to look good. At the end of the day I changed out of my farm duds and put on sexy clothes. I asked him how his day went, complimented his bass playing, and let him come and go as he pleased. But something was feeding his hostility toward me. I could hear it in his voice. For the first time in 30 years, he had a short fuse.

"Bil!" He barked at the kitchen sink. "How many times do I have to tell you to keep the sink strainer in the drain? You're going to let all those food scraps clog the sink and then I'm the one who has to fix it."

"I tilt it like that because when the water runs out, it pulls the plug down and blocks the flow."

He gave me a nasty look. "Maybe if you weren't so lame, you could figure out a way around that."

"*Lame?*" I stopped scraping crud off the stove and turned to face him. "Did you just call me *lame?*"

"You heard me."

My head exploded and I shook with the release of emotions bottled up for months. "Are you fucking kidding me? *LAME!?* If there is one thing I am not, it's *lame.* I may be pushy, bombastic and myopic. But I am not fucking lame! Where does that word even come from? That is not a word you use. Who are you? Even your vocabulary is a stranger to me."

"I don't know who I am," he said taken aback. "I really don't know."

"What does your therapist say?" I dried my hands and put all my attention on him.

"She says you're a boss cow and I need to assert myself."

"Your therapist called me a boss cow?"

"Not exactly," he said. "I called you a boss cow."

"You think I'm a boss cow?"

"That's your archetype."

"What a shitty thing to say."

"But you get my point."

"If I'm a boss cow, what does that make you?"

"A concierge."

"That's your archetype, a concierge?"

"That's what it feels like."

"Really, this is what you talk about in therapy — the boss cow and the concierge?"

"Yup."

"Holy fuck."

He sat down at the kitchen counter and dropped his head in his hands. "Everything I do every day is for somebody else. Everything I care about is shoved to the side so I can make other people happy."

"Maybe you need to have an affair or something to boost your ego." I was trying to be funny.

He sat upright and looked startled, arched an eyebrow at me, and shook himself.

"Chet, I'm just kidding," I said, seeing his confusion. "You choose the life you want to have. You don't have to be a concierge. Stop doing things for other people. Things can be different."

"I don't see how."

I put my arm around him and kissed the side of his face. "Things are a state of mind. You choose what you do, and you choose how you feel about it."

"It doesn't feel like I have a choice. I feel trapped."

"You are not trapped. You are not my concierge. We are partners. I love you." I hugged him. "I want you to be happy. I want you to be happy with me. I don't want to fight with you. I'm trying really hard to please you, but I feel shut out."

"I know you're trying," he said, dropping his head in his hands again. "I'm just really depressed. Nothing is what I thought it would be."

That was the end of our discussion. I kissed him on the forehead and went back to cleaning the kitchen. I didn't want to alienate him by being critical. It never crossed my mind that there was another woman in the background twisting my husband's heart. At this point they had been having an affair for almost two years and she had him by the balls. I felt sorry for him because he was sad. I made excuses for him because he seemed lost. I was high on farming and, with the exception of my marriage, quite happy with my life. He was depressed. I told myself that people get depressed. A midlife crisis was a normal thing for a man in his 50s. I believed he would figure it out with his therapist. So I moved on to the next task on my to-do list.

11. Purple Spandex

In June 2008, two and a half years into his affair with the Juicer, my parents were living in their RV in our driveway, taking care of the farm for us, and Chet was admitted to the hospital with multiple tumors. After the biopsy of his bronchial tube, the results confirmed it was lung cancer. The surgeon showed me pictures of the tumor, shook my hand and said, "I'm sorry." We met with an oncologist to talk about cancer treatment. Chet would have to go through several months of chemotherapy. At the end of our meeting the oncologist shook Chet's hand and said, "I'm sorry."

The radiologist thought this cancer could be the result of the radiation treatments Chet had had for Hodgkin's disease 30 years earlier. His doctors agreed that radiation therapy back then was applied too broadly and at too high a dose. After some searching to get those old health records from Boston, the doctors in the Berkshires told us that Chet's spine had already received the maximum dose of rads, so radiating his tumors was not an option. The radiologist shook Chet's hand and said, "I'm sorry."

The neurosurgeon said the tumor on Chet's spine was a gelatinous mass crushing the vertebrae, but he was confident he could eliminate most of the pain. The surgery wouldn't cure the cancer or remove all the cancer cells, but it would remove most of it, which would slow the growth of the tumor. The risk was damage to Chet's spine, which could leave him paralyzed from the neck down. But that was the risk with or without the surgery. The very real possibility of his entire body being paralyzed stared Chet in the face.

"Let's do it," he said.

The neurosurgeon shook his hand and said, "I'm sorry."

Chet spent June 21st, 2008, his 54th birthday, in the hospital. I took a hiatus from my paying gigs and volunteer work. All my attention was focused on my husband. Everyone understood. Once I said the word cancer, people knew what I was going through.

~ : ~

After the surgery, Chet came home from the hospital tethered to an oxygen machine that filled the house with an industrial rumbling. Moisture slurped through the tubing in a sickening visceral reminder of his fragility. I flashed back to Maurice curled on the hospital bed in the dining room with the three curved-glass china cabinets. *Righty tighty, lefty loosey.*

Lying beside him in our bed in the dark, his oxygen machine became the soundtrack for my first panic attack. A charge of electric adrenaline flooded me with fear. Fear of the next day, fear of life without him, fear of being alone, fear of missing a mortgage payment, fear of dealing with the house, fear of running the farm by myself, fear of the fear of the fear, falling, falling, falling. I wanted to scream.

Then a familiar voice said, "Everything's just fine here."

I had brought my mother to the farm and we went for a walk in the snow until she stopped because her feet hurt. She wore only little rubber boots, but I thought she was wearing shoes inside those little boots. When she absolutely couldn't walk any further, I sat her on a frozen log to see if she had a rock in her shoe. Instead I found her frozen bare feet. There I was alone in the woods with my elderly mother with frozen bare feet. I knelt in front of her and lifted up my coat and put her feet on my bare stomach until they didn't hurt anymore. Then I took off my socks and put them on her and put her boots back on, and we ran as fast as we could back to the farm. All the way there she chanted, "Everything's just fine here. Everything's just fine here."

Those words stopped my panic attack, but I knew it wasn't true. Everything was not just fine here.

The next morning sitting with Chet on our bed, I said, "Why do you think this is happening to us?"

"I don't know," he said.

"You must have been absorbing some incredible stress to be this sick. Was it me? Was it the farm? What's going on inside of you? I know you've been really unhappy. But I thought things were getting better."

He looked off into the faraway. "I don't know, Bil," he said. "I don't know why this is happening."

"It must have been something," I pushed. "Disease doesn't come from nowhere. Living in a way that makes you unhappy every day could make you sick. You've had so much resistance to the farm for such a long time."

"Stop it," he said. "It wasn't the farm."

"I would do anything, anything we can think of to change this, to roll back the clock to our past life."

"It is what it is," he said.

I didn't know what to think about his stoicism, so I just accepted it. His refusal to let me into his state of mind was a wall between us. I thought about what it must be like to feel the approach of death, and I imagined him trying to manage his own emotions and mine. I didn't want to be a burden to him. I didn't want my name on the list of things he needed to avoid in order to stay in control of himself. So, I shut myself down and consciously backed off from the inquiry.

"I love you, Chet," I said. Meanwhile my mind was spinning through every memory looking for answers to my question. *Why? Why? Why? Why was this happening?*

"I know you love me," he said. "I love you, too."

The next day he passed out in the bathroom. I found him collapsed on the floor and called 911. An ambulance took him back to the hospital. They scanned his chest looking for signs of a heart attack and discovered a new tumor growing around his lung, a quart-sized gelatinous mass that threatened to pressure the lung into collapse. That tumor was inoperable. So even though the incision from surgery on his back had barely begun to heal, the doctors started him on chemotherapy.

~ : ~

The oncologist was emotionless when he told us that Chet had several brain lesions, all extremely small, but there was a possibility of him having a stroke or seizure at any time.

"At this stage there is nothing more we can do," he said. "We watch and wait to see what the disease does next."

"What stage is it?" I asked.

"Stage 4," he said. "I'm sorry."

I researched Stage 4 lung cancer online and read everything I could find on diagnosis, treatment, nutrition and alternative therapies. Then I felt I had to tell Chet what I had learned. We put his oxygen tank in his backpack so he could wear it outside, and I held his arm to keep him steady. It was summer on the farm and the land was in its uproarious green glory as we inched slowly up the road. The cows were munching on grass and grooming each other. Hens gaggled about. The rooster crowed. Our goats, Wendell and Berry, looked up at us and bleated hello.

"Pretty cool, huh?" I said, pointing to Chet's vegetable garden, where I had planted his asparagus.

"I need to get out here and weed," he said wistfully.

"Did you know you're supposed to wait a couple years until you pick your first crop of asparagus?"

"That's ironic," he chuckled. "I guess I didn't read that far in the book." He scanned the horizon. "There are so many things I want to do."

"This place will wait for you," I said. "Right now, you need to stay chilled and upbeat."

"I have cancer. How upbeat do you want me to be?"

"I want you to be as upbeat as you can be for the rest of your life."

"My life sucks."

"I know. I've been researching Stage 4 lung cancer online."

"And?"

"It's terminal, Chet. It's the last stage." I paused to watch his face. "They think it's going to kill you. I guess that's why they keep saying 'I'm sorry'."

"What about the chemo?" he asked.

"It's just buying you time. Maybe... Sometimes it doesn't work. If it does work, you'll be really sick from the poison for a few months, but maybe you'll live a few more years."

"I don't feel like I'm going to live a few more years."

"I know. I can tell."

We walked over to the wood pile and sat on a log. The chickens scrambled into the bushes and disappeared. Henry stretched out to snooze on the grass. The rooster crowed again.

Chet's eyes searched the sky. "There must be a hawk in the trees."

"I'm so mystified by this fate," I said, watching his mind drift away from me. "Ever since you had Hodgkin's we've done all the right things. You eat well. You exercise. You live a beautiful life. You're surrounded by people who love you. You have a great job. Your depression seemed like you were managing it. I know our financial situation put some pressure on you. I know the farm is a burden. But none of that seems drastic enough to cause this. Where did this come from? Why is our life turning out like this? I don't get it." I put my face in his shoulder and cried. "Oh, Chet. I've tried to take such good care of you. How did this happen?"

He cried, too. "I don't know," he said. "I don't know."

"I'm so sorry about the farm," I said. "All the drama I caused in our lives. I am so, so sorry."

"It wasn't the farm, Bil. I love the farm."

~ : ~

The first work party at our farm was organized for mid-October 2008, just two weeks after the Juicer had made her debut in my life. That whole experience, learning that Chet had been cheating on me, was stowed neatly in the back of my mind where I just wanted to forget it happened and move on with my life. My husband was dying, and I had a farm to run. The future was bearing down on me like an avalanche. So I compartmentalized my trauma and forced myself to focus on survival. I had a list of projects I hoped to accomplish with the help of friends, tasks that took teamwork and tools. I invited a dozen Berkshire friends to come over on a Sunday morning and, while Chet slept, we worked together for several hours, completing projects and crossing them off my list.

They helped me switch from summer systems to winter systems for fencing, food and water; took apart the network of hoses and coiled them in the cellar; set up the hay feeder in the paddock in front of the barn, and walked the fence lines, trimming away the brush. They relocated the water trough, built a new shelter for the goats, and split firewood. It was exhilarating work. Afterward we had festive beverages and a potluck dinner, and talked about the restorative energy of the farm, the purposefulness of the chores, and the sharp angle of the sun. Someone said it felt like church.

The following weekend Chet and I had another work party, this time with a crew of friends from Boston who had known each other for many years in music, film and theater. It felt like a family reunion with 14 people sleeping in the house and a crowd around the table for meals. Again, I had a list of projects I hoped to accomplish. They brought their own tools and prodigious skills and replaced the rotten wood decking on the front porch, cleaned the gutters, put Chet's vegetable garden to bed for winter, and planted garlic. Another couple of cords of firewood were split and stacked. The coop and the barn were mucked clean. And finally, we got to the last item on my list — Burt's funeral.

Burt had been in the freezer in the barn for five months, recently joined by bags of Lisa's meat and bones. I thought it would be a fun group project to plan Burt's funeral celebration and put him in his final resting place. We were all used to doing art projects together, and this was going to be our last show. Some focused on the funeral pageant and others on preparing the grave. To dig the hole, Chet gave backhoe lessons on the tractor, and enthusiastic gravediggers lined up as though the tractor were a carnival ride.

After dinner the night sky was clear, and the stars were bright. Though he was pale and bald, and moved like a very old man, Chet was jolly and animated. We lit candles and got flashlights and lined up for a procession from the house to the barn. The musical instruments came out: Martha's accordion, Laurel's trumpet, Brian's saxophone, Chris's guitar. They launched into a bluesy New Orleans dirge and we paraded across the barnyard to the freezer.

Four solemn pallbearers made great ceremony of taking Burt's white box off the shelf and carried it from the barn to the apple tree in the field across the road. As they lowered the box into the hole we stood in a circle around the grave and prepared to perform in honor of Burt.

Jim began the program with a tender whistling of the theme song from Lassie. Then Beth led a cheerful sing-along of B-U-R-T-O based on the famous camp song "B-I-N-G-O", and Burt-O was his name, O! Joe read a passage about dogs from the Book of Isaiah. Sam recited a limerick she wrote just for Burt. Chris sang a verse of "Amazing Grace" followed by Jim's parody of "Pore Jud is Daid" from *Oklahoma!* Annie read a short children's story about a dog. Rich chanted a Sanskrit prayer and affirmations from the Veda. And Joe recited the Mourner's Kaddish in Hebrew. Finally, it was Chet's turn.

"You have to wait and see," he said to me earlier when I had asked him what he would perform. "It's going to be perfect."

Standing in a circle around a dirt hole in a dark farm field, the night hid our faces, but the anticipation was electric as we turned our attention to Chet. He raised his arms as if to include all of us in his song. Then he hummed his starting note and sang out a cappella into the crystal air.

The worms crawl in
The worms crawl out
The ones that crawl in are lean and thin
The ones that crawl out are fat and stout
Your eyes fall in and your teeth fall out
Your brains come tumbling down your snout
Be merry my friends, be merry
Be merry my friends, be merry

His voice was beautiful, smooth and self-assured. I was proud of him. When he finished there was a loud cheer, hooting and hollering. We each took a handful of dirt and threw it on Burt's box. Then the musicians cranked up a gospel song and we drifted noisily back to the house, each silently caressing the memory of Chet singing those words.

~ : ~

The following Monday morning I left for two weeks to attend the Slow Food 2008 conference in Turin, Italy. Months earlier friends had urged me to sign up for the trip. They committed to watching over Chet so I could take a break. The first week would be filled with conference activities. The second week I planned to do a final edit of my essays for submission to a publisher interested in my writing on local food systems and the politics of farming. Most of my expenses were paid by Slow Food and a non-profit. I felt like I owed it to myself to go.

Although my essays were mainly about agriculture and public policy, the publisher was intrigued by the role of the farm and food in Chet's end of life story. She suggested I infuse my essays with personal anecdotes. She thought my stories would give the wonky text a wider appeal. I struggled to put such recent experience into words and draw connections between my private life and my public opinions. I wrote dutifully, but I couldn't find my voice.

Alone in Turin I thought back on the last time I was in Italy, vacationing with Chet in 1997, and I was miserable. This was my dress rehearsal for widowhood, being alone in the world. I got lost on a city bus and felt helpless. I knew how to speak Italian, but I couldn't function. For a couple hours I rode the bus and just watched people pass. Then desperate for connection, I called Chet.

"Bil, you're in Italy," he said. "Have fun with it."

"I don't know how to have fun."

"Get off the bus in a nice neighborhood. Go to a cafe and have a shot of Jack Daniel's."

"I'm in Italy. I'm supposed to be drinking wine."

"Fuck what you're supposed to do. Do what you feel like doing. It sounds to me like you need to chill and have a shot of Jack. Go do it. Take care of yourself."

"I wish you were here with me."

"I wish I was there, too," he said.

That night in my hotel room I toyed with my cell phone and sent my first ever text, a message to my husband.

"in bed thinking of u" I wrote.

To my surprise he responded instantly. "ditto"

"my head is a mess"

"u need sum good head" he wrote.

"where do i go 4 that?"

"u don't go u cum"

"is this text sex?" I asked.

"what r u wearing?"

I didn't reply. He was obviously in the habit of texting the Juicer and assumed my message was from her. Sex was no longer part of our repertoire. Chemo really had addled his brain. I didn't want to embarrass him, didn't want to bring her into the conversation when we were so far apart, didn't have the will to confront him. So I let it go and never mentioned it.

~ : ~

Shortly after I returned home from Italy, I woke up in the night to see Chet sitting up in bed, texting on his cell phone.

"Chet, you're cheating on me while we're in bed together?" I was incredulous. "It's like she's in bed with us."

"Texting is not cheating, Bil." He was matter of fact. "It's texting."

I let it go.

A couple weeks later, the beginning of December, we went to clean out his office at the college. He didn't have the stamina or the mental acuity to do his job anymore, so he was forced to resign. I filled boxes with things from his desk drawers and put them in the car. There were spent votive candles, a hand painted souvenir mug from Rome, and an unopened bottle of my favorite kind of grappa, the grappa he and I drank on our trip to Italy in 1997.

"She gave you all this stuff?" I asked.

"Yeah," he said nonchalantly. "She went to Italy to a lot of the same places we went."

"You mean you told her about our trip, and she did what we did?" Her apparition was taking the shape of a doppelganger living my life in hopes of replacing me.

"Yeah," he said. "She's fucked up like that." His tone was casual, disconnected from the revelation of his words, as though we were just chatting about a mutual friend who had problems, as though he didn't realize I was his wife and he was talking about his girlfriend.

I thought I could let it go. I really did. I intended to manage myself, compartmentalize, skip the drama. I didn't want every moment I was with him to be about her. But this was too much. My doppelganger was racing through me with a flaming Zippo, charring my sanity, like she wanted to kill me. Or she wanted me to kill myself.

As I drove toward home, I started shaking and had to pull over. My vision blurred and I felt like I could have a seizure.

"Fuck you!" I shrieked at him, splitting the skin in the back of my throat. "Fuck you for dying and leaving me with this big steaming turd in the middle of my life. Finding out you cheated on me right before you die, when there's no time to figure out what really happened." I could taste blood on my tongue. "Your fucking brain is so rotten with drugs you can't even explain it. There's no time. I'm never going to know. I'm never going to know what really happened. I'm going to be haunted by this for the rest of my life."

I fell forward onto the steering wheel with my arms around my head and heaved gut racking sobs, while my husband turned his face away from me and said nothing.

That night as I washed dishes with my back to him, he sat down at the kitchen counter and our eyes met in the reflection of the kitchen window over the sink. Pain hung like black curtains. "I love you, Bil," he said. Then he turned off his cell phone and set it on the windowsill in front of me. "You can have this. I won't be needing it."

~ : ~

After the chemo failed, he thought he would try high tech laser radiation on his brain. Even though it wouldn't cure him, it might buy him time. Strapped to the table with his eyes pressed shut in a mask, and people moving around him talking, he had the very real feeling of being paralyzed. The voices of strangers speaking about him as though he wasn't there gave him a preview of his death. In that moment he decided to stop all treatment, and a few days later he enrolled himself in hospice.

He had a living will so his family and healthcare proxies would know how he wanted to be cared for in the event he was unable to express himself. His instructions were clear that he wanted to die at home, and he wanted his ashes spread on the farm. A palliative care physician came to see him at our house and explained the hospice process.

When the two of us were alone sitting in bed, he said, "We should put at least as much thought into planning my death as we put into planning our wedding."

That was an interesting idea. We planned our wedding to exclude our family because we didn't want the drama of their presence. I loved the way we got married with just the two of us focused on each other.

"Okay," I said. "What do you want to wear?"

"My purple spandex pants."

I laughed. "Really?"

"No," he said. "I wouldn't do that to you."

"I'm sure I could get them on you if that's what you really want. Although you could just put them on now yourself. That would be easiest."

"I think they would just melt in the oven," he said. "What did Gandhi wear?"

"He was probably naked," I said. "Wrapped in linen or something."

"That's what I want."

"Okay. What else?"

"Just because I'm dead doesn't mean I'm not here," he said. "I don't want to be a carcass. I don't want to be kept like meat in cold storage. I don't want my dead body to be handled by strangers. I want the people who love me to take care of me just the same as if I was alive."

"Wow, Chet. That sounds pretty cool, but I wonder if it's legal."

"You're going to have to figure that out," he said. "Just promise you won't dial 911."

"I promise," I said. Then I called our attorney to find out what I was supposed to do when my husband died.

"Just dial 911," she said.

"Why would I do that?"

"They'll take care of everything."

"Like what?"

"The police will come, they'll confirm he's dead, and then they'll call an ambulance to take him away to the morgue until you figure out what you want to do with him."

"If he's already dead, it's not an emergency," I said. "I don't want the police involved. I don't want a bunch of strangers in my house right after my husband dies."

"That's all I can tell you," she said. "It's what people do."

When I related the conversation to Chet, he said, "It's not what I'm going to do. I want to die at home and stay at home until you put me in the oven."

~ : ~

We planned the holidays to be a celebration of his life. He made a list of the people he wanted to see, and I coordinated the visits. A couple weeks before Christmas his mother and sister, Cathy, came to stay with us. They had not seen Chet for a year, since before his cancer diagnosis. All they knew about his condition was from telephone conversations and email. He kept them at a distance intentionally because he didn't want to be dragged down by their emotions. He loved them and he knew how much they loved him. But the memory of their fighting when his father died made him mistrustful of their behavior in the presence of his own death.

They didn't know when they arrived that we were inviting them to our house to see him for the last time, and then sending them away before he died. It was up to him to explain that to them. He knew it. He was clear that he didn't want them there when he was on his way out. He was orchestrating his final performance and he couldn't trust them to play along.

When his mother arrived, I could see from her dazed eyes that she was buzzed on tranquilizers. She took valium every day, calling it her nerve pills. When she walked into the house, she gave me a dizzy hello hug and the first thing she said to me was, "Are you going to remarry?"

"No," I laughed. "I'm planning to kill myself."

She didn't hear me. Her mind was drowning in thoughts of losing her son. I took her and Cathy to the guest room and helped them unpack. Once they were settled in, Chet wanted to have a conversation with his sister. While his mom made herself at home puttering in our kitchen, Chet and Cathy sat on the couch in front of the fire and chatted about their lives, their father's death, and Chet's end of life plans.

No one in his family had ever been cremated. Even though they weren't practicing Christians, they associated fire with the flames of Hell. It didn't feel right to them to burn Chet's body. Also, since Chet was dying at the farm, they wouldn't have a funeral service to host back in Columbus, and no big lunch at the VFW hall like they had had for Maurice. They would miss having that kind of closure. Without a grave to visit they didn't know where they would go to remember Chet.

It was inconceivable to them that they would see him for the last time ever when they left the farm to go back home to Ohio. All this they learned on the first day of a two-week visit, two weeks when his mother would be a grief zombie in our house, appalled by the music and laughter, offended by the celebratory meals and unamused by the death jokes.

~ : ~

While Cathy kept an eye on Chet, I went to visit my mother with a bouquet of roses. When I got off the elevator, she was standing at the end of the hall looking like a forgotten movie star. Her hair was curled and combed, her nails were Jungle Red, and she wore a pair of Jackie O. sunglasses with her chin up to keep them from sliding down her nose.

"You look fabulous," I said to her.

"Thank you," she said, taking the roses from my hand.

She was wearing clothes that were not her own; a baggy white blouse, a pair of too long bright blue slacks, some stolen necklaces, and a man's shoes. We filled a plastic jug with water to use as a vase and put it in her room. In the soupy mind that didn't care which bed she slept in, or whose clothes she wore, she was precise about how to arrange flowers. When I attempted to assist her, she clucked her tongue and shook her head, correcting my mistake, adjusting the stems to perfection. Her last expression of herself was an intuitive sense of style.

She was born a lady with a hat and gloves, and a purse and shoes to match. She sat with her knees together, her ankles crossed, and her hands folded in her lap. She had wanted me to be a lady, too. She taught me how to decorate the house, how to draw a charcoal still life of the fruit bowl on the kitchen table, and how to put an outfit together and pack a suitcase. We went for walks with field guides and she taught me the names of birds and wildflowers, and how to make cornbread on a campfire. My life was molded from her interests. In so many ways she had been the ideal mother, and now, when I really needed her, she was gone, and I was tired. Being in her room, watching her arrange the roses, felt like hiding from the rest of my life.

"Mom, remember Chet? ... He's not doing very well," I said. "I think he's going to die soon. I thought about getting you guys together one last time, but I don't think I can. Not that you're going to miss him much. But I just thought I'd let you know. In case there's a shred of awareness left inside you, I thought you would like to know. Chet is really sick and he's going to die. ... He doesn't know what's going on with you either. I didn't want to depress him. ... God damn it, you guys are depressing."

I cried for a while and dug around her bedside table for a tissue to blow my nose.

~ : ~

In the end it was her uncompromising sense of style that got her kicked out of that nursing home and moved to another one nearby owned by the same company. They said it was for her safety. Evidently, she was taking clothes from other people's closets, and she was willing to fight for her choices, including slapping another woman and pushing her to the floor.

In the new place she came down with an infection that gave her chronic diarrhea. She had been on antibiotics for the past year because, after a few years in the nursing home without oral hygiene, she had a mouth full of decaying teeth, and she wouldn't let the dentist work on her. She tried to bite him. The government didn't want to pay for general anesthesia and oral surgery in a hospital. So they gave her antibiotics instead of removing the infection in her mouth.

It wasn't long before the nurses observed that the antibiotic pills weren't working anymore. My mother had a constant low-grade fever and she had to be given antibiotic shots every day.

When I showed up to see her at the new place, there was an orderly lying on top of her trying to hold her down, and a girl in scrubs on the floor beside her, trying to grab her arm as she flailed violently like a wild animal trying to escape her captors.

"What the fuck are you doing!" I yelled.

The two startled employees ran out of the room, and I sat beside my mother and held her in my arms. "This is too much," I said as I cried and rocked her. "It's just too much. I am so sorry, Mom. I am so, so sorry."

A nurse-like person appeared in the doorway of the room.

"You have to let them give your mother the shot," she said.

"I don't have to do anything," I snapped.

"If you want your mother to stay here, she has to have the shot."

"I'm not opposed to her having the shot. I'm opposed to treating her like an animal."

"The aid was having trouble finding her vein and she refused to hold still."

"Look how frightened she is," I said. "Look at her arms. They're covered with bruises. What are you doing to her?"

"She has to have shots a few times a day," the woman said. "She has C. diff. That's why she's in a room by herself."

"C. diff!" I shouted. "I should have been told that when she got the diagnosis. How is it possible that you are telling me that now?" I stood up and leered at the woman. "I know what C. diff is. It's in the news. There's no cure for it. People are dying. Do you even know what it is?"

"It's an infection," she said, taking a step back from me.

"It's the last infection," I hissed in her face. "It's extremely contagious, and it's fatal for old people like her. That's why it's in the news. Am I the only one here who knows that? Really? You could be a bunch of mass murders. That orderly was lying on top of her. They weren't even wearing gloves or a mask. How many other people here are going to get sick because of you?"

"We do the best we can with what we've got," she said, inching toward the door.

"Does anyone here know anything about medicine?" I yelled as loud as I could. A remote area of my brain registered how good it felt to yell that loud. "Good god! If she has C. diff she shouldn't be here." I went on yelling. "You people don't even wash your hands. I suggest you call a doctor and get her admitted to the hospital before I report you to the board of health."

My mom was admitted to the hospital later that day.

~ : ~

Chet required constant attention, he couldn't walk by himself, and I was glad for Cathy's help. I phoned my parents in Florida and asked them to come back to the farm for a while. A kind neighbor who was away for the winter let my dad and Peggy live in their house. As soon as they arrived, we settled into the routine we had developed during the summer. They took care of the animals so I could focus on Chet and my mom.

Our home was starting to feel like a religious shrine. Visitors brought cherished objects, flowers, incense, music, pictures and books. Chet was surrounded by gifts that symbolized the divine. People sang for him. On a snowy day he sat in his chair looking out the window at the farm when a group of friends arrived to sing Christmas carols for him. They lined up outside his window and sang songs of the season as he listened in tears from the other side of the glass.

He made his best effort to wrap up relationships in a way that conveyed peace and comfort. Each word was final. Sometimes his own emotions exhausted him. He knew his steroids exaggerated his feelings. It was another moment when we talked about his dad and wondered if Maurice cried so much around the time of his death because he was on steroids. Chet said they made him feel the way he imagined my menopause mood swings made me feel. He wanted to know the emotions he was experiencing were really his own, not the side effects of a drug. So he stopped taking his steroids.

When his fingers didn't work well enough to use his laptop, he had to abandon it. We knew that meant the tumor was pressing on his spine again. I could see the Juicer's text messages piling up on his cell phone. Her phone number was on the missed calls list over and over again. She left voice mails begging him to call her, inviting him to watch the full moon with her, telling him she would find him in the afterlife. When she got no reply, she sent me an email asking to come to the farm and see him one last time. Then she mailed us a check for $1,000.

I asked Chet if he wanted to thank her for the money, which we badly needed. He didn't take any time to think about his answer. "Oh, Bil, I can't talk to her," he said in a tone of voice that conveyed his exhaustion. Those words resounded in me. She was shut out. I took satisfaction in emailing her to say he was unavailable. I told her he wanted to be remembered as he was the last time she saw him, when they kissed in the driveway in front of our house. She pleaded with me, and I said no, resolutely. It was easy for me to say no to her. But I knew what she was feeling.

The hospice nurses came to meet with us and gave their full support to our plan for Chet to die at home. They provided medicine and supplies, and a pain management plan. They sat with us and explained how to interpret his pain, the side effects of the drugs, and how to ameliorate them. Chet's mom sat in on those conversations, and when she and I were alone, she said, "Bil, are you going to give him those pills? I could not give them to Maurice."

"Of course, I'm going to give him those pills," I said. "They're pain pills."

"They'll kill him. You'll be killing him if you give them to him. I could not have that on my soul."

"He's dying of cancer. Cancer will kill him. The pills just make dying easier."

"Dying isn't supposed to be easy," she said. "It's not right to kill a person."

"So, you let Maurice be in pain," I said. "You let him lay there curled up in a ball in your dining room, and you listened to him beg for relief when you could have taken his pain away. You thought that was right?"

"I could not have that on my soul. I could not do it."

"I'm not going to stand by and let my husband suffer. I wouldn't let my dog suffer. Death is not a punishment."

"Yes, it is. You're supposed to suffer when you die," she said. "That's what death is."

"Death is whatever you want it to be."

"You always think you know everything, Bil. But it's not right."

"It's not your decision," I said. "It's Chet's decision."

~ : ~

When we took our last bubble bath together, Chet sank into the hot water and said, "Now that I have your attention, there are a few things I'd like to discuss with you."

"What do you mean, 'Now, that I have your attention'?"

"You're buzzing around this place like Donna Reed on steroids."

"Your mother has been living in our house for weeks. The closer it gets to be time for her to leave, the more freaked out she is."

"I don't want to talk about my mother. I want to talk about dying."

"What about dying?"

"I really want to die."

"I know."

"I want to die now."

"Chet, don't you dare die while your mother is here. Michael will be here exactly one week from today. You have to say goodbye to him."

"I don't know if I can wait that long."

"You have to wait. If you die while your mother is here, it's going to wreck everything. She'll freak out and I'll be forced to take care of her, because you'll be dead. Please don't put us through that. I want to be with you when you die. I don't want to be dialing 911 for your mother."

"Okay, but I can't promise anything."

"I know. Whatever happens, I'll deal with it."

~ : ~

One of the great ironies of Chet's condition was the pile of drugs on his bedroom dresser. He had always enjoyed a recreational buzz.

Now he had all the drugs he ever dreamed of and he didn't want to use them, because they made him feel out of control. One night after a dose of morphine, he suddenly got his legs back and popped out of bed so fast I had to chase him around the house. He was naked, but he was determined to take a leak off the long porch. Fortunately, all the doors were locked, and his fingers were too numb to unlock them.

"What are you trying to do?" I asked, blocking his way.

"I'm going outside to pee."

"You can't go outside."

"Watch me."

"No, really, Chet, you can't go outside."

"Get out of my way. I have to pee."

"You need to use the bathroom."

"I'm going outside."

"No, you're not. It's too cold to go outside."

"I'm just going to pee."

"No, you're not."

"Yes, I am."

"It's too cold."

"I'll be the judge of that." He put his hands on his hips in exasperation, and I couldn't help but smile at how cute he looked, naked and defiant.

"Please use the bathroom," I said sweetly.

"Where's my wife?" He was indignant.

"What do you mean where's your wife? I'm your wife."

"Then open the door." He pointed to the doorknob.

"No. You'll freeze to death before you get your dick working."

"I think not."

"I think so."

"Get out of my way."

"Chet, you're insane. You're too messed up to go outside. You're not mentally competent."

"Prove it." He put his hands on his hips again and scowled at me.

"Okay, what's your name?"

"You're my wife?" He gave me a long snide look. "And you don't know what my name is?"

~ : ~

My mom's hospital nurse asked me to come for a consultation. When I got to her room, she didn't seem to know who I was. We made eye contact, I squeezed her hand and she squeezed back, but she didn't speak, and she wouldn't eat or drink.

The doctor came into the room and said he was considering a feeding tube. I told him I wouldn't approve a feeding tube. Fortunately, I was my mother's healthcare proxy, and she had put her advanced directives in writing. I knew she wouldn't want a feeding tube forced into her body. When the doctor tried to talk me into it, I was curt.

"Let's enroll her in hospice," I said.

Of course, it was my experience with Chet that gave me such certainty in coping with my mother's end. He and I had discussed these same issues. The idea of giving a dying person a feeding tube seemed inhumane to me. It disrespects a process that should be serene. It forces a person to digest food when their body wants to discontinue activity. It fragments a dying person's energy at a moment when they should be condensing, a moment when their life force should be focused on a peaceful transition into death.

I knew this was contrary to the doctor's training. My ease with death discomfited him. It made him skeptical of my motive. He took me to a quiet room and interrogated me, as though I had a sinister plan for my mother.

"Tell me about your relationship," he said.

"I love my mother and I want her to die a peaceful death."

"We are here to save lives. I want my patients to enjoy their quality of life for as long as possible."

"How is a feeding tube quality of life?"

"Life is life," he said. "Every death here matters."

"Life and death are statistics," I said. "I know you don't want to look bad, but people come to hospitals to die."

"Not if we can help it."

"People die. That's life. A feeding tube isn't going to keep her from dying. It's just postponing her fate."

"Our mission is to help people live as long as they can."

"You should be helping people die a beautiful death. A feeding tube is grotesque. It's completely unnatural."

"Often patients rally with that kind of assistance."

"Rally for what?" I asked. "So, she can feel her incontinence? So, she's aware of the plastic tube in her throat? Because she isn't going to rally and suddenly remember I'm her daughter and she's my mother. A feeding tube isn't going to cure C. diff. A feeding tube isn't going to save her life. It's cruel to put her through that."

"I think a feeding tube at this point is appropriate treatment."

"I think a feeding tube at this point is disrespectful."

Finally, he agreed. He had no choice. They relocated my mother to a local nursing home with hospice rooms and a staff that was experienced with C. diff. The hospice agency that took care of her was the same one that was taking care of Chet in our home. Occasionally, the hospice nurses that came to our house would update me on my mom, because they had seen her earlier in the day.

12. Last Call

The first week in January 2009 was time for Chet's mother and sister to leave. They had celebrated Christmas and New Year's Eve with us and our friends. Perhaps celebrated isn't the right word. They went through the motions. They ate and drank and wore the obligatory party hats. But his mother stood on the sidelines of the festivities as though we were enacting some perverse satanic ritual by having fun, blowing noisemakers, and dropping a tinfoil ball at midnight. The more we enjoyed ourselves, the more Chet was entertained and distracted, the more monstrous his mother's horror.

Finally, on the morning of their departure their anguish was unbearable. The idea that they would never see him again was agony and they couldn't pretend otherwise. To them our acceptance of his fate was wrong. They fought against it. Chet tried to soothe them, but he had no energy. Emotionally disconnected by his medications, lying on the couch, he listened to their last sobbing words as they bent over him and cried into his chest, but he couldn't match their level of emotional intensity.

"My job is the easy part," he said. "All I have to do is lie here and die. Your job is the hard part. You have to go on living."

We hadn't thought of our plan from his family's point of view, and it's unlikely we would have changed the plan if we had. Chet had a vision for his own serenity. My first duty was to support him in that. Sending his mother and his sister away while he was still alive seemed cruel to them, and perhaps it was. But my head was splitting, and his mother's wailing was more than I could handle. I felt like a volcano with a cracked cap. The danger of having these women in my house was scaring me. I understood their pain, but their inability to control their hysteria in Chet's presence made me angry.

I watched them pull at him as though they could bring him back from the edge of his intentions. They wanted him to believe that he would get well, and they wanted to stay with us to see it. They couldn't comprehend how their point of view invalidated ours. I loved them, but I wanted them gone. I thought their attitude was selfish, but I knew they thought the same of me. My own hysteria was cresting just below the surface, and I didn't want them to drag me into their abyss. I held Chet while he waved goodbye to them from the front porch, and that's the last time they saw him.

~ : ~

Finally, Michael arrived. He and Chet were in bands together when they were teenagers in Columbus and studied music together at college in Boston.

"Wake up, Chet," I said. "Michael's here."

He opened his eyes and looked around the room. "I can't believe I'm going to die before I paint this bedroom."

I laughed. "How do you feel?"

"I feel like shit. But I have cancer. How do you feel?"

"I'm exhausted. I'm not sleeping very well, and I'm an emotional wreck." I looked at myself in the mirror. "I have these big bags under my eyes, and I'm getting fat because I'm eating all your food."

"Don't worry," he chuckled. "Your vanity won't allow you to be self-destructive for too long. You'll come out of it."

I gave him a kiss and helped him out of bed into his wheelchair. We had put a hospital bed in the living room for him so he could be social. As I wheeled him through the hall, he looked up at me with a wry smile and said, "Mr. De Mille, I'm ready for my close-up."

That evening the guys from Chet's jazz band came over. They stood around with Michael, hovering over Chet in his hospital bed between two couches, talking about music. Chet appeared to be sleeping. Then he raised his arm and pointed a finger to the audio speaker on the wall. "The horns are sharp," he said. The guys listened and laughed. He was right. The horns were sharp.

As they chatted, I sat watching Chet slip away, and I had a conscious feeling of his muse floating through the ether and filling me. In a gusty psychic whoosh, a poem landed in my head, whole, already composed. I could feel the words pushing at my fingers to transcribe them, a feeling I hadn't had since high school when, in my darkest hours, poetry was my palliative. The guys looked cross-eyed at me as I pulled my computer off the coffee table into my lap. But I had to write. The words in me were coming to life.

~ : ~

The widow's song is not her wish
Like night sweats, raspy breathing and stained sheets
 it is a song that scuffs across the floor on the edge of dementia
 soundtrack for a nosedive
The coyotes wail an operatic serenade
 in the blackness the swan shrieks her song

How simple death
 wash, wash, chapped hands
 fold, fold, fold, broken fingernails
Hiding pills in vanilla ice cream
 just a spoonful
Florence Nightingale on crack
 for the already gonzo
Cherry Ames hospice nurse
 May I escort you to the door?
A Girl Scout is always prepared
 Did I get my First Aid badge for this?
The bride's surprise
 Was this my marriage vow?

How would Donna Reed do it?
Should I be wearing pearls?
Tending a dying fire this task has befallen me light as air
and I am crushed by it

The widow's song floats to the sky and brings down tears
a chilling rain spatters mud on her shoes
Her wet skirt clings to her legs
Her mascara runs like rivulets of mud taking the life from her eyes
She imagines herself beside him in the dirt
washing down the hillside
floating out to sea
To become tears again and soak the mascara that stains her cheeks
trickling to her mouth
a smudge of red craving a kiss

The widow's song is the crack of a woodsman's axe
in an orchard where no fruit is born
And trees give themselves blossomless to the fire

~ : ~

On a whim I emailed a professional photographer friend and asked him to visit us with his camera. Jason had photographed the farm many times before. He and Chet knew each other, and Chet was a fan of his work.

That night I slept in the living room on a twin airbed pushed flush against Chet in his electric hospital bed. It was almost like sleeping together. During the night he slid out of bed without waking, and walked over to the woodstove to relieve himself, as though he were in the men's room at a night club. I smelled his pee sizzling on the hot soapstone as I pulled him back into bed. His weight was hard for me to manage. I groaned and struggled to slide him up onto his pillow. Skin to skin, muscle to muscle, he could feel my exhaustion.

"Oh, Bil," he murmured. I knew what he was thinking. He was thinking he was a burden and he was all done here.

In the morning I returned from barn chores to find Jason sitting beside Chet's bed with tears in his eyes. I went about my morning housework and he photographed us. Chet didn't wake.

A few hours later Jason left, Michael arrived to say goodbye, and Chet was still in a hard sleep. Then as if on cue, his breathing became raspy. Michael decided to stay a while longer. The hospice nurse arrived for her daily visit and told us Chet would die soon. She and I shuffled him around on his bed to change the sheets, and he woke up looking grumpy until he saw my face.

"Oh, it's you," he smiled at me and closed his eyes again.

Michael and I spoke softly and played music as Chet's breathing rattled on. The irregularity of it kept our attention. When it became quite loud, I squeezed an eyedropper of morphine onto his tongue. My parents visited him and left. Chet's face lost color. Michael held one of his hands and I held the other. Suddenly he lurched up at Michael and glared at him. Then he turned and lurched up at me, glaring. I could see his face relax as he recognized me.

"This is it, baby," I said. "This is it." This was the moment we had been preparing for all these months. I smiled at him. He knew from my tone everything was okay. He settled back into his bed and relaxed. A few more breaths and he was gone, soft, warm, and limp.

Michael left me alone to fuss over my husband the way one fusses over a newborn baby, kissing him, touching him, removing his clothes, straightening his bed covers. Then I folded his hands across his chest and sat down beside him and cried.

~ : ~

Death's symphony crescendos in aching bones
  a warm heart becomes a cold stone
Through an infinite archway a lonely ghost races above the floor
  from nowhere to nowhere
Between the flying buttresses where cobwebs cast long shadows
  past the sleet chiseled trees
The sun flutters on yellow leaves
  and the ghost becomes dizzy
Chasing his tail from auricle to ventricle

trapped
The beauty here touches no one

A spiral staircase beckons in a long unstoppable slide
violins scream down the banister
The bottom rushes up and disappears
on the glistening arms of drummers
Over and over again in a false finish
falling through clouds
Until Pan's flute sings

Spinning a thread of golden notes
slicing the ghost into wisps
He escapes through the filigree of time and space
into the ether
Where a tiny bird sits on a conductor's baton
and stares in silence at the music
A cello plays the sound of wings ascending
tympani rumble in the distance
And the bass fades in a tentative mist

~ : ~

I felt his last breath. I saw his face relax. He was finally at peace. He was where he wanted to be. He looked angelic. No more pain, no more struggle, no more frustration, no more Chet. The price of life is death. No more kisses, no more bubble baths, no more walks in the woods, no more cheeseburgers and martinis, no more life partner, no more co-farmer, no more soul mate. There is no consolation for such loss.

Chet Allen Cahill died at the age of 54 on the afternoon of Friday, January 16th, 2009, the beginning of the Martin Luther King, Jr. Day three-day holiday weekend. A hospice person came to the house a few hours after he died to make an official record of his death. The jazz guys returned to pay their respects. My parents came and went. I walked Henry. The house was still.

That night I collapsed in the same place where I had slept the night before, on the twin airbed in our beautiful living room with my dog on the couch and my dead husband beside me on the electric bed. It was the first night in months that I slept the whole night through. No cries of pain, no night walks, no slippers to fetch, no sheets to change, no pills to swallow. Henry, Chet, and I — the three of us slept side-by-side all night long.

Saturday morning, I gave Chet's gold earring to Michael. We said goodbye and I was alone with my thoughts. I emailed Jason to let him know he had captured Chet just hours before he died and now the same scene took on new meaning. We talked about the coming flow of events and I gave him permission to continue to document our process. Chet wanted to be a role model and through Jason's photographs he would be.

~ : ~

A month earlier I had contacted a funeral director to make arrangements for Chet to be cremated. Now I called her on a Saturday morning to make an appointment for the hearse to take his body to the crematory. But the crematory was operated by the city of Pittsfield only on weekdays, and not on holidays. And the medical examiner required before cremation in our state was not available until Tuesday.

Yet I had promised Chet I would keep his body in my possession right until he was delivered to the crematory. I promised him he wouldn't be shipped around like lost luggage and left to sit alone and uncared for on a shelf in cold storage. I promised him I would take care of him just as though he was still alive. Moving as fast as government would allow, he would have to be home with me until at least Wednesday.

Keeping an un-embalmed body in the house for five days set off alarms at the funeral service and hospice, both of which advised me to move Chet to cold storage at the funeral home or get a big order of dry ice and keep him packed in it. The funeral director managed the paperwork, made the appointments, and scheduled the hearse.

I couldn't envision keeping his body in the middle of our big sunny living room for five days with or without dry ice. But I wasn't ready to put him in a box and send him to sit in a refrigerator until his paperwork was processed. I wasn't finished being with him. The funeral director understood. But she warned as delicately as she could of the unpleasantness to be expected if he was not kept at the proper temperature.

In the midst of all this, Chris arrived, a longtime friend from Boston. We decided to move Chet to the coldest room in the house, the den, and put him on my twin airbed between the couch and the TV. I got a thermometer to manage keeping the temperature at 40 degrees. Then we sealed off the hallway with big wool army blankets and opened the windows a crack to let in the winter air.

A shrine materialized on the coffee table beside Chet as we gathered the spiritual icons, candles, art and flowers from the living room. Intuitively the den was transformed into a sacred space. I sat wrapped in a blanket on the couch beside him, feeling his presence, watching his body stiffen.

Sunday morning, I emailed friends to share my story and invite them to visit for a few hours that afternoon. It was Chet's grand finale. We were busting taboos about death and dying, about corpses and what a human body looks like after life, about social norms and how people interact with the dead. We were keeping it real.

Not long after the email went out, a dozen people showed up and made a spontaneous party for themselves. They sat with Chet in the den listening to music, reading poetry, and contemplating existence. They were at home in our kitchen. My spirit was lifted by their presence, and I saw how Chet's vision for his end took on meaning in their experience. The circle was unbroken.

In the next two days, alone with time for my own contemplation, the juxtaposition of Chet's cold body in the den with the churn of life on the farm was an epiphany. He was still with me. His muscles tightened his face into a slight smile. His member stiffened into a bulge in his groin. His face meerschaum, his ears violet, his body cold as river rock. He evolved from life into death to become a sculpture of himself.

Yet, he was still my sly Chet. He was here and the farm was still the farm. Everything was flowing in one direction. Life didn't stop when Chet stopped. I could feel life and death at the same time. It was all one thing.

~ : ~

The medical examiner came to the house at 8:00 Tuesday night to sign off on Chet's cremation. At 8:30 Wednesday morning, the hearse pulled into the driveway and attendants from the funeral home carried a white cardboard cremation box into the den. The crematory was an hour away and I wanted company for the ride. I had never been to a crematory before and I didn't know what to expect. I rented the funeral home's limousine and rode with my parents, the jazz guys and Jason to Pittsfield.

The crematory was in an old cemetery adjacent to historic granite buildings and the caretaker was an elderly man who worked for the city. He rolled Chet's box out of the hearse onto a gurney that rolled inside the crematory where he pushed a button to open the oven door and lined up the box with the roller that would slide Chet into the brick chamber. It looked like a pizza oven shaped like a shoebox, a place you might sleep if you lived on a submarine, a transformative space, go in raw, come out cooked.

"Who wants to do the honors?" the caretaker asked, pointing to the box.

Instinctively I stepped forward and gave Chet a forceful push into the oven. As his box sailed away from me, I had the feeling of ejecting him into the Cosmos.

From the crematory, I went to see my mother at the nursing home. For days we didn't know who would die first, Chet or my mom. Her room was neat and quiet. There was a little white teddy bear with angel wings on the bed beside her. I squeezed her hand and she squeezed mine. She opened her eyes for a moment. "Hi, Mom," I said. Then she receded again. After a while I kissed her goodbye and went home.

I couldn't stay beside her bed. I couldn't bring her to my house to be her caregiver in her last hours. I couldn't have her die in my living room where Chet died. Not so soon after Chet. My heart was not an assembly line. Her death was not performance art. She was not conscious of the process and she would not want to be on display as she died. I couldn't manage another corpse. My mind was fully occupied by Chet. I couldn't focus on my mother. My head was banging hollow. I needed to sit down and close my eyes.

~ : ~

Nine days after Chet died, January 25th, 2009, my mother died. Her body was moved from the nursing home to the mortuary at the funeral home. For her cremation I made the same arrangements with the same funeral director and had her packed into the same kind of white cardboard box. I rode in the same hearse with the same driver to the same crematory with the same little old man, who wheeled her up to the same oven and pointed to the box with the same question.

"Who wants to do the honors?" he asked.

"I want to open the box," I said, carrying an armload of fresh flowers that had been sent to the house for Chet.

"I'm sorry, we can't do that," the driver said.

"Sure, you can," I said. "You just pull the little plastic tab."

"I'm sorry," the driver said. "This is not a viewing facility."

"I just want to say goodbye to my mom."

"I'm sorry, but we don't—" the old man started to say.

"Okay," I interrupted him, smiling sweetly. "Maybe you guys could go and stand in the other room and let me have a few minutes alone here." They looked relieved and backed away. "Thank you," I said, smiling again.

With the men outside smoking cigarettes, I opened the box myself. Mom was in her Sunday dress with the little white teddy bear tucked under her arm. The funeral home had styled her hair and put make-up on her. She was in sweet repose. I covered her with roses and fragrant white lilies, breathing in their scent. *Only one of us can smell this*, I thought. But she would have liked the idea.

"Thanks for being my mom," I said to her. "I know you tried your best. I know you loved me." I kissed her on the forehead. "I love you, Mom." Then I put the lid back on her box, and I gave her a push into Heaven.

~ : ~

Death is the ragged edge
between the fabric of the Cosmos
and the dirty dishes by the sink

A haunted valley between the known and the unknown
the most frightening predators
your innermost fears
A carnival of emotions in shadows and light
your body a costume
your mind a funhouse mirror
Center stage a kitchen sink

Bits of dinner, cold coffee, breadcrumbs, a crust of toast
your last meal
You are in your bed
your eyelids move as you dream
you are spilling over the edge
Like a steep waterfall it feels like chaos
but everything is flowing in one direction
you become a beam of light
Light wraps you in a brilliant cocoon
your light becomes the light of the world
And you shine
brightly, beautifully into my eyes
as I peer over the ragged edge

13. Red Pajamas

My dad and Peggy kept the farm going in the weeks after Chet died while I spent my time looking out the window, lost in the surreal scape of my mind. Time was broken into pieces, slithering away from me in a Salvador Dali painting. Before Chet, after Chet. With Chet, without Chet. He died. He is dead. My husband died. My husband is dead. Chet died. Chet is dead. Standing alone in the desert my skirt swept the sand and I begged the sun to take me, too. No one wants to be left behind, certainly not the last person on Earth. I was a prisoner living a death sentence, stranded in a field of fallen trees, strapped to a withering dream, all my stories lined up before a firing squad, my past burned to the ground, my future riddled with bullets. I had not contemplated life after Chet except to fear it.

The crematory packed his ashes in a plain brown metal box with a generic label archiving the details of his disposition. I put my hand in the box looking for a feeling of familiarity. His bone dust coated my fingers as I dug into the lumps, my fingers a ghostly grey. Dust to dust, he was on me. Was I going to wipe my husband on my pants? Should I wash my husband off my hands at the sink and rinse him down the drain? I sniffed my fingers and licked my hand clean, and he was inside me one last time.

A metronome of mundane tasks kept time for me, syncing me with my new circumstances. Get the death certificate. Return the oxygen tanks and the hospital bed. Put the port-a-potty in the barn. Toss the wilting flowers in the compost. Turn the death room back into the living room. Death is over. Keep moving. Keep busy. Focus. Stash the medicines. Open the sympathy cards. Take the trash to the dump. Move on to the next thing on the list. The laundry. I need to buy toilet paper. Feed the dog. Water the plants. Feed the chickens. Collect the eggs. Throw hay to the cows. Plow snow. Just keep moving.

Then my grief drew me into a chair where I collapsed and scrolled through photos on my laptop, reliving my history, reshuffling my memories. As my finger clicked the arrow key, my eyes stared hard at each image, burrowing into that moment in the past, remembering all that would never be, trying to understand what happened. When did it start? I searched the photo gallery on my laptop for traces of the Juicer.

My history was divided before Chet died. Before her, after her. Maybe there was no after her. She was there to the very end. But I needed to know when it started. I wanted evidence, confirmation of my suspicions. How much of my past was polluted by her? I thought I could find clues in the date stamped archive of my photos of Chet. My eyes drilled into him as my brain twitched between anguish and rage.

There was a third thing I was coping with, other than my grief and his infidelity. His death event had become a legend, and word of it was spreading beyond our circle of friends to people who heard about it and wanted to know more. I was getting phone calls from people who barely knew me but wanted to ask questions about how we did it, how to have a home funeral, how to keep a body cold, how to die in peace. Chet would have been pleased with the way his reality show played out. Jason's photos were the crowning exhibit, a portrait of my divine man as he became a divine corpse in sacred repose, right down to the exquisite purple capillaries lacing his ears. We did it. Yes, we. It was my mission, too. I took it on. I believed in it. It was beautiful. I was proud to have been part of it. Mission accomplished.

~ : ~

The full moon dangled on a pendant of stars outside the bathroom windows. I was drunk, slugging down my third martini in the bathtub, listening to *Turandot*. *Nessun dorma*. Then I got a pair of scissors and hacked my long locks to the edge of my skull, prison style. How appropriate. After the new hairdo, I stumbled over to my pajama drawer and saw my red silk pajamas, and the martinis said, "Too bad you won't be wearing those again."

Really, I thought. *I don't get to wear my red silk pajamas. Because I'm a widow? Really? Am I being punished?*

The widow word had been bugging me. Since biblical times widows have been mistreated, enslaved, stripped of their social status, forced to give up their possessions and sometimes even forced to give up their children. They have been married off to their husband's brothers and forced to become breeders for his family. In Egyptian lore a widow could be buried alive in her husband's tomb. In India a widow could be burned alive on her husband's funeral pyre. In Nepal widows were forbidden to wear red because red is the color of joy. A widow is bad luck. Her income plummets. Her assets disappear. She loses the farm. This was not a cohort I dreamed of joining. This was a curse.

Wherever I went I had a black letter W on my forehead, a title conferred upon me without my consent. Being a widow is a lower social caste than being married. It's a pity card that comes with its own set of patronizing facial expressions and a tone of voice that says your ticket has been downgraded. "I'm so sorry. You no longer have a seat in first class." Expectations for my future were diminished. I was damaged goods. I had to wear those red silk pajamas. It was a matter of self-respect.

~ : ~

The fruit basket is nice
  But I'd rather have my husband back
His ashes sit in a box beside the spent candles and white flowers
  I sit by myself across the room
There is an empty space beside me
  Wherever I go I am followed by empty space
Someone used to be there warm and kissable

But the wind blew
The sands of time stung our eyes
Our dreams were swept away by a raging tempest
in our beautiful teapot
And now here I am
Alone with a fruit basket

~ : ~

My girlfriends tightened the circle around me, and I loved them for it. They were smart and caring, and I could feel them weaving a safety net with my name on it. They dropped in to visit me and invited me out to dinner and kept me socially engaged. They included me on holidays, remembered my birthday and gave me gifts. We had dinner together and I shared my poems and showed them Jason's photographs. I talked with them about my day-to-day life, the farm and my animals. They bought my eggs and my beef, and they helped me promote the farm. It was healing for me to be with them. But I didn't tell them about Chet's affair. It was too complicated, too disruptive, too out of character with their impression of my marriage. And I knew once I let it out, the story would take on a life of its own. I didn't want to lose control of the story. It was my story.

After 32 years living with a guy who loved tools, I had become a dependent. Plumbing mystified me. I didn't know how a doorknob held a door shut. Cleaning the gutters and swapping out the storm windows and screens were tasks that were never on my to-do list. My paint was chipping, and I had squirrels in the attic. I had an exterminator take a look and he said I had a colony of flying squirrels living over me, handsome nocturnal creatures with big round black eyes. I followed him up the ladder to see them with his flashlight and they smiled at me as though I were a guest in their house. They were my parallel existence. I decided to let them stay. Having squirrels in my attic was no longer a metaphor. It was my reality.

I didn't hear machines until Chet died. He would be awakened in the middle of the night by the sound of the water pump in the cellar cycling on and off because I left a hose running somewhere outside. I would sleep through it. He spoke the language of the furnace and the washing machine and the icemaker. I was oblivious. Now these machines were mine and they frightened me with unfamiliar noises. They came to me in dreams where I was thin and starving because I failed to understand a row of blinking LEDs on a digital control panel. Tools lined up like can-can dancers and taunted me for my failure to understand points of leverage. I opened an instruction manual and all the pages were blank. I couldn't figure out how to use the fire extinguisher and the house burned down. Without Chet, I began to hear the machines. Anxiety opened my ears.

Sleeping alone was particularly difficult. I missed the soft rhythm of another set of lungs. I missed the body heat and the tender touch. I missed the night words and the intimacy. I missed being hugged and held. I missed kissing and sex. I missed the assurance of a warm human beside me who shared my fate, who would look out for me and keep me safe. A roof leak could keep me awake all night traumatized by the price of fixing it and my imminent financial doom. Economic humiliation was the wolf at my door. Missing a mortgage payment would be the ultimate collapse of the social compact between my ego and me. One of the many stages of grief is fear.

~ : ~

Our friends were looking forward to a gathering in Chet's honor where they could share their memories and comfort each other in their loss. I wanted to do this for them. So I planned his memorial celebration to be on his 55th birthday, June 21st, 2009, six months after his death. I needed to talk about what I had learned as a caregiver and a widow. The day would include storytelling, Jason's photographs, my poems, a feast, and the spreading of Chet's ashes on the farm. It would be an occasion to talk about dying a conscious death and plant seeds in people's minds for how to make death a celebration of life. It would be the conclusion of the mission.

Writing poetry had become my therapy. I needed poetry to help me process feelings that were beyond my verbalization, beyond sentence structure, streams of emotion gathered in words. It wasn't about art. Writing was my salvation. My poems were the excrement of an imprisoned mind. I needed to get them out before they poisoned me.

139

At the same time, Jason's photographs were visceral, and I didn't want them to seem vulgar or exploitive. I needed to put them in the context of Chet's vision for his death and explain how they fulfilled his desire to die differently. To prepare for the program, I scripted a slide presentation of the photos and made a notebook of the script so I could rehearse it.

Once written for my script, Chet's story was a compelling read and I was inspired to publish it as a commemorative art book called *Dying Beautifully*, featuring Jason's photos and my poems. Meanwhile Chet was so well liked at the college that the administration offered their black-box theater for his memorial service. Then friends of his suggested we make a video of the program. That inspired me to stage my talk, organize props, and costume myself in those red silk pajamas. As it happened, Chet's memorial service was a performance as much about me as him.

Friends from Boston and the Berkshires helped me organize a pig roast at the farm to take place after our gathering at the black-box theater. We planned a barbeque for a hundred people. Then I designed and mailed the invitations, which featured my favorite photograph of Chet and me, taken on our romantic weekend in Boston in February 2008, a year before he died.

~ : ~

For two years after the band reunion Chet and I were estranged. Then President's Day weekend, mid-February 2008, my friend Annette was visiting Boston on a business trip with her husband, Kevin, and invited us to stay with them in their hotel suite, high above the city for the holiday weekend. I got a farmsitter, and Chet and I drove to Boston together for the first time in years. It had been so long since he and I spent time with each other relaxing that it felt like being on a date with someone new. The four of us had a late lunch in the hotel bar. Then we meandered across the snow covered Public Garden where Kevin snapped a photo of Chet and me on the bridge above the frozen pond, rosy cheeked and beaming, the perfect photograph of the perfect couple on the perfect winter day.

The city was effervescent. We held hands, kissed and laughed, lighting up the night. It was as though Chet and I had stepped back in time, back into the couple we used to be, before our years of estrangement. We had dinner in an Italian restaurant in the North End, shared the chocolates on our pillows, and watched an old movie on TV. Then we made love between the sheets, and again the next morning in the shower.

That night was the highest I have ever been in my life. Happy doesn't begin to describe the electric joy that lit every cell in my body. He loved me again. I could feel it. We were united. Our sex was extraordinary. In the shower, we devoured each other like hungry animals. The starvation experience of his depression was over. My life was back on track. My stars were aligned again. I could be happy again. Whatever had gone down, we had overcome it. And we were together once more. Husband and wife. Lovers and best friends.

On the way home from Boston to the farm, we took a side trip through the city, and passed each of our former houses, reminiscing. "I'm glad we don't live here anymore," Chet said. "It's cool. But it never felt like home to me."

"I know what you mean," I said. "None of our city places felt like home the way the farm does."

"Sometimes the farm feels like our child," he said.

"It is our child, Chet. It's a living organism we made together."

"I never thought I would have a place like that."

"We're so lucky," I said. "Lucky to have each other and the farm."

"I wish my dad had lived long enough to see what we've done with the place."

"He would have loved the cows."

"He would have loved the whole thing. It's like we're living the life he didn't get to have."

"When you think how far we've come and what we have now, it's like our dreams have come true."

"I know," he said. "I love you, Bil."

"I love you, too, baby."

Finally, the man I married was back in the skin of the man in my bed. My lust for him filled me. I had no idea what had changed in him, but I was elated that it had. The next morning at the farm, before he returned to work, we exchanged a passionate kiss. But by that evening when he came home, he was sinking again. He couldn't look me in the eye. He wouldn't talk. He didn't want to touch. But this time I reacted differently. I didn't blame myself. My inner voice said, *It's not my fault. He's not depressed because of me. He loves me. It's not my fault.* And I resolved to wait for him to ascend from that swamp even if it took years.

That trip to Boston, a year before he died, was the last time we had sex. And because of that invisible fact, the photo of us on the bridge in the Public Garden symbolized much more for me than just a romantic weekend. It enshrined the resurrection of my marriage, the best sex I ever had, a renaissance in our love, the perfect restart of our perfect lives. That's why I chose that photo for the invitation to Chet's memorial celebration. It's how I wanted people to remember us. It's how I wanted to remember my husband.

~ : ~

I hear you singing
Long after my eyes cannot see, I hear you
The melody of splashing water and fragrant soap
White towels without a backbeat
But for the wings of birds keeping time in the sky
Carried on your breath an airlift of music delivers me to the clouds
Where I find you
Peeing off the long porch and counting fireflies
In the first days of summer
When you join the night songs and give voice to the melody
That came to you in the shower

~ : ~

The invitations were mailed in April for the memorial in June, and people were getting excited about gathering at the farm. At the end of May, I was sitting with a friend in my kitchen, planning the program for Chet's memorial at the college, and we got to swapping stories about Chet's work life, analyzing his years of depression, and how his unhappiness affected our marriage and me. Then the friend admitted he knew about the Juicer. In fact, she had been in touch with him.

"I'm really sorry," he said. "Chet made me promise never to tell you. But I was so angry with him for putting me in the middle of his big lie. He forced me to choose between him and you."

"So, you knew all about it?"

"Those weekends he was supposed to be staying at my house while we did the doc shoot — he didn't stay at my house."

"He stayed with her."

"I can't believe I'm telling you this. He made me promise. But I feel so guilty. And I want to help you. You need to get through this. You need to know the truth. I know it's really bad. I was shocked when he took her to Maine."

"Maine? *He took her to Maine?*" I felt as though I had been punched. A deep hole opened in my gut and all of me fell through it. The thought of Chet taking the Juicer to the resort where we had spent our honeymoon and staying with her in the timeshare condo we bought for ourselves as a wedding present, that thought was a bullet through my soul. Blood splattered on my most sacred memories. I died. My vision blurred, I got dizzy and collapsed.

"Oh, god," he said. "I thought you knew."

So that's where the fancy bathrobe came from. He took her to Maine for a week at the end of February 2008 after our weekend in Boston, and they went shopping together. Or maybe it was a gift from her, like the grappa. Why had I not been more suspicious when he pulled it out of his suitcase? Why did I let go of such an obvious clue? Because I didn't see it as a clue. He went to the resort for his art sabbatical just two weeks after our romantic weekend in Boston. At the time, I believed he loved me. When he came home from Maine depressed, I felt bad for him. He seemed so lost. I rationalized the bathrobe as a symptom of his midlife crisis. If he needed to buy himself a fancy bathrobe to make himself feel better, I could relate. I had 50 pairs of shoes, most of which were purchased in a moment of retail therapy. I projected that onto my husband. Yes, it was very weird that he bought himself a fancy bathrobe. But I did not suspect another woman in the picture. Not for one second. Six months passed between the appearance of the bathrobe and the Juicer's visit to the farm.

Now a critical piece of my story had fallen into place and I was beginning to understand what had happened to me, why the afterglow from our weekend in Boston was so short lived. It was as though a curtain had been drawn over this stage of my life and I couldn't see it until I had that one piece of missing information. Then the curtain opened, and Chet's malaise was revealed. While he was making love to me in Boston, he was planning to make love to her at the resort. That duplicity was inconceivable to me. It was impossible. My head exploded.

Two weeks after our weekend in Boston, two weeks after the last time we had sex, two weeks after the resurrection of our marriage and the renaissance in our love, two weeks after the perfect photo of the perfect couple on the perfect winter day, my husband took his mistress to the resort where we spent our honeymoon. For a week they ate in the restaurants where we ate, walked on the beach where we walked, cooked in the kitchen where we cooked, sat on the couch where we sat, screwed in the bed where we screwed. That doppelganger had been shadowing me for years, stealing my life for herself.

I couldn't stop from trying to fit the pieces together. I mapped the events I knew about on a calendar to visualize what I had missed. Our weekend in Boston in February 2008, after that his trip with her to Maine, then the pain in his back in March, couldn't plant his asparagus in April, couldn't lift the new calf in May, couldn't drive the tractor either, then his diagnosis and surgery in June, then the arrival of the expensive stainless-steel juicer at the college in July, then the greeting cards and the photographs of her, then her phone calls to his friends, her texting him in July and August, then her visit to the farm in September, then my trip to Italy in October when he was obviously texting with her, then him texting in bed beside me in November, then her freak out when he stopped communicating with her after my meltdown in December, then the many voice mails and texts she sent right up until his death in January 2009. Over and over again I replayed the list until every injury was memorized.

~ : ~

My cheek makes a shallow grave in the mud
Cold wet bags of sand are placed all along my body
pressing me deeper into the sludge
My breasts, my hip bone, my knees, outline my future
I am sinking never to return
  like a dinosaur in the lava flows
  an insect in amber
Captured for eternity in my most desperate moment
Remembered in a passive state, still
  I succumb to this disaster quietly
I will not be humiliated by hopelessness
  my silence is homage to my loss
I am a relic of my heart
The broken home of my soul

~ : ~

I can only imagine how it must have haunted Chet to know that I would one day find out the truth of how he spent the last few years of his life. No wonder he couldn't make eye contact with me. He had crossed over to the dark side. I was starting to feel like she was his cancer, like she killed my husband.

My organization skills went psychotic and I tore through years of archives in our tidy office, demanding conclusive proof. Every file folder, every piece of paper, his computer, his cell phone, his photos, his emails, his documents, his browsing history, his contacts, his calendars, his receipts, his journals, and his trash, I inspected and itemized all of it. Nancy Drew on acid.

File cabinet drawers gaped, manila folders spread eagle on the bed, tiny scraps of paper piled by year and date covered the desk. I quickly discovered he had a code for himself using her initials. The breadcrumbs were all there. I couldn't sleep until it was finished. I stayed up all night reading itty-bitty text and making red checkmarks on printouts of credit card statements. I dozed on the floor for a while. Then I cross-referenced everything I found in his stuff with my own calendars, receipts, emails and journals.

My sleuthing confirmed the worst. He and the Juicer had been carrying on for three years, from the band reunion in Boston in January 2006, until he gave me his cellphone at the end of 2008, a month before he died. Three years.

Knowing that didn't make me feel better. I thought it would put my mind to rest, but it didn't. There was no big healing moment when heavenly light shined on the piles of paper in my office and I was suddenly freed of the burden of suspicion. There was no epiphany where I thought, *Oh, that's how it happened. Oh, that's what his words meant. Oh, that's why he was gone on the weekends. Oh, that's why he couldn't look me in the eye. Oh, that's why he couldn't get it up when I touched him. Oh, that's when he must have been thinking about her.* No, there was none of that. No cleansing enlightenment gave me peace. Once I knew the extent of his deceit, I crashed.

I felt so stupid. If I missed all that action, what else had I missed? If I believed he loved me through all that betrayal, what else did I believe that wasn't true? How could he have loved me and been with her at the same time? Maybe he didn't love me. Maybe I wasn't loveable. Maybe I was a fucking loser. This is what happens to losers.

My mind was out of control, but I didn't tell anyone. I did not reveal my nights of madness in the office, going through years of receipts and emails to prove to myself my husband had cheated on me. I was an embarrassment to myself. I didn't talk about it. I felt like it was my failure, my mistake, the result of my bad judgment, a black mark against my name. She was a shit stain on my life, and I intended to hide it. People thought Chet and I had the perfect relationship. Looking at us made them feel good. They idealized us. We were cute together. It was a lie, but I wasn't ready to give it up.

~ : ~

By the time I found out Chet had taken the Juicer to Maine, people were already RSVPing to the invitations for his memorial celebration. The art book I created for the occasion, *Dying Beautifully*, was already at the printer. Folks across the country were making travel plans. I had put events into motion that I couldn't stop unless I took the extreme action of cancelling all of it. And how would I explain that? I had a choice. I could maintain the charade of my perfect life, or drop a bomb into my world, shattering myself, and the memories of so many other people.

I didn't have the fortitude for a bomb. I was already broken. I was a widow and I missed my husband. I was living alone for the first time in my life and I was uncertain about my future. Getting a grip on the ordinary consumed me. I couldn't handle the chaos of exploding my social life with the truth about my marriage. I needed stability.

My life was already ruined on the inside. I didn't want it to be ruined on the outside, too. I needed someplace to go in my world where I could feel at peace. Even if it was fake peace. So I went on with the plan for Chet's celebration, and swallowed the many compliments about the beautiful photo on the invitation. I smiled and nodded when people told me they had that picture up on their refrigerator where they could see it every day because it reminded them of Chet, and what a cool couple we were. Our love inspired them, and they dreamed of having what we had.

There was no way I could talk about what really happened. I thought about telling my friends the truth, but it didn't sound true. The story of Chet's death was beautiful. The story of his affair was ugly. I wondered if people would believe me. Or would they turn on me and accuse me of wrecking my own life? Would they think I was mentally ill? Would they savage me with gossip and hairy eyeballs in the grocery store? I couldn't face that. On the outside everything was perfect looking, even in death. But my brain was a crime scene. So I put my emotional gore in that lockbox in the back of my mind, and I didn't look at it.

~ : ~

June 21st was a lush day on the farm, verdant and sweet smelling. The theater was filled. I performed my script in my red silk pajamas in front of a huge screen displaying Jason's photos. In the receiving line afterward, as people expressed their condolences, they spoke of the importance of the story and how much they enjoyed the telling. They treated me like a war hero. Copies of *Dying Beautifully* were distributed and those books carried on the mission of Chet's death as they went out into the world. It was gratifying. I knew Chet would have been pleased.

The barbeque at the farm was cacophonous. Friends helped prepare and serve fabulous food. A flower farm sent boxes of fresh cut peonies to decorate the tables and the house. I engaged a bagpipe player for the spreading of Chet's ashes. After lunch, he climbed the hill above the barn in his plaid kilt and began to play. The melancholy moan of bagpipes filled the air, drawing our shared sadness to attention. I walked carrying the box of Chet's ashes to the barnyard and the crowd gathered around me.

"Take a handful of Chet's ashes," I said, opening the box so they could see inside. "He wanted them spread on the farm. Carry him to the places where you remember him and sprinkle him there."

It was a new kind of communion. Person after person put their hand in Chet's ashes and took a fistful of him. Then with the bagpipes serenading us, we sowed him across the land. People walked in his garden and around the pond, through the barnyard and the woods, into the pastures, each person acting out their memory of him, placing his ashes where they found his spirit. It was catharsis, the group journey we hoped for, just as Chet wished.

Chet's sister, Cathy, came to his memorial service and put her hand in his ashes, and walked alone across the barnyard crying. I was glad she came to see his vision complete. Chet's mother did not attend. A program with a slide show and poems was not her notion of a solemn funeral. The idea of putting her hand in his ashes seemed eerie. She didn't call it creepy, but that's what she was thinking. Still, she was curious about how the day went and wanted me to call her when it was over. As soon as she picked up the phone, I could hear the TV. She was on her rocking loveseat anesthetized by a dose of nerve pills, smoking.

"What's going on?" I asked, wearing my headphones so I could do dishes while we talked.

"Oh, I was just sitting here watching a baseball game," she said. "This isn't really the one I want to watch. I want to see the one that comes next. But it doesn't start for another hour. So I started watching this one. Then my sister called, and we got to talking about her surgery, and I got up to get myself a ham sandwich. And do you know, I've walked through that kitchen door a million times, and I tripped and spilled my can of pop. You can't see it because the carpeting is so damned dirty. I try to get that cleaning lady of mine to rent one of those carpet cleaning machines, but she has to take her daughter to DUI school on Tuesdays before she comes here, and she says she doesn't have time to pick up the machine in the morning, and I'm not paying for an extra day just because her daughter drinks too much and isn't smart enough to let someone else drive her home from bingo. Anyway, I don't know what she's going to do about it, but she's going to have to do something because I can't have a rug that dirty in my house. You know what I mean, Bil?"

"Yes," I said, dishtowel over my shoulder, pacing the kitchen with a wet sponge.

"I mean, really. You pay people good money to do good work and you expect it to get done. But things just aren't the way they used to be. No one wants to work for their money anymore. Everyone wants a handout. I can't even watch the news. It just makes me mad. All these people on welfare. The blacks are taking over. And I don't even know who the Hispanics are. I mean, what country do those people come from? And why are they here? I wouldn't even know what country to send them home to. And now that Barak Alabama is president, I'm scared. I mean I'm really scared. Aren't you scared, Bil?"

"No, I'm not scared." I didn't tell her how much Chet loved Obama, and how I thought for sure he would live to see that man inaugurated as president. I was planning on him living that long. I wasn't ready for him to die on January 16th because I had it in my head that he was going to die on January 21st, after we watched the inauguration together. "How are your knees?" I asked.

"My knees are fine as long as I don't walk too much. It's not my knees that are bothering me. It's my left hip. I can't even get comfortable on the couch anymore. Yesterday when I went to the hairdresser, I sat down in that chair and I yelled out loud. It hurt that much. Then when I got home Arlene came over and I was telling her about it, and she said she thinks I should try moving the TV. But you know Bil, I've had that damn TV in the same place for 50 years and I'm not going to move every piece of furniture in my house just because my hip hurts. When you get to be my age something new hurts

149

every day. You just get used to it. I'm telling you, Bil, don't get old. It's awful. Last night I had chest pains so bad I thought I was going to die right here in my living room. But I guess that's just how it is. I sat in a chair and rocked until the pains went away. I told Kelly about it this morning and he thinks I should go to the doctor. But what's the doctor going to do? I'm 88 years old."

"Are you depressed?" I didn't need to know her answer. Since Chet died, she was high whenever I called, and I could see the logic of it. If I hadn't had the farm to grip me, sliding into addiction would have been easy.

"I don't know if I'm depressed or not," she said. "These pills the doctor gives me are supposed to make my anxiety go away, but they may not be enough to get me to whistle *Dixie*. I miss Chet. I just can't believe he isn't going to call me again. Some days I wake up and think, 'Oh, maybe Chet will call today,' and then I remember he's dead. A woman isn't supposed to live longer than her son. It's not right. There were so many things I wanted to say that I didn't say. I just wish it would have been different. I wish I had done more to help you while I was there. I would always do your dishes or clean your stove or wash your refrigerator. But this time I just couldn't do it. I was too upset. Watching him shuffle around the house like his father. I'm so glad Maurice was already dead because it would have killed him to see Chet sick the way he was. He was so brave. Wasn't he, Bil? I couldn't do what he did. I don't think I could. I couldn't just die like that. But I guess it was the drugs that killed him anyway. Not the cancer. You know what I mean? I watched Maurice in all that pain, but I knew if I gave him the morphine, I would be killing him, and I just couldn't do that. I'd be afraid to. I don't understand hospice. It doesn't seem right to me, killing people with drugs instead of letting them die the way they're supposed to. But everything else is changing. I suppose death is gotta change, too. Anyway, I'm not dead yet. Just to prove it, I get up off the couch and give a Tarzan yell. I beat my fists on my chest and holler just to prove I'm still here. You know, like this —"

And she gave a long high warbling holler into the phone just like Tarzan in the jungle.

~ : ~

My performance at Chet's memorial service, and the photo book, *Dying Beautifully*, were encapsulations of Chet's story, highlighting the seminal ideas, like planning his death the way we planned our wedding, enrolling himself in hospice and dying at home, and having his dead body cared for by people who loved him. I told the chronology of events, the complication of him dying on a holiday weekend, and the experience of having his corpse in the house with me for five days after he died. In 2009, his approach was radical, and our story was exotic. For many people it was also oddly comforting.

Standing under theater lights in my red silk pajamas, I shared my experience of witnessing him, being his primary caregiver, and fulfilling my commitment as his wife. I talked about the cultural history of widows and why I was wearing my red pajamas. "Red is the color of joy," I said. It was my mission to find the beauty in my experience. That was my script.

Afterward several women spoke with me about doing the reading of my script again. My story resonated with them and they wanted to share it. They were having their own experiences with people they loved resisting death, and they wanted their husbands and friends to hear what I had to say. Some of them were caregivers for dying men and they identified with my mixed feelings of sorrow and obligation. Some of them were already widows and my poems helped them process their grief. This reaction made me feel like telling Chet's story was the right thing to do.

Show business friends who had been to Chet's memorial service encouraged me to carry on with telling his story as a one-woman show. It was inebriating to receive so much positive feedback at a time when I was feeling so low. The idea of a one-woman show filled the empty space in me with a sense of purpose and overshadowed my obsession with the other events surrounding Chet's death. My ego was vulnerable to persuasion that Chet's story was my mission because I was helping other people cope with death. It was easy to slip into this scenario, like changing clothes. It gave me a sense of order and direction, and a distraction from the cognitive dissonance threatening my sanity.

I rewrote my script to suit a public performance, including humor about the massive numbers of Baby Boomers who would be dying soon, the need to bust taboos about death, and my hopes for my own inevitable end. The title became *The Widow Wears Red Pajamas*. A small experimental theater gave me their venue for three nights. At the college, Chet's colleagues heard about the show and I was invited to reprise the performance for faculty and students. An art gallery in Pittsfield that doubled as a maker space invited me to present the show on their gallery stage. Then friends in Boston invited me to perform the show at a music venue there. Then the regional hospice association invited me to perform at their annual meeting on stage in front of a few hundred people. Then an ashram invited me to present an education program on dying a conscious death.

It happened so fast and there was so much back pressure behind it. People told me again and again how much it meant to them to hear Chet's story. For months I was very busy doing unlikely combinations of things. I was in two one-woman shows, one on the farm and one on the stage, practicing my lines while I moved cows and collected eggs.

As word of mouth spread about my show and the details of Chet's death, I became a de facto death consultant. More people called me to talk about death and dying, how to manage death at home, and how to encourage loved ones to see death as a celebration of life. Those phone calls were like therapy sessions. I was shipping copies of *Dying Beautifully* and I could see the possibility of a career move. I could be a death celebrity. Talking about death could be my life's work, Chet's vision could become my personal mission. People wanted me to go in that direction. It was an open door. All I had to do was step through it and forget everything else that had happened to me.

~ : ~

My performance was easy for me because it was a story I knew, and my emotions were real. I was not an actress. Each time I gave a performance I relived the real experience of Chet's illness and death. It was cathartic for my audience to listen to me while they looked at images of a happy couple, a beautiful home, and a dead man. But I was lying, and I knew it.

What began as a script of extraordinary facts became a script of extraordinary lies. Between shows I was discovering more evidence of the affair. I was forwarded an email written by the Juicer, bragging about her weekend on the farm with him, picking wildflowers with him in the woods, detailing how she tried to give him a blow job until he pushed her away, carving their initials in the soft wood of the barn wall. The email was so explicit it was as though she intended for me to read it.

The barn was my very special place. I loved working in the dusty light and listening to the roof creak in the heat. I found solitude in the cavernous hay mow. My barn cat lived out there, and I often snuggled with her in the hay. The cows and the goats knew the barn as their food place, and they came when they heard the big doors sliding along the metal track. I loved farming and I loved my barn. The idea that yet another part of my life was violated by my doppelganger ripped at me.

I humiliated myself hunting for those initials. I took my most powerful flashlight and scoured every inch of every post and beam, wall and door. Chet and I had never carved our initials anywhere. I couldn't believe he would do something so juvenile with her. But I had failed to see so many other things that really happened. I had missed so many clues.

Wearing my reading glasses, I pressed my face to the wood looking for chiseled letters. It was mind pollution. I had a mental infection. She was a cancer in my life. My one sacred place, my beautiful barn, was not safe from her. I couldn't stop thinking about it. My barn was haunted. If it hadn't been full of food for my cows, I would have burned it down.

Forcing myself to continue to do the show was splitting me. Who was that woman performing *The Widow Wears Red Pajamas*? It wasn't me. An actress could have faked another person's story. She could have acted the romantic sadness and poignant grief, untainted by my resentment and hostility. But faking my own story had me balancing on the edge of a knife. I could feel myself breaking down. Red is the color of joy. *Right.* One night I had a fantasy of standing on stage and screaming for 90 minutes, blood coating my tongue and dripping from the corners of my mouth, until I collapsed under the lights unable to acknowledge the applause, the thunderous applause of a million mes.

I realized then I couldn't be telling stories anymore. I cancelled the last few shows and went into hiding on the farm.

~ : ~

I have tasted dust
in the billowing wake of a train wreck
a big bang collision
fragments blasted from the center in perfect symmetry
pieces of pieces of lost relationship

I can see the picture in my mind
I know each piece of the puzzle
all 5,000 pieces, intimately
they are the children of my dreams
moments in time disconnected

I reassemble them in clusters
the sky, the heart, the bed, the scream
a ruby galaxy covers a kiss
I match two pieces
my fingers drip perfectly round red

Knives balance on edge blade to blade
an exquisite stainless-steel sculpture
if you listen long enough, you'll hear the sound of the train
the slow wooden whistle of the locomotive
the frightened bird brakes, the crash

Stories explode and fly in clouds
too far from their beginning to ever return
the emptiness of god settles on the land
dust coats your nostrils
and you taste the past

14. Couples Therapy

Listen up, Chet, wherever you are! You fucked me up, man. You got away with something and we need to talk. When I kill myself, people are going to shake their heads and mutter how impossible it seems that someone like me could do such a thing. She was so smart, she was so good looking, she had so many friends, what a beautiful house, what a beautiful life, how could this happen?

Remember your Grandma Carmen's third husband? He stuffed a rag in the tailpipe of her sedan, closed the garage door and deep breathed exhaust. When she found him, she was pissed because the car was out of gas and he left a mess on the seat. The smell in her car was his final comment on their relationship. Revenge suicide is an obvious choice for an angry lover.

I remember when my Uncle Frank killed himself. After 50 years of marriage, he had to institutionalize his wife because she was demented, and he couldn't take care of her. He was a World War II vet home alone for the first time and he didn't even know how to cook. He was lost without her. So, *pop!* He blew his brains out in the shade behind the garage. I thought he did the right thing.

My grandmother said suicide is a sin. She worried that she wouldn't see Uncle Frank in Heaven because people who commit suicide go to

Hell. All the big religions are against suicide. Seems self-serving to me. I think I have the right to kill myself.

I plan to use your drugs in a vanilla ice cream shake to settle my stomach. My worst fear is puking up the death potion and not dying. It would be just my shitty luck to survive my own suicide and be forced to live the rest of my life with brain damage. Although it could improve my mood.

I'm going to grind up your pills and mix them in the blender with the ice cream. Then I'll take your last few fentanyl patches and put them in my armpits and my groin. I wish I hadn't thrown away your morphine, but the eyedropper got a little icky putting those last few drops in your mouth while you were gurgling yellow foam. When I cleaned up the living room, I tossed the whole morphine bottle in the trash. You know me, always cleaning in a frenzy. I'll never understand why I didn't just wash the eyedropper.

Once the shake is made, I'll get in bed and drink it, and fall asleep and die. I want to die in bed. Or maybe the bathtub. Not in the woods or the barn. It just seems more practical. Someone will eventually find me. Then into the box and into the oven, just like you. It won't be a beautiful death like yours, but it will do the job. Finally, I can turn off this noise in my head.

My brain is a pain factory. When a moment becomes still enough for me to hear my own thoughts the atonal clank of rage drowns out my sanity. I am beyond grief. I'm mentally ill. I compulsively review my past as though I expect one more analysis to result in a different outcome. I intend to crack the code on your infidelity. I know now that you were gaslighting me to the very end. I have to reconsider every moment of my life in light of your affair. The trail of evidence you left behind is provocative.

All your life you had secrets and hiding places. I realized you needed to have time unaccounted for to feel free. I believed you loved me, and I was certain whatever you were hiding was something idiosyncratic. There was an amusing charm in your need for privacy. I felt like it was an act of love for me to give it to you without suspicion, without complaining, without a challenge. I never read your mail or went through your files or touched the stuff on your desk or looked in your dresser drawers or dug around in your workshop or went through your pockets or read your calendar or looked in your wallet. I'm doing all of that now.

I believed in you. I believed in us. I believed in love. I feel like you pulled the pin on a live hand grenade and disappeared before it exploded. Now I'm trying to clean up the mess, but I don't even know what I'm looking for. I'm no longer sure what was inside me in the first place. I may not even be here. How would I even know me if I saw me? Some days I think the best way to clean my closet is to burn down my house.

"Nothing is what I thought it would be." That's what you said. And I know just what you mean, because nothing is what I thought it was either.

In the last year of your life, you lied to me every day. How can I ever get over that? If you were here, we could take months to analyze our couplehood and rationalize our behavior. We could have great make-up sex and laugh at what jerks we are. But you are not here, and I have no way to process this situation other than the boiling inside me and the steam coming out my ears. You are not who I thought you were. You are my crisis of faith, motherfucker.

15. Mucking Around

Late summer, after Chet's memorial celebration, when time yawned and I looked for ways to keep busy, I harvested the garlic from his garden and hung it from the ceiling in the bungalow. The room had been his workshop, a wooden building with a screen porch overlooking the pond. The task immersed me in his world. Like his dad's basement and his recording studio, Chet's workshop was outfitted with sundry gadgets, tools, machines and supplies, a masculine space for smart hands.

All around the room his pegboard of tools, the jars of nails, the cans of paintbrushes, and his collection of broken clocks whispered to me in his voice. I thought about kissing him, the feel of the muscles on his face, his perfect tongue, and a river of sadness swept through me. For a while I just sat in a chair and cried in the dark.

He would have loved that night. The air was smooth and dry. The pieces of his unfinished projects were scattered about. After I hung the garlic, I reorganized the room from top to bottom, fiddling around long into the night with the feeling I was dissecting my husband and labeling his parts. Screwdrivers beside hammers and channel locks, sandpaper on the shelf with steel wool, spools of wire on the shelf below, zip ties on the shelf below that, plumb bob with the levels, cleaning as I went, wiping, dusting, polishing.

I was deep in silent dialogue with him, explaining what I was doing, when I found the half empty grappa bottle hidden in a barrel with his vacuum attachments, a twin of the grappa bottle I had found in his office at the college. That was a kick in the face.

In my mind I was with him while I was cleaning. I was in his world. At the sight of the grappa bottle, I gasped and doubled over to catch my breath. He may as well have hit me with it. I guessed it was from her weekend in September at the farm, when they spent the night on the screen porch talking. Or had they rendezvoused at the farm on another occasion? In any case, he knew how upset I would be if I saw it because he knew I would recognize the label as my own favorite kind of grappa. So he hid the evidence of their affair and forgot it. My doppelganger had shadowed me into my own house. I was so pissed-off, I stood right there and drank it. All of it. *Fuck them.*

~ : ~

This is me typing the Edvard Munch Scream
    listening to a Bartók concerto
    raw meat spoils on the kitchen counter
I am slipping, slipping, slipping
    a locomotive off the tracks
    tumbling down the walls of a canyon
    a moth caught in a crow's mouth
    ink washed off the page by rain
A howling beneath my pillow
    my ears bleed
That our last breath should be sweet is a dream betrayed by fear
    I tremble
The smell of smoke settles into the rug
    ashes become dust
I disappear in the tailwinds of a passing storm
    leaving my shadow to burn in the sun

~ : ~

Four months after Chet died Ayla gave birth to April under the pines on the hill above the barn. Until then I hadn't seen a cow give birth, but I remembered how Chet was there to help Ayla calve Rouge. So when I saw the tiny hooves peaking from under Ayla's tail, I took a seat beside her to watch.

She breathed patiently. The pumping action of each successive breath inched the hooves into the air, then the round end of the nose appeared, then a few minutes later the head, then a few minutes later the thick tubular body. Then *plop!* The weight of the falling torso pulled the hind legs through, and the 60 lb. blob of slime lay still on the ground. Ayla turned around to investigate with her nose. Then she began to lick off the placenta until April was revealed.

The biochemistry of licking forever imprints the identity of newborn on mother and mother on newborn. The force of Ayla's tongue cleaning her child jiggled and rocked the motionless calf until consciousness surfaced on her face, and she took her first look at the world. Nature may have equipped April with the capacity for life, but her mother's nurturing tongue and warm breath were the loving welcome that promised life was worth living.

Life goes on, I thought, as I watched these two women become their future selves. *Life goes on with or without us.*

A calf must stand on its legs by force of intuition. After nine months of amniotic sleep, her body parts must realize their true purpose and act. Ayla's nudging, licking and lowing were encouragement, but it was up to April to find her legs and use them. One at a time, each limb unfolded, stretched and pressed a new hoof to the ground. She experimented with standing on two legs at a time, first raising her rear, then falling. Then raising her chest and falling. The process was similar to watching a child learn to ride a bicycle. The sense of balance has to become so intuitive that it can be learned once forever. April teetered and tottered for half an hour until she was up on all fours. Then she had to find Ayla's udders.

A newborn calf is looking for something hidden in the warm body of mom. Ayla turned and nudged April's rear in a delicate dance pointing the calf's nose toward her first meal. Then the calf would get lost in her mother's legs and Ayla would turn and nudge her again. Nature's preprogrammed instructions keep the cow from stepping on the calf, even when she can't see her, and keep the calf seeking the udders that she has never known. Finally, the calf puts her mouth on the teat and punches the bag with her forehead to bring down the milk, another essential step in the process hardwired into a cow's brain — using her head as a tool for getting what she wants in life.

Nature takes care of herself. I can take care of myself.

~ : ~

Like my mother-in-law, I reveled in my newfound independence after my husband died. Without a resident man, I had no limits, no checks and balances, no second opinion. I was completely free to make my own mistakes. I didn't have his skepticism, or his commitment to practice, or his apprehension of mud. No one was there to talk me out of it when I decided to relocate the hay feeder to the front of the barn, where I could just drop hay down into it, instead of carrying bales out to pasture.

Grief is a pervasive feeling, but it's not the only feeling. It co-exists with a circus of emotions waiting to play out in action. In my head, even though I was tragically sad that the love of my life was gone, there were certain things I knew I would do as soon as he wasn't there to stop me. I knew it before he died. And I launched into action as soon as I could find the time and muster the motivation. Changing the set-up for feeding the cows was on the top of the list of things I intended to do after Chet died. I had a plan, and I didn't consult with anyone. I just did it.

To set up the new feeding area, I planned to use the tractor to re-grade the slope in front of the barn. I had become friends with Chet's Massey Fergusson and enjoyed doing tractor work, especially landscaping. I wanted the sloped area in front of the barn to be big and level enough to make a U-turn with the tractor.

To level the slope, I planned to get a truckload of rocky fill and cover it with topsoil. After a bit of research, I called a guy who had some fill that I could get cheap. He told me he had some ground-up cinderblocks from a demolition job. He was certain they were just what I needed.

A couple days later I had a mountain of broken cinderblocks in front of the barn. They were not fill and they were not ground up. They were chunks of concrete block broken just enough to be useless for masonry. The bucket of the tractor could not push them or scoop them or scrape them, and to move them by hand would have crippled me. This was a mistake Chet would not have made. He would have gone to look at the "broken" cinderblocks before he had them dumped in front of our barn.

I was pacing around my new cinderblock mountain, fretting over the situation, when two guys I knew from the highway department drove by in the excavator they used to maintain the gravel road. I flagged them down and they confirmed it would be impossible for me to move those cinderblocks with my tractor. Thankfully, in 15 minutes they solved my problem with their powerful machine, pushing the broken concrete blocks into a thick layer across the slope in front of the barn.

It took two truckloads of topsoil to cover those cinderblocks, and hours on the tractor to push that dirt around and grade the slope into a flat area. The tractor was a little big for me, and the driver seat was rusted into place. To reach both the floor pedals and the joystick that controlled the bucket, I had to sit up very straight and extend my right arm all the way out to grab the black ball on the end of the joystick. After hours of micro movements with my arm extended, the tendons in my right shoulder were shrieking, but the front of the barn looked just how I wanted it. I was in pain, but I thought I did a great job. Chet, however, would have been horrified for reasons I would soon learn.

~ : ~

The new hay feeder setup worked pretty well at the start. Chores took less time and effort, and I could watch the ruminants eat without leaving the house. But with the cold came the wet, and without the slope to drain the land, water collected around the hay feeder and in the new topsoil across the front of the barn. The cows spent a lot of time standing there, and their hooves mashed their manure and hay droppings into the topsoil, making a patch of spongy muck.

An adult cow produces about 20 lbs. of manure a day and I had a few cows. It was more manure than I had time and tendons to shovel, especially in winter when daylight was in short supply. So the muck got deeper as winter progressed. It didn't freeze because the manure was warm, and the composting action of the manure and the hay droppings kept it warm. That's why it's ideal to have cows living out on pasture where they can spread their manure in a more efficient manner over a much larger area. And of course, that's why Chet didn't want to feed the cows near the barn.

By mid-winter the cows stood knee deep in muck that made loud farty sucking sounds with each step. The goats hated it and climbed into the hay feeder to keep their feet dry. The sheep were a mess. When I walked through the muck, my boots were sucked down into it, and I had to pull up hard with my leg to take each step. Then I struggled to pull up my foot and lost my balance. My foot slid out of my boot and I wobbled on one leg with my sock in the air before I fell backwards into the foul pudding. My whole body sank into poo goo, and I was looking up at cows. Chet howled, "You wanted mud. You got it."

It took a few loads of laundry, a shower, and wiping down the mud room to make all that muck disappear from the house. To soak up the water collecting around the hay feeder, I spread a thick layer of hay on the muck. The cows loved that. The new layer of hay insulated the warm manure, and the cows loafed around the hay feeder even more than they had before.

It wasn't long before the layer of new hay formed a dense thatch over the bottom rungs of the hay feeder. The thatch was so strong that I couldn't move the big metal ring. When I tried to use the tractor to move it, the thatch was so tightly woven over it that the metal rails bent and broke. Chet said, "So you broke the hay feeder trying to get it out of the mud? Nice work, Bil."

~ : ~

When spring came, and the cows were finally back out on pasture, and the muck in front of the barn was dry enough for the tractor to have traction, I hopped on the Massey Fergusson and began to clean up the mess I made. I scraped off the top layer of muck and moved it to the compost pile. Then I started getting tidy around the edges. I was getting good at using the tractor in small spaces.

Near the end of the chore I was scraping the section closest to the barn foundation, getting every last bit of muck into one last load. As I maneuvered, I got the tractor into a tight spot between the fence and the barn wall, with the bucket heaped full. I had only inches to spare without hitting the barn, but I didn't want to dump that bucket and spend the time to refill it.

There's a little picture on the side of the tractor under the word DANGER! It shows the full bucket lifted in the highest position over the engine block and tilted toward the driver. Regardless, I lifted the full bucket of muck to the highest position over the engine block to create more space between the front end of the tractor and the barn. Then I shifted gears and gave it some gas.

The tractor lurched, the bucket tilted toward the driver, and the entire load of muck dumped, just like in the picture. The engine block was covered, my legs and feet were buried, I had manure in my eyes and hair, on the dashboard and the steering wheel, my feet slid off the pedals and the engine died. For a moment I was in shock and just sat there realizing what I had done, listening to Chet's laughter rock the Cosmos. Fortunately, it was not a load of cinderblocks.

Twice I found myself covered from head to toe with cow manure because I was intent on doing things my way, and twice Chet laughed at me from the Great Beyond. Falling down into the muck and sinking was humiliating, but it wasn't that dangerous. Dumping the bucket on my head was one of the biggest mistakes I had ever made on the farm. Thinking about how I could have killed myself gave me the chills. Toying with suicide gave me a soothing sense of options, but crushing myself under a load of rock was medieval. If there had been anything solid in that muck, my life on the farm could have come to an abrupt end. Of course, Chet was right about fearing mud. The words Pig Fever echoed in my mind. From that moment on, I consulted my inner Chet before I started projects and Chet remained my co-farmer in my head.

~ : ~

When Henry's hips started to fail, I was unprepared. The bullmastiff breed is known for having hip problems. When we got him as a puppy the vet warned us that his hips were going to hurt him. The first sign was an awkward stiffness, as though his hind legs were sticks. Then he jumped off the porch and fell on his face. He stopped hopping onto the couch, and he had trouble getting in the car. He weighed 150 lbs., more than I could lift. He was deeply depressed, and I suspected he was in constant pain. Finally, he couldn't lift himself up off the hardwood floors. He was humiliated.

After Chet died, Henry was my constant companion. He was always with me doing barn chores, feeding the chickens, mending fences, walking through the woods, sitting on the long porch. I talked to him, hugged him and cried into his warm neck. He was my comfort, the one animal I could kiss. Eleven months after Chet died, I remembered what he had said about his own death, about not wanting to be humiliated by the process.

The vet came to the house to give Henry the shot, because he couldn't get up off the floor and I couldn't get him into the car. All the emotional control I had exerted during Chet's end of life care was used up. I was raw. I begged for my dog's life. I howled the way Chet's mom and Cathy howled. But there was nothing the doctors could do. He died in the living room right where Chet died, and I kept him there for 24 hours, curled up just as he would have been if he were sleeping at my feet.

Yes, it was weird to have my dead dog in my living room for a couple days. But not any weirder than having my dead husband laying around. My heart was gaping. Death was starting to feel normal, like just another thing that happens. I didn't hate death. I hated the pain.

Henry's absence changed the barnyard dynamic. My friend Catherine helped me bury him in the pasture beside Burt, and I think the circle of predators around the farm knew he was out of commission. That's when Chet's favorite rooster, Big Gay Al, became a target for the fox. Big Gay Al was huge, but he wasn't very interested in the hens, and his crow never matured from the tin alto of a toy rooster. He was not a great guardian of the flock, but he was very friendly, and he would occasionally follow Henry around the lawn.

"We can't kill him," Chet said. "He's a special needs bird." So we kept him, even though he was useless.

I didn't see the attack. But seeing Big Gay Al afterward, I could imagine what happened. I found him wandering aimlessly with his neck folded over and his head dangling at his side. His neck was stripped of feathers, but the skin wasn't broken, and he could still see, although he couldn't get his beak in position to eat. It seemed as though his neck muscles and tendons were torn, but his spine was still working. I'm sure the fox was thrilled to have such a big bird in her mouth, and then very disappointed that Big Gay Al's neck didn't snap as easily as a hen's. And I can see Big Gay Al running madly across the barnyard, trying to escape the fox fur collar around his neck.

I could have mercifully killed him, but all I could think of was Chet playing with his goofy rooster, trying to teach him to crow. When Henry's hips disintegrated, his death was extremely traumatic for me. I wasn't in the mood for one more death, and Big Gay Al didn't seem to be in pain. It was just that his head was in the wrong place. I could relate to that.

With rubber bands and a rolled-up terrycloth washcloth I made a neck brace thick enough to hold his head up, but loose enough so that he could look around and swallow. He lived in the breeding apartment in the coop for a couple months, until he didn't need the collar to hold his head up and eat. It was an interesting experiment in chicken first aid. His head never sat proud again, and he never made a sound, but he was mobile enough to enjoy ranging on the lawn. Then one day Big Gay Al just disappeared.

~ : ~

The full moon bestows a brilliant blackness
A solitary chair holds the world in its arms
*   the small, small world of teaspoons and pocketknives*
a silver coaster, my grandfather's ashtray, a hat

Here scrolled stories
Light projected on a wrinkled sheet
*   faces blur, colors run together and pool in a fold of cloth*

Remember the indecision of the hickory tree
to grip the rocks with boney fingers
or climb with crooked limbs to the sky

A white blanket pulled over the farm
up to her chin save a tiny hole burnt by the moon
How many times we walked here
to see that pinspot part an invisible curtain on crusty snow

~ : ~

I thought my dad and Peggy would come back to the farm and visit me. I had enjoyed working with them while Chet was sick. But they didn't want to come back to the farm. They didn't want to revisit the scene of Chet's death and resurrect those emotions. They felt they had fulfilled their obligation to me. Farming was not their thing. They thought I should sell the farm and they didn't want to support me in keeping it. They didn't approve of my choice to farm alone. From their point of view, it was too risky on too many levels.

I experimented with having a farmhand, even had a helper live with me for a while. But I found I needed silence. There was an abacus in my head slamming beads back and forth along a wire, measuring my losses. It took 100% of my attention to follow along.

Polite conversation was an effort. Being in the presence of other people amplified my mental isolation. I went through the motions of socializing, but I returned to myself feeling wounded. Farming was a costume that covered my disheveled emotions. I didn't want to be a widow. I wanted to be a farmer. The farm gave me something to do, something to talk about, a reason to go home, an excuse for not attending, a refuge from prying eyes.

By the very act of farming, I made the farm mine. It was not *our* farm anymore; it was *my* farm. Farming soothed my rage. My animals distracted me from fantasies of suicide. The more engaged I was in farm work, the better I felt, even when I was dumping manure on my head. I cleaned until the skin peeled off my hands. Organizing validated my existence, even if I was folding socks on a falling airplane.

Taking care of the farm was my religious ritual. I crawled on bloody knees through my Twelve Stations of the Frozen Hose.

Friends volunteered to help me with the gardens. I hired strong hands for some big projects, like fencing a new pasture and splitting firewood. I continued to have work parties to help with the change of seasons in May and October. But the farm was my passion and my art project. I wanted to do the work myself because I wanted to have the experience. The bruises and sprains, cuts and rashes, spider bites and blood blisters gave me a sense of physical connection to the system I intended to master. I wanted to disappear into Nature and be swallowed up by her.

~ : ~

Spring 2010 came like spring always does. It had been a year since Chet died. I started thinking about the calves that would be born, my gardens, and getting a new flock of chickens. It was warm enough to have the windows open and the grass was greening. I missed Henry, his warm affection and his fierce protection. He was my sentinel and my alarm system. The house was too still without him. So I decided to get a puppy. Now for sure, I thought, suicide is off my to-do list. You can't get a puppy and then kill yourself. It's not right.

When I found the dog I wanted, my friends saw it as a positive sign and passed the hat to help me buy him. Moon changed my brain chemistry. He was a six-month old Weimaraner, leggy and coltish. His demand for exercise got me hiking again. He wanted to chase sticks and balls. My sullen adult self had to learn to play. I had to be nimble to keep up with him. The lawn started to seem small. I shortened the east pasture by 30 feet to make the lawn bigger so he would have more room to run.

Puppies are funny. The first time Moon made me laugh I felt my old face crack and fall off. I couldn't remember the last time I had laughed like that. Not a dark laugh, like laughing at Chet's death jokes, a happy laugh from having fun. Fun. Before I got Moon, fun was incomprehensible to me.

Moon was a good kisser and he was good in bed. He liked to cuddle. He went to bed when I went to bed, and he got up when I got up. He

168

did not text. He did not go away for the weekend. I never had to ask him to be with me. He was always there. When the breeder said he sold most of his dogs to women who were replacing the men in their lives, I wanted to kick him. It was in Moon's interest to love me. He wasn't faking it. He wasn't trapped in a depressing marriage. Our arrangement wasn't a social construct designed to make our family and friends more comfortable. The bond between Moon and me wasn't a plan. Moon didn't have any plans.

Like Henry, Moon loved the farm. I thought I could teach him that the chickens were his sisters, but the first time he saw a coyote chase a hen across the lawn and catch it in her mouth, he became obsessed with the sport. He was jealous that the coyote and the fox got to play with the chickens, and he didn't. Sometimes he successfully chased off the fox and then killed the chicken himself. His jaw trembled, his eyes opened into throbbing yellow circles, and prey drive took over his brain. It was in his DNA to kill chickens. He would sniff them sweetly when I was present. But if I left him alone in the yard for too long, I would find a half eaten carcass by the back door, or in his bed, or on the kitchen floor.

I had free range chickens for seven years before I got Moon. It was a costly way to raise a flock because mortality was so high. But the eggs were superlative, and my customers were willing to pay the premium. I raised the price until it hit $8 a dozen and $5 for a half dozen. Even at that I wasn't making a profit, just covering direct expenses. Still there was glory in it — the sight of beautiful birds roaming the landscape, the mounds of pastel eggs, and those exquisite orange yolks. Then came Moon. He and the chickens shared the lawn. The more he killed, the more he wanted to kill. It was his favorite game. So I had to choose between free ranging my chickens or free ranging my dog.

As I fetched the roll of electric mesh fencing from the barn, the same roll that Chet bought years earlier for the chickens, before we put up the electric fence around the barnyard, I thought about how we argued, how I was always willing to fight for my ideas about farming, the sacrifices I was willing to make. With perfect hindsight I could see the cascade of decisions: get the goats, let the goats keep their horns, have the chickens and the goats share a fence, switch from the mesh fence that was best for the chickens to the high tensile fence that was best for the goats, forget about fencing the chickens, accept the predator problem, brand our eggs as free range, sell very expensive eggs.

Now I was giving up free ranging my flock for my dog, swapping out one kind of love for another. Moon launched a new cascade of decisions. Chet would have tried to talk me out of getting a hunting dog for the farm. "A Weimaraner?" he would have said. "Aren't they bred to chase animals?"

He would have said, "You shortened the pasture by 30 feet to make the yard bigger for a dog? Are you kidding me? It's going to cost more to feed the cows and more to mow the lawn."

As I built a pen around the chicken coop with Chet's electric mesh, I heard him say, "I can't believe I didn't live long enough to see you fence in the chickens."

He would have said a lot of things. But he had his love. Moon was mine.

~ : ~

With the chickens confined to the new pen around the chicken coop, the manure that used to be spread across the land began to build up on the floor around the nesting boxes and mucking out the coop became a weekly chore. I went to the barn for a tool and left the window open where I was shoveling chicken manure out into a wheelbarrow. Then the sudden cacophony had me running back to the job. Hens were piled on top of each other in the corner under the nesting boxes, flapping and screeching in panic. On the floor beside them a Cooper's hawk pulled the skin off their sister and took a bite out of her breast.

"You motherfucker!" I charged. "Get out of here! Get the fuck out of here!"

The hawk's eyes were clear and cold, free of the emotions that ripped through me. I grabbed the manure shovel and started swinging. In a space the size of a big bathroom she out maneuvered me. I swung. She dodged. I swung. She moved like a Kung Fu master. Our eyes met but there was no exchange. I didn't penetrate her the way she filled me She was all focus. She had no doubt. She wasn't afraid. She was magnificent. I couldn't do it. I couldn't kill her. I dropped the shovel and she flew past me through the open window.

The hens on top of the pile were just fine and scrambled out of the coop into the barnyard. Others were crushed. I held their breasts in my palm and bounced them in my hand, as I lifted their heads and stretched their necks long and straight. I was doing chicken CPR, trying to get them to breathe. It worked on a couple birds, but five of them were dead. The rest of the day was spent dressing five hens for the freezer. As I counted the egg yolks inside them, I was annoyed by the loss of production. But the experience of being that close to a hawk was thrilling. My mind replayed the flash dance of the fight and the stoic wildness in her eye. I felt the wind from her wings and the cut of her fearlessness. I wanted to be like her.

~ : ~

Many other voices emerged to take up the banner of sustainable agriculture. I was not a leader anymore. My anthology of essays was old news and never made it to print. My resume had a hole in it. In the summer of 2010, I took on managing a local farmers' market to get myself back in circulation. Then I tried office jobs. In my first job interview, my prospective boss said, "I've read your resume and you've done so many things. Who is the real Billie Best?" My eyes squirted tears and I couldn't speak. I was an Olympic bullshitter, but she had asked me the one question I couldn't answer. I sniffled. My nose ran. She passed me a box of tissues and I didn't get the job.

Walking down the road crying in a pity party for myself, I ran into one of my neighbors in his pick-up truck, a fat old Cajun man, swarthy, crude, and incredibly smart. He used to trade dirty jokes with Chet, and the winter after Chet died, he gave me five cords of firewood to help me out.

"What's the matter?" he asked.

"I'm missing Chet," I whimpered. "I'm missing the life we had. It was my dream life and now it's gone."

"I'm sorry your husband died," he said. "But you had your dream life. Some people never get to live their dreams. You did. You should be thankful for that."

He smiled and drove off, and I knew he was right.

~ : ~

A great man is missing
  but it hasn't made the papers
There is a crater in my chest
  you could drive a truck through it
But the police haven't come
  sirens are screaming in my head
The neighbors haven't noticed I've been robbed
  I search the milk cartons and the posters in the general store
Have you seen this man?
  he was handsome and so well loved
Then one day he was gone
  snatched from his home by thieves
All that's left is his wedding ring
  and a crying wife

16. Swipe Left

If I was Buddha's daughter, I would have learned that expectations and attachments are the root of suffering. Desire is friction with reality. When we let go of our attachments we swim through life like a fish through water, without resistance. When we stop pulling on desire, life comes to us freely. Whatever. I'm not Buddha's daughter.

I was a love junkie in withdrawal. Millions of bacteria had swarmed between Chet and me with skin to skin contact and the exchange of bodily fluids, swapping and sharing our essence. Two bodies, one biome. My body and my brain attuned my life force to his. Our neural networks integrated. We could feel each other's thoughts. When he died my body was cut off from its other half. My physiology craved him, and when I lost him, I became physically and mentally ill. I had the feeling of being unnecessary. My biology was without purpose.

Love gave me purpose. Love is Nature's strategy for survival. Monogamy is not love. Marriage is not love. Breeding is not love. Love cannot be negotiated, imposed or stolen. Now that it was missing in my life, I could see the scope of it. Love changes everything. Being together with Chet spoon-fed our neurotransmitters with contentment. His scent shimmered through me and buoyed my spirit. His touch released the tension in my body. His voice nourished me. The comfort of his presence in my life had a Butterfly Effect that rippled through my heart to my soul. Love is unity. I was empowered to become my wildest dreams because I was strengthened by his love.

Living alone on the farm all I wanted was the love I had lost. I wanted the man I had lost. Since that wasn't possible, I thought maybe I just wanted a man. A new man, someone to give me that feeling I had with Chet, that sense of purpose, that experience of unity. But there weren't many options for dating in the rural Berkshires. I lived alone on a dead-end gravel road on the edge of a forest in a town without a stop light. There was no bar scene where I could explore my options for men in my age bracket who were both single and desirable.

As a last resort I went looking for a boyfriend on a matchmaker website and set up a coffee date with a cute guy my age who had a very well written profile. He seemed smart. He was interested in classic cars and bluegrass music and lived a half hour away. Then over cappuccino he blithely told me he had four children from two previous marriages, and he was looking for his soul mate. My brain seized up. I didn't know what to say. I lacked the social skills for a completely phony conversation. All I could think of was, *Give me a break, asshole.* But I didn't say that. I just politely cut him loose.

I already had one soul mate. Although he was dead, he occupied infinite space in my mind, stinking up my lockbox with his gangrenous romance. I could smell it, but I would not have admitted it to anyone if they asked. I thought about it all the time. There was no escape from it. I carried the photographs in my head. The crime scene was still taped off and boarded up. The chalk lines around the bodies were still on my floor. The bathrobe still hung in my closet beside those red silk pajamas.

My emotions were perfunctory. I was learning to live by myself, but I wasn't healing. I wanted companionship, but I couldn't carry on a conversation about myself. I wanted sex, but sex with another person scared me. The idea of someone thinking I was their soul mate triggered my rage. Still, I scrolled through lists of men.

At first sliding down the page through search results for my ideal guy was like scrolling through a list of vacation destinations. I tried to imagine being there, what I would wear, things I would do, how good I would feel in this fantasy place. I imagined being rescued from my life by another person with a much better life. I could just disappear into him and leave my painful world behind. It would be like never having to do laundry again. All my dirty laundry would just take care of itself.

But after my one coffee date, scrolling through lists of men on dating websites was more like looking at used cars. I checked their age first and I was skeptical of anything too perfect. I wanted to see a complete report of the physical condition of the vehicle and the repair history of the engine. To avoid repeating past mistakes, I wanted a clean bill of health, a full body scan that showed no weird shaped moles, no fatty liver syndrome, no diabetes, and a working penis. The worst thing that could happen to me would be to get into a new relationship with a cool guy and have him breakdown and kick the bucket. But history repeats itself.

~ : ~

My high school boyfriend, Sac, came to visit me on the farm in 2011, two years after Chet died. It was an easy thing to fall back into. He was a divorced Mr. Mom. We were good friends and he was a great kisser. But he wanted to watch TV and I didn't own a television. I wanted to talk politics and he wanted to watch the game. He sat on the couch while I did farm chores. We went to a sports bar so he could watch baseball. He was happy snacking on junk food. I cooked three meals a day. He didn't enjoy fine dining. I didn't own a microwave. He was annoyed by gourmet restaurants. I refused to eat fast food. It wasn't a perfect relationship, but I was hooked on his body and willing to keep him as my pet man.

Sac had visited the Luna House in Boston in 1977, when I first started working with Orchestra Luna. He knew Karla. He had met Chet, watched the band perform, and helped the roadies move equipment. Chet liked him. They shared a sense of humor and an interest in sports. It was comforting for me to have Sac at the farm because he knew me. Forty years after that first French kiss in high school, we slid right back into being a couple again, spent the Christmas holidays together, and I introduced him to my friends. But it soon became apparent that he was not well. He had no energy. He was out of breath. He wasn't able to shovel snow. He couldn't go for walks in the forest. I thought he just needed to exercise more and eat a healthier diet. But no amount of nursing and nutrition gave him strength.

After a few weeks he had to return to Illinois to see his doctor. Then he was diagnosed with Stage 4 lung cancer. The coincidence of that was a paradigm shift for me. My worldview spun around my head like flying pizza dough. Sac was going to die soon of the same malady that had killed Chet. He had a tumor on his rib and started chemo. *Keep it real,* I told myself. *My boyfriend has cancer. Shit happens. And then really weird shit happens.*

"I'm not going to die," Sac told me. "You would have to be the unluckiest woman in the world if God took me away from you right now."

But of course, he was going to die. I knew that.

He said, "Who knows how much time I have left? Even the doctors don't know."

In a phone conversation a couple of months later, he said, "I'm going to die. There's nothing more they can do for me. Once the chemo is over, the cancer is going to come back again."

"I'll help you any way I can," I said. "What can I do?"

"I want to know about life after death. Which religion do you believe in? What about karma and the next life? Will I come back as something? Is there a place we go? What should I prepare for? How should I do it? What will it be like?"

He wanted to know all the same things Chet wanted to know, asked the same questions. I didn't mind explaining my own thinking. I loved them. I have a spiritual life. Ideas guide me. Beliefs inspire me. But Chet and Sac did not have a spiritual life. They both had the intuition that death was about more than biology, but they took no interest in their own metaphysics until the Grim Reaper wrecked their party.

"So, you want me to be your death coach," I said. "Over the phone."

"I know you're married to the farm," he said. "I wouldn't ask you to come here. Just tell me what you know."

I told him everything I could think of, everything I went through with Chet, everything I believed about Nature. But I did not go to Illinois. I looked that choice in the face and I had to reconcile myself as I consciously chose not to see Sac again. I didn't want to go through a reprise of the big emotional death thing. I didn't have the strength. I wasn't done crying for Chet. And Sac was right — I was married to the farm. Given the choice, I chose the farm. Sac's death gave me clarity on that.

~ : ~

Around the time Sac died, Chet's mom died, and my grandmother died. I relapsed into deep grief. Poetry was my only therapy.

17. 57

Today I am 57
    Time is a galloping horse and I'm riding bareback
My legs are the legs of the horse
    The lines on my face are the waves on the beach
The waves on the beach are the lines on the road
    The lines on the road become the spokes of a wheel
The spokes of the wheel become the bars of my cage
    The bars of my cage become fallen trees
The fallen trees become matchsticks
    The world is on fire

I squint in the light
    My sightlines become crow's feet
My crow's feet become a map
    The lines on the map become a web
I walk the strands of the web and lose my balance
    The waves on the beach become a smile
The lines on the map become a ladder
    The spokes of the wheel become milestones
The bars of my cage become a basket

The fallen trees become my arms
And the matchsticks light my way

I know where I am
  Even when the world is on fire, I know where I am
Because I know my lines
    Because I am 57

I have 57 secrets and they are all hiding inside of me
  This year I'm kicking them out
They are freeloaders on my psyche, and I want my space back
    They are 57 mistakes I've made hiding in the basement
Each mistake has a regret, each regret has a resentment
    I harbor resentment here for all that is imperfect about me
My inner voice is my biggest critic
      I prop up my mistakes like little dictators
Stomping through my brain waving their swords
        Threatening to hang me from the highest tree if I so much as forgive myself
There is no forgiveness for secrets, they are their own poison
        They fear the alchemy of truth, huddled in the corner of eternity

My secrets are chained to me, they sing the song of slaves in a black hole
    They allow me to romanticize my regrets
But now I want them out
    I set them free with these words
I have lied, I have cheated, I have stolen things
      I have harmed and hurt and blasphemed
I have been unfair, I have been unkind, and I have been selfish
      I have been jealous and I have been angry
I have betrayed love and broken hearts
        And my own heart has been broken
I will hide it no more

It's time for each secret to have its story told
    For each chain to be broken, for each slave to sing its own song
For each little dictator to step down and seek asylum
      My secrets are no longer secret, I have no regrets

Because I am 57

I have 57 dreams, rare dreams, unspoken dreams, renegade dreams
They are my laundry waving in the wind
They are the silver cape that billows from my shoulders
They are the deck of cards I deal to each hand
Some of my dreams have torn corners, some are shiny pennies
*   Some are rats in my hair, some have rings in their noses*
Some of them have come true
*   Some are lies*
My dreams are stones on a path
*   When I stand on a stone it's the only moment in time*
Stone by stone I connect the dreams that have become my life
*   Stone by stone I move from here into the future*

There was only one path to this moment and it is the path I took
*   I followed my dreams to be here*
I rode a galloping horse through time and space to be in this moment
*   Each birth, each death, each hunger*
Each joy, each loss, each victory
*   Is a sign along the way*
A sign of my time
*   Warning me, welcoming me to my dreams*
At 57 I have finally arrived

My brain is a museum with 57 exhibits
*   The exhibits are treadmills that power my ego*
Some are made of seashells and feathers
*   Some are made of snow and sand*
Some are made of wooden spoons
*   Some are made of steel and glass*
When all 57 treadmills twirl, I light up, tequila shoots through my veins
*   I see god and she is me and we get along*

I have an old boyfriend treadmill
*   Guys from high school, sugar daddies and suits jog in a line dance*
Round and round they go, electrifying memories of hickeys and miniskirts

Beach vacations and kisses stolen in an elevator
I have an arch enemy treadmill
My fourth-grade teacher, a hairspray rival, a groupie smoking a cigarette
I've got these women cuffed at the ankle
Cussing at me, they slog through perpetuity one stiletto at a time
I have a best poems treadmill, text files float above me in tongues of fire
On a good day they ascend into heaven in a glitterati vortex
On a bad day they groan and swirl down the toilet

Each treadmill needs two feet to turn, one in agony and one in ecstasy
I am writing the natural history of balance
In 57 exhibits I interpret my experience
Then my treadmills become pinwheels
The wind blurs my epiphany into my litany and my epitaph
I am a flower gone to seed, carried off to far places
I start over because I have momentum
Because I am 57

I have 57 loves
Each of them has a swoon line
A phrase that reels me in, knocks me over, and gets me high
A black haired boy writes me love letters
A godfather gives me a gold necklace, a musician sings "Moon River"
A gangster sends me perfume, a nice guy soothes me with humility
An old love sweeps me off my feet
I am beginning to see a pattern here
In this parade of saints, beaux, and gigolos
The swoon lines become the lines on the road
The lines on the road are made of stone
The stones mark my way from dream to dream
Each dream is a lover, each lover is trapped in a bottle on a shelf
I sip them and swill them galloping bareback
Past forgotten secrets and rusting treadmills
Through a field of languishing regrets
Into the wilds of my imagination
My legs are the legs of the horse
The waves on the beach are the lines on my face

The lines on my face are the spokes of a wheel
The wheel tangos over a bed of coals
The bed of coals is my bed

My horse flies
From the clouds I see 57 fires that lit my nights
57 kisses that made me whole
57 hands that held my heart
57 dreams that came true
And I believe
I believe in fire
Fire is love and love is time
And the fires of time belong to me
Because I am 57

18. The River

It took a few years after Chet died to get my life on the farm under control. My systems were designed around my skills and they were manageable. I settled into a groove and the routine was comforting. My animals were my partners. My neighbors looked out for me and my friends were my safety net. On good days it was a good life, and I knew I was blessed to have passed through the eye of the needle and come out whole. I wrote grants and built websites to pay my household bills. My farm finances were still rickety, but my beef sales paid my hay bill, and my egg sales paid for my chickenfeed.

Farm work built my strength, hauling hay and firewood, pounding fence posts and clearing brush, shoveling manure and snow, carrying 50 lb. bags of chickenfeed, lugging stone, digging holes, and pushing a wheelbarrow. Chores took a few hours every day, five days a week, and I spent most of my time on weekends doing projects. The constant activity improved my coordination and my stamina.

All around us, the forest beckoned Moon and me. We took up animal tracking. He killed whatever he could catch, raccoons mostly, occasionally a possum or a woodchuck. I put in a small vegetable garden of raised beds beside a pasture fence near the kitchen. In the long light of summer, I often pulled weeds there until dark. The cows in the pasture would amble over to the fence and commune with me.

I would smell their breath and listen to them chew, and we would talk cow talk while Moon ate snap peas.

My depression subsided as I rationalized my history. I knew I was not unique. Cancer is epidemic. What happened to me happens to a million people every day. Wallowing in it was unattractive. I turned off my self-pity with stories of people who had it way worse than me. My anger and my grief untangled. Of course, I missed Chet. He was alive in my dreams. I heard his voice in my head. I wanted him. Nothing was going to change that.

He was a man disillusioned by his circumstances. The Juicer was a boost to his ego and a distraction from his fate. I relegated his bad judgment to a three-year period of our 32-year relationship, from 2006 through 2008. Lots of men in middle age needed sex with a younger woman to remind them who they could be. Sadly, Chet was one of those. I had to accept that.

If I hadn't been so enthralled with my own pursuits, the affair might not have happened. Maybe I could have prevented it by behaving differently. Maybe it was my own narcissism that had brought this betrayal into my life. It just didn't seem right to blame it all on Chet.

It was a tidy explanation, and as I repeated it to myself, it became factual. I felt the tension inside me ease when I opened up about it to a few friends. Each of them had a different reaction, and it was instructive to witness their feelings. Mostly they were sympathetic. But some of them said some pretty nasty things about Chet. I appreciated their loyalty, but I didn't want to hear that. So I went back to my strategy of silence and continued to keep the affair a secret.

Hate did not fit with my self-image. I did not hate Chet. But I hated her. I wanted to grab her by the throat and throw her up against a wall. It didn't make me feel great about myself to admit that. But I had to be honest if I expected to heal. Then a voice in my head would ask, *Heal from what? What had Chet's affair cost me that was so valuable? What injury had I suffered?* The litany of offenses played over and over. Storm clouds hung thick in the back of my mind, and my anger rumbled like distant thunder.

~ : ~

I had moved the cows to a new pasture, and I left the old pasture gate open to walk the fence line. While I was fiddling with a wire, Moon took off on his own and I lost track of him. Back at the house I called him, and I could see him running toward me, but he didn't look like my dog. He was the wrong color. As he got closer, I could see he had rolled in a fresh cow pie. A thick layer of wet manure coated his silver hair. And he was thrilled about it. He galloped and pranced in the yard, bucking like a happy bronco, showing off his marvelous wrap.

"Oh my god, Moon!" That was my first mistake. He knew that voice. It was my dead chicken voice. He ran to the farthest corner of the yard and watched me. "What the fuck did you do?" I hollered. His ears laid back and he cowered as I pulled out the garden hose and put a spray gun attachment on the end.

Moon hated the hose. Hose water was very cold. His hair was thin, and he had no insulating body fat. He didn't even swim in the pond because it was never warm enough for him. He preferred a sponge bath with tepid water, scented shampoo, and a soft washcloth. But I was in no mood to pamper the little bastard. Getting him clean was going to be a nasty job, and I did not plan to do it in the kitchen, and for sure, I was not bringing him into my bathroom. There was no way to clean him without spreading manure everywhere. I knew I was going to have manure on my hands and my clothes and my shoes, and I was furious. So I went after him with the hose set on jet spray because that setting had the most power.

Moon was a sprinter and the yard around the house was an acre. I ran trying to squirt him clean and he bolted just out of reach of the water jet. As I chased back and forth, the hose got wrapped around bushes and pinched, but I kept after him. I was missing lunch with friends because there was no way I was letting him in the house, or my car, until he was clean. Worse — Moon and I slept together. I had to get him clean and dry enough to be in bed with me. The whole thing made me nuts.

I don't know exactly how long it was, but it seemed like a really long time. I was getting tired of running. Moon had fear in his eyes. Still I kept squirting. The one creature I loved most in the world was afraid of me, but I didn't care. I was relentless. I wanted to punish him. I knew this was no way to train a dog, but I couldn't stop myself.

We were both panting. I could feel the sweat on my scalp. Moon was sad, but he wasn't coming near me. He paced the fence and I could see him thinking about running away from home. Then he backed into an electric wire and yelped. His sadness turned to panic, and he ran aimlessly howling around the perimeter of the yard. I knew the electric jolt must have been way worse with the wet manure on his back. He was really hurting. Instinctively I dropped the hose and ran toward him, but he dashed away from me.

Seeing my dog run away from me when he was hurt broke me. *Oh, my god*, I thought. *What am I doing?* Tears swamped my eyes. "Oh, Moon, I'm so sorry," I cried out to him across the lawn. He knew that voice, too. That was my dead Chet voice. "I'm so sorry, sweetie." I sobbed so hard I had to sit down. He took a few steps toward me. We were both confused. *Who am I?* I thought. *What am I doing? Get a grip.*

~ : ~

One morning, after hours of clearing brush, I filled myself with eggs and home fries and collapsed into a deep sleep on the couch. They must have knocked a few times. My car was in the driveway and the windows were open, so they knew I was home. It was Moon's barking that forced me to get up and answer the door. My muscles were stiff, and my eyes were half closed until I saw them with their little pamphlets.

"Don't tell me you woke me up from a nap for a fucking Bible lesson," I snapped. They wore plain clothes and their faces were soft and pale. "Are you fucking kidding me? You think you know more about Jesus than I do because you go to church? Get out of here! Get off my land!" I opened the door to rush them off the porch as the old man took his elderly wife's hand and helped her down the steps. Then I went back to the couch and dropped my head in my hands and cried. I hated myself.

Even my dreams were angry. Chet was standing in front of me with indifference on his face, like he didn't care what I thought. He was on trial, and he was going to be declared guilty. He already knew that.

"I want to see it," I said.

He took off his shirt. A dog's head was tattooed on his torso, a huge black muzzle painted over the long scar from his Hodgkin's disease surgery, and he had a dog collar tattooed around his neck. Then he dropped his pants to show me the paw prints tattooed up and down his legs, some of them just outlines, as though the tattoo artist had run out of ink, run out of time, just run out.

"How could you?" I cried. "I love this body. How could you vandalize such beauty?"

His eyes froze in a dead stare. Then he said he liked it. But I knew he was hiding something, a lethal habit, a toxic moral contradiction.

"You kept that bitch a secret," I said. "She ate a hole in your virtue, gnawed on you until she killed you."

Then my eyes slammed open. Yes, Chet was on trial. I was a wraith in flowing black robes sentencing him to death even as I begged him not to leave me.

~ : ~

Eventually I had the emotional capacity to break down his man cave, the home plate of his soul. On his shelves he had stacks of paper that had been there since we moved from Boston, his Real Book, his sheet music, his arrangements and compositions, his college papers and music textbooks. I wanted his jazz bandmates to inherit this historic archive. So I carried the stacks into the kitchen and invited the guys to come over for cocktails and sort through them. It was a gin-soaked evening, listening to music and reminiscing about Chet.

The next morning as I was picking up the flurry of leftover sheet music for the recycling bin, I found a handwritten letter from the Juicer that must have been hidden in the stacks. She had put pen and ink to lined paper with a snapshot of herself holding a cat and looking provocatively over her shoulder. The letter thanked Chet for suggesting she see *The Piano* — a film he and I had gone to see in the theater twice. Then she made a tender reference to her pussy, and exclaimed, "What a beast you are in bed!"

The Piano came out in 1993. Five years before we bought the farm, 16 years before Chet died. It was one of our favorite movies. 1993.

Life is a river, not a grid. You can't keep a river in a hatbox. A river does not fit neatly in a row of cubicles. A river does not hold its shape. A river is not tidy. The 1993 letter was only a piece of paper, but it changed everything. Even now I ask myself why it hurt so much. But it did. It took me down. I didn't know what to think, so I thought the worst.

My whole marriage was a lie. All my stories about my life and Chet had to be rewritten. The recently reconstructed me — the one who had accepted that her husband had had a three-year affair — that me was a fiction. That me did not exist. My husband was having an affair in 1993. Maybe he never stopped seeing her after we got married in 1985. Maybe my marriage was always a threesome.

Negative emotions burned through me and a wildfire of hate charred my heart. I did not cry the sweet tears of grief. I did not listen to love songs and weep. I did not reminisce. My mood was an improvised explosive device. The biochemistry of violence flushed my muscles with tension. I had a hair-trigger temper and I was looking for a fight. Knives found their way into my subconscious. I wanted to kill somebody. I called a gun dealer and had him come to the house to buy all our guns because they were chanting my name in shiny metal voices promising relief.

Suddenly I hated my house, blamed my house for betraying me by hiding secrets. The Museum of Chet & Billie lost its mandate. I intended to inspect every item I owned for hidden lies. No more out of sight, out of mind. No more collections of the forgotten. No more boxes closed for 30 years. No more stacks of the unknown. No more shelves too high to reach. No more spaces too icky to crawl into. If our stuff was the encapsulation of our history, I aimed to rewrite the past by exterminating the present.

It took a couple years of redecorating — moving furniture, painting rooms, eliminating clutter — but it was very satisfying. The house was more modern looking, less sentimental, and so was I. When the process was complete, I saw myself differently. My views on love, sex and marriage were changing. I was 60 years old and still clinging to my emotional past. I needed to get rid of my mental clutter. How silly I had been. There I was in 2014, a grown woman behaving like a schoolgirl, getting all frizzy about the simple misplacement of my husband's penis. *Why?* I asked myself. *Why do I care? What difference does it make?*

Chet said, "Bil, it's just a juicer."

But clearing her from my mind wasn't as simple as taking out the trash. Five years after Chet died, I needed visualization therapy, a cartoonish fantasy of annihilating her, like on that old MTV show, *Celebrity Deathmatch*.

~ : ~

Ladies and gentleman! Welcome to *Celebrity Deathmatch*, where tonight we have a duel that's been in the making for 30 years, a match made in the fury of a woman's scorn, the mother of all chick fights, the matchup of a cold calculating She Machine against the wrath of Mother Nature.

This is going to be messy folks, so cover your hotdogs and hold on to your napkins, because tonight on *Celebrity Deathmatch*, we bring you the food fight of the century between Nature's own bloviating bovine beauty, and the super sleek, everybody's got to have one, stainless-steel crusher.

Introducing, in this corner, the Boss Cow! Fifteen-hundred pounds of muscle and milk armed with a monster forehead, and udders firing on all four cylinders, powered by pure animosity. It's going to be a horrific showdown, folks. She's a mad cow!

And in this corner, our challenger, the Juicer! She's the coveted home appliance of those who can never be too rich or too thin, armed with three power settings, a splashguard, and blades strong enough to liquefy her opponent.

This is it, ladies and gentlemen, the *Celebrity Deathmatch* you've all been waiting for — the Boss Cow and the Juuuuuuuuuuuicer!!!

There's the bell. The Boss Cow is pacing, sizing up her opponent. The Juicer plugs in her power cord and turns on her motor. The Boss Cow is circling. The Juicer is fiddling in her corner. What's this? What is she doing? She's got something. She's got an extension cord! Is that cheating? We don't know, folks. The Juicer could be cheating, but it's too late now, the fight is on. She's got an extra 25 feet of mobility. Let's see what she does with it.

The Boss Cow sniffs the extension cord and continues circling. The Juicer pivots. The Boss Cow steps over the cord. Snap! The Juicer has tripped her. The Boss Cow stumbles. The Juicer bashes her. She stumbles again.

The Boss Cow is snorting. Her head is dropping. She's moving her forehead into position. The Juicer whips her extension cord against the Boss Cow's hooves. The Boss Cow drops her nose and charges. The Juicer whips her cord. That forehead is a killer, folks! The Boss Cow bashes against her. The Juicer slides across the ring. She's against the ropes. The Boss Cow charges. It's a direct hit!

The Juicer's splashguard is demolished. She's got no protection from liquid now. She ups her power setting to the max. The Boss Cow charges again. The Juicer runs to the other side of the ring. Is she running scared? No! Her extension cord trips the Boss Cow. She's running circles around her! Having four legs is not an advantage in this fight, folks.

The Boss Cow stumbles. She's down. The Juicer circles her again. She's tying up her legs. The Boss Cow is on her back. She's down. She's down. Down for the count! The bloviating bovine is on her back! This is a crisis, folks! It's an upset! Who knew it would end this quickly?

The challenger is smug now. She's tightening the cord. You can see the pressure building inside the Boss Cow. The Juicer leans over her and gloats. She circles with the cord one more time.

But wait! What's this? Those udders are standing up like missiles. What's happening here? The Juicer doesn't see it. She's already doing her victory lap. The Boss Cow moos. God almighty, that's a loud cow! The Juicer stops. The Boss Cow fires. It's milk! Oh my god, I've never seen anything like it. Those udders are shooting milk like a fire hose — four fire hoses! It's a milk monsoon!

The Juicer is covered in milk. She can't see. Her crusher is filling. She's foaming. Milk is filling the ring. The Juicer is splattering milk everywhere. It's a frappè. No, it's whipped cream. NO — oh my god, folks, you're never going to believe this — it's butter. It's BUTTER! The Juicer can't stop herself. She is turning the Boss Cow's milk into butter!

What a turnaround! What a mastermind! The Juicer is slipping and sliding. Her extension cord is slack. The Boss Cow is on her feet again.

She's circling her nemesis. The Juicer's motor is shrieking. Now it's smoking. She's overheating. What's going on here? Is this a trick? What's happening? She seems paralyzed. Is that fire? It is! The Juicer is on fire. Flames are shooting out of the Juicer.

Oh, my god! It's a grease fire! The Juicer is overheating and burning the butter. Her motor is sputtering! Her cord is melting! She's against the ropes. She's out of control. There's melted butter everywhere. She's burning up! Flames are shooting out of her. Who knew butter could burn like this? What a mess! What a smell! She's choking. The Juicer is choking on the smoke. The Boss Cow is lowering her nose. One more smash with that forehead will put an end to this once and for all, folks.

But wait! The referee is in the ring. And who's that with him? It's the fire marshal! The fire marshal is stopping the fight. He sprays the Juicer with his fire extinguisher. The referee is talking to the Boss Cow. He calls the fight! He's calling the fight! He unplugs the Juicer! It's all over, folks. This fight is over! The Juicer is unplugged. What a turnaround!

Ladies and gentlemen, you saw it here tonight. You had to see it to believe it. The victory of milk over machine. It's a historic moment, folks. The Juicer is being carried out of the ring by her dishwashers. The Boss Cow wins! I've never seen anything like it. She crushed the crusher with milk. It's a victory for the beautiful bloviating bovine. Look at her strut around the ring like she owns it. That is one big cow, ladies and gentlemen. That is one big beautiful Boss Cow.

19. The Curse of Abundance

Streamlining my material world was a high colonic for my psyche. I established a new order — the order of Me. I was officially no longer a we. No more referring to myself like I was part of a couple, saying our this and our that. Everything was mine. Going forward my life was my own. I owned it. No negotiation, no compromise, no Chet. I couldn't control the space he occupied inside me, but I could edit him from my sight and my stuff.

After I found the 1993 letter, every closet, drawer, shelf, cupboard, box and bag was under suspicion for hiding secrets. Weaponized with a trashcan, a recycling bin, and a flame, I marched through my house with the intention of annihilating history. I didn't want to be reminded that I was once married, once in love, once had a soul mate. It wasn't just anger. It was alchemy. I systematically got rid of one third of everything I owned, and my husband's stuff was at the front of the line. Every item was scoured for secrets and counted. One, two, three, you're out. Gone. I ran classified ads and had tag sales. I brought in dealers and pickers to go through the house and buy stuff. I donated, gifted and abandoned. Then I recycled and trashed the remainder.

When I went through the process of purging Chet from my house, I learned that our antiques and collectibles were out of fashion. Stuff we thought was worth a lot of money was worth peanuts, and stuff that had sentimental value was worth nothing. So many of the things we kept were intended to be passed on to the next generation. But there was no next generation waiting to inherit my grandmother's silver service, or the oak desk my grandfather refinished, or the eight-day clock Maurice had restored, or the wool rug hooked by my great-great grandmother.

Parting with things that had sentimental value felt like giving up pieces of myself. But I had to do it. I had to draw the line somewhere. At one time in my life accumulating possessions was self-expression. I was curating my status, expressing my values. I intentionally acquired things that I thought were cool, I received gifts from loved ones, and I inherited family treasures. Now I was going through the opposite process, undoing all that emotional attachment and letting go. Maybe I was disappearing myself. Little pieces of me were walking away at my tag sales. I was dismembering myself. At the end of Chet's tool sale his bungalow workshop was empty, and my heart ached.

Then I had a dream where he was playing bass with his band on the edge of a lake, and when it was his turn to take a solo, he rowed a boat out onto the water where everyone could see him. A pallet of stuff fell from the back of the boat and we watched as all his boxes sank into the blue haze. His CDs became a school of shining silver donuts floating through a reef of tape decks and guitars. He laughed into his beer as his stuff hit bottom and with Christ-like calm he raised his arms to speak. "The process is the destination," he said. "It's only stuff. Have your tag sale. I'm still here."

It was just a dream, but once again, he knew exactly what I was thinking.

I could feel my great-grandmother's hot breath as I sold her doilies for one dollar each on a picnic table beside the driveway. In my family, the women that came before me spent long hours doing needlework. They embroidered, cross-stitched, crocheted, knitted and hooked. A fine home was adorned with fine needlework. Dresser scarves and doilies, pillowcases and bedspreads, quilts and monogramed handkerchiefs were their contribution to the family legacy in a world where men worked, and women stayed home. They had baskets of needlework beside their chairs with a bright light that shone down into their lap where their skilled fingers produced holiday gifts, wedding presents, and baby bonnets — things I couldn't give away at a tag sale where the neighbor ladies chatted about how they had similar stuff in boxes in their homes, and nobody wanted that either.

Getting rid of so much stuff made me feel like I was throwing away my time. I was throwing away my money. It slayed me to see how much of my life was invested in the acquisition of status symbols that had no status. How did that happen?

At the peak of my success as a desk jockey I had bought myself a cushy black leather desk chair. Evidently, desk chairs are the new buggy whip. When motorized vehicles replaced draft animals as transportation, the market for buggy equipment collapsed. Buggy whip factories closed, people were unemployed, and draft horses were sent to slaughter just the same way we send a car to the junkyard. My desk was designed for managing paper-based systems, reading, writing and storing files. When I bought it, my black leather desk chair was status.

Mobility killed the desk. Today you can rule the world with a smart phone in your pajamas on the couch. Liquid labor markets have created a mass migration of workers who don't want the ball and chain of stuff. Stuff is a drag on mobility.

The people who came to my tag sales at the farm walked right past my leather desk chair without a glance. It was not cool. No one even asked how much I wanted for it. At the end of the sale, I left my black leather desk chair at the town dump and gave a passing thought to the life of the cow that once inhabited that skin.

Even thrift stores and charities didn't want a lot of my stuff because their shops and warehouses were already full. There was a time when I thought hoarders were sympathetic mentally ill people. But when I realized most of my stuff wasn't worth anything, I saw that Chet and I were hoarders. Our house was full of stuff for the sake of stuff.

Television birthed a nation of hoarders. Stuff came in contact with our egos, drained our wallets, and multiplied to consume all available space. Stuff is a communicable disease. Our hunter-gatherer selves evolved from the meadow to the mall, and stuff became pandemic. That's the curse of abundance — our stuff is killing us. We behave as though the purpose of life is to get stuff, the purpose of work is to get the money to buy stuff. We endure a lifetime of stress for the status of stuff. When life becomes uncertain, we reach out and touch our stuff, and it gives us comfort. Our stuff is always there for us, a permanent reminder of who we are and what we have achieved. But the security of stuff is an illusion. That's why chickens don't have stuff.

~ : ~

Once I had the house looking stylish and organized to sleep eight guests, becoming a bed-and-breakfast inn seemed like a way to generate income from my fabulous hemorrhaging asset. My finances were still way out of balance. The expenses of home ownership were constant and escalating. I had too much stuff to take care of and not enough hours in the day to earn the money it took to maintain all of it.

I had walked away from a six-figure income when I chose to farm instead of returning to the corporate world after 9/11. But the house I lived in was designed for that level of income. In 1998 we had renovated the house from cellar to roof, put in all new systems, and purchased all new appliances. By 2014, it seemed like everything I owned was breaking down.

I had a dinner party for my favorite women and cleaning up afterward they discovered my dishwasher was broken. I had been living without a dishwasher for months because I just didn't have the money to replace it, and I didn't want to add to my credit card debt. That choice set off alarms among my friends. My precarious finances became public knowledge, and for my birthday they took up a collection and gave me a new dishwasher. Not long after that, the motherboard on my digital stove fried, and I had to replace the entire appliance because the manufacturer was no longer making digital replacement parts. Even my appliances had a shorter lifespan than I expected.

To experiment with running a bed-and-breakfast inn, I signed up for Airbnb and became a host. Guests stayed in the first-floor master bedroom suite while Moon and I moved into a smaller bedroom upstairs. Some of my guests came from far off places, but most of them were couples from New York City looking for a weekend getaway. It was validating to see urbanites appreciate the farm, and I enjoyed chatting with them about the animals, the food and rural life. It was a reminder of how my own understanding of Nature and history had evolved since moving from Boston to the Berkshires.

One of my guests said, "Your lambs are so beautiful."

"Those are calves," I said.

"Oh," she said. "What's the difference between a lamb and a calf?"

"A lamb is a sheep and a calf is a cow."

She smiled, amused with herself. "I've seen pictures of cows, but this is the first time I've ever seen one in real life."

Another guest was curious about the icehouse. I took him outside to inspect it and explained that it had double walls with sawdust insulation between them. Ice blocks would be cut from the pond in winter and stacked from floor to ceiling in the insulated room. That's how ice was stored before refrigeration. He squinted at me as though I was playing a joke on him. "I doubt that," he said, and walked away with his hands in his pockets, annoyed by my preposterous story.

A charming young couple from Queens stayed at the farm to celebrate their wedding anniversary. When they came in the house, the first thing they said was "We've never been in a place without streetlights before." As gifts for the occasion they had given themselves iPads. I watched out the window as they walked down the road, holding their tablets up in front of their faces to photograph the farm. It was as though the farm was a digital game, and they didn't know how to experience it without the interface between them and the land.

~ : ~

It took a season of Airbnb guests for me to learn that renting the master bedroom suite on weekends would not be the solution to the imbalance between my income and expenses. The number of hours in the day was the same, but my workload was increased. Airbnb paid me better than farm chores, but I loved farm chores. With Airbnb I was a hotel maid in my own house. To get high ratings from my guests, the entire house had to be immaculate. I enjoyed cleaning as an obsessive-compulsive disorder, but the obligation of cleaning to maintain my five-star rating on Airbnb did not assuage my neurosis, and it wasn't enough money for the time it took. I was better off building websites.

Once again, I was confronted with the option to take on a housemate who could rent a bedroom and a bathroom on a monthly basis. But I didn't want the hassle. I didn't want the chitchat. I didn't want to live with a TV watcher. I didn't want to share my kitchen. It had been six years since Chet died, and I was settled into being alone. I didn't want the friction of being with another person every day. When it came to the choice between having a housemate and becoming economically sustainable, or living alone and sliding further into debt, I saw the truth of it. My debt was a lifestyle choice.

I had spent a lifetime accumulating possessions the way squirrels spend a lifetime accumulating nuts. However, squirrels have only one currency to pay for their stash of nuts — their energy. They cannot collect more nuts than they have the energy to collect. I had another currency, an imaginary source of limitless unearned income: Debt. Debt was a way for merchants to sell me things I couldn't afford. It was the magical thinking that encouraged me to keep spending even when my bank balance was zero.

Chet had seen what I didn't see: my addiction to farming was really an addiction to debt. I lived alone in a large three-bedroom two-story farmhouse with a bungalow, a barn, a chicken coop, a car, a tractor, pets and livestock. All those things had maintenance costs. Without my big city job, my household income was not enough to pay my total cost of ownership. I had become a slave to my spending habits, disguised as they were by altruism, advocacy and love.

~ : ~

I knew I was in trouble when I used gaffer tape to repair my vibrator. I had drained my savings, cashed in my retirement accounts, liquidated my life insurance policy, and maxed out my credit cards. I was proud of being land rich and cash poor. Wearing torn pants and frayed jackets was a badge of honor. But I was burying myself with only one way out of the hole. And debt wasn't the only risk I was taking.

I didn't have health insurance or someone to run the farm if I was incapacitated. I didn't have a person in my life that would be my caregiver if I became ill. And my stamina was ebbing. Fourteen-hour workdays on the farm dwindled to eight-hour workdays, and then to six-hour workdays, and then I was spending more time recovering from my chores than accomplishing them.

The tractor work — using the lever to raise and lower the mower, and the joystick to dig holes and plow snow — inflamed the tendons in my right shoulder. After a day of fencing my hip could feel like it was pierced by a railroad spike. If I dressed too many chickens or pulled too many weeds, I had to put my aching hands in ice packs to stop the swelling. Cleaning flared my carpal tunnel syndrome. And the cartilage in my knees threatened to snap.

When this wave of realization hit me, I reorganized myself to conserve my energy. I stopped selling beef. To pay for hay, I sold some cows to a livestock dealer. I didn't purchase new chicks and I stopped selling eggs. I bartered grazing rights and storage space in my barn for firewood and tree work. And I kept doing Airbnb.

For another year this approach stayed my debt. But the imperative to downsize was there again the next year, 2015. The exterior of the house needed to be painted and the chimney needed repointing. The furnace was almost 20 years old. The oil tank sprang a leak, and I needed to replace the broken steps on the long porch. In a few years the house would need a new roof, and there was rotting wood around every window and door.

I could see my future cost of living on the farm was going to be far out of reach. The math was bubble popping. Somehow, I had taken on all these obligations without calculating their total cost. And their cost wasn't just money, it was time. I had reached the point in my life where time was worth more than money, and I didn't have enough of either.

I applied for a high paid desk job working for the government. My corporate marketing background qualified me for the position, and it seemed like it was going to happen. But when my prospective boss got wind of my writing about agriculture and my criticism of globalization, he didn't want the baggage. He refused to even meet with me. My days as an activist were a matter of public record that I couldn't hide. I didn't want to hide. But now I could see how in addition to the math on ownership of stuff, I had failed to calculate the total cost of owning my opinions. Turns out self-righteousness has a very low market value.

~ : ~

It was impossible for me to imagine life after the farm. I wasn't compelled by another vision for my future. But I was out of options. The only thing worse than being old was being old and poor. That was the thought that pushed me to take the steps I knew I must take to survive. No one else was going to take care of me. I had to take care of myself.

I put the house on the market at the end of 2015 when I sold Cinco. It was my ten-year anniversary of owning cows and I had only two left, Cinco and her daughter, Vista. I kept Cinco for eight years because she produced perfect calves. She came when she saw me, and she licked me and lowed with pleasure when I brushed her. She was a cheerful animal who kicked her hind feet in the air when she ran through the lane to fresh grass. I loved her.

The cattle breeder was a farmer looking for the best genetics for grassfed beef. When I produced a report on my cows' lineage going back four generations he was impressed and offered me a very good price. On a chilly December day, Cinco and Vista walked onto his livestock trailer to eat the apples I threw there. I never thought I would do that, let my beloved Cinco disappear into the uncertainty of another farm. I would have felt better killing her out behind the barn and knowing she came to a beautiful end. But I had worked so hard to raise perfect cows, and her genes deserved to be passed on to future herds.

Over the years the farm had become a vine-covered pastiche of rust, wire and wizened fence posts. When I gave some real estate agents a walk-through, they frowned, and I heard the phrase "deferred maintenance." They didn't see what I saw, the mystique of peeling paint and lichen, the flourishing ecosystem, the heroism of working land. Authenticity wasn't a feature their buyers sought. Perhaps some buyers wanted farm charm, but few, perhaps none, wanted a working farm. Some of the people who came to look at the house didn't even walk out to see the barn.

Their criticism was hard to hear. They didn't care about agriculture. They didn't care about Nature. For them the meadows were ambiance, something to appreciate from a distance, on the other side of a wall of insecticide. They weren't interested in saving pollinators. The pond looked weedy to people who enjoyed golf courses and had no other frame of reference for wild water. No one wanted to hear my frog stories or look at my pictures of salamanders. One particularly anxious real estate agent asked me to refrain from mentioning snakes. Habitat was an idea people had heard of, but they didn't want to actually live in one. They didn't see a working landscape as a benefit to the community. They didn't want community. They wanted status.

A finance guy wanted to turn my barn into his corporate headquarters. Several lookers wanted to cut down all the trees. A suburban couple wanted all the fencing removed as a condition of the sale. A family wanted to fill in the pond with dirt so they could build a playground for their kids. A developer wanted to subdivide the land and sell the pastures as house lots. My real estate agent told me if I wanted to sell, I would need to let go of my ideas and unfarm the farm.

"Are you fucking kidding me?" That was Chet's voice inside my head when I had a carpenter build new porch steps from chemically treated wood. I heard his words loud and clear, but that moral dilemma was a lifetime ago. I couldn't afford cedar steps, and buyers didn't know the difference. The expense of preparing the house for sale drained the last of my resources. I spent thousands of dollars covering chipped paint, replacing rotten wood, fixing gutters and downspouts, filling cracks with mortar, hauling away my compost piles, and evicting mice, squirrels, snakes and bats. All things I could have done in the 18 years I lived in that house, but those improvements never rose to the top of my to-do list. Until I had to sell.

~ : ~

My plan was to downsize and start over. My Boston crew came for the weekend and helped me fill a small storage pod with just enough stuff for a one-woman life. I kept the things I treasured, and the remainder disappeared.

I gave away my chickens and made arrangements for Wendell and Berry to live with my neighbors until I found a new place. I intended to keep them. They were 12 years old and the vet said they could easily live a few more years. When I left them in my neighbor's unfamiliar barn, they were skeptical and anxious. Hearing their voices cry to me as I walked away triggered all my other feelings of loss. That familiar ache hardened my face. I couldn't look back.

The farm was to be left broom clean. As I swept through the heart of the barn, moving from chamber to chamber, the energy flow of a hundred years of farmers rushed through me, and I slid backwards through the process of becoming a farmer. It was the final familiarity, like touching Chet's body in the hours after he died. I was losing another love. There was much to do, my lists were long, and my hours were dwindling. I didn't have the luxury of grief. I had to box up my sadness along with everything else I owned.

When my grandparents' generation farmed, the power of people and draft animals set the limits of production. Farms were sized to the available muscles and feeding those muscles every day meant growing diverse plants and animals. When my parents' generation farmed, machines replaced muscles, and there seemed no limit to how big a farm could be. They maximized their profits, and feeding people became the grocer's job. Chet and I farmed a dream of living in harmony with Nature. We wanted a new way of being on Earth. Unity was the beauty we sought, and it is the beauty I left in my wake.

I thought I would live on Crazy Wife Farm for the rest of my life. She was my womb, my child, my proudest achievement, my sister. Now she was going into a box in a row of boxes, each tied with a long piece of twine trailing into a starless universe, connected to a word, a song, a picture, a familiar task, a smell that opens the box, and pulls me from the present into the black hole of memory. My sadness was for all that I had lost, including myself.

20. Hunting Unicorns

On July 18, 2016, I sold the farm — seven years, six months and two days after Chet died. I had $500 left in my bank account and $60,000 in debt. If the sale had fallen through, I would have had to borrow money to make my August mortgage payment. That's how close I cut it. No one else knew it, but I humiliated myself in my own eyes.

Selling the farm by myself was a complicated ordeal that took all my focus and didn't leave time for me to organize a new life for myself. I had put some stuff in storage, but I didn't have a place to go to, and the closer I got to selling the farm, the less I was able to think about getting a new home. I wasn't ready for a new life. I was still in love with my old life. I was finally ending my story as a wife. That me would be gone with the farm. At age 62, I was starting over as a single woman in a new world. Before I could find a new place to live, I had to find a new person to be.

For lack of a better idea, I decided to go on a road trip and packed my car with the things I thought I would need — some casual clothes, bedding, supplies for a camp kitchen, a set of tools, my laptop, and Moon. In my last hour on the farm, I walked around my gardens and collected my favorite rocks, the ones I could carry, and put them in my car. They're my lucky rocks. I also packed Maurice's last undershirt and a pair of Chet's boxer shorts in case I needed a swimsuit. I was traveling with the underwear of the dead men I loved, along with my muck boots, my tractor tow chain, and my favorite Christmas ornament velcroed to the dashboard. It was a witch's brew of possessions.

Part of my blur in those last weeks on the farm was caused by a hurricane-force revelation that I had yet to fully process. My houseplants were among my prize possessions, a few of them I had had for almost 30 years. I pruned them and preened them, transplanted them and looked forward to their blossoms. Selling the farm meant getting rid of them, putting them up for adoption, or finding someone to keep them for me until I had another home. One plant in particular had sentimental value, a fern Chet had given me as a gift in the early 1990s. Was it 1993? I really don't remember. But just that thought was enough to send me down a rabbit hole of suspicion.

In 2016, as I was preparing to give away my fern, I remembered how I got it, and suddenly I asked myself, *What was he trying to hide?* I remembered being surprised when he gave it to me out of the blue, for no special reason. I was charmed when he hung it in the window of my Boston home office because he knew I loved plants. Now the facts of my fidelity forensics were fuzzy and heavily influenced by my quest for sanity. I was sitting on the floor of my farmhouse in the Berkshires looking for ways to blame my husband for my unhappiness when I tripped over a recollection I had long ago swept under the rug.

In 1993 Chet and I were 39. It was eight years after we had eloped. I was working in the marketing department of a large corporation hacking through the jungle of office politics. My boss let me know he was attracted to me with long looks and groping hands. I don't know why I tolerated it. To keep my job perhaps. That kind of behavior was common back then. He took me out for a picnic lunch in the park. We chatted as we sat on the grass watching boats on the river. He kissed me and I kissed him back. He kissed me some more and I let him give me a hickey. That's all it was. It was stupid. It was wrong. I didn't think of it as cheating, but I did know it was a mistake. It was a mistake for many reasons. And today I see that it was cheating.

I came home and went straight to the bathtub, feeling dirty and ashamed.

Chet said, "Bil, that's a hickey on your neck."

I said, "No, it's not."

He turned his back and left the room. That was it. We never discussed it further. End of story. I thought I was off the hook.

In retrospect, reviewing that brief moment of conversation, I could see how he would have assumed I had sex with somebody. Anyone would have assumed that. But at the time, it didn't occur to me that he would assume anything. At the time, I was just dreading how I was going to explain myself, and I was super relieved when I didn't have to. I didn't think about the harm of not talking about it. Life was busy. I moved on, whistling past the graveyard, thinking I got away with something, thinking the problem magically went away.

In 2016, sitting on the floor beside my very old fern, pinching her brown stems and fluffing her potting soil, I told myself this story and I found it hard to believe. A.) What the fuck was I thinking back then? and B.) Why was I just remembering this now? It was seven years after Chet's death. For seven years this memory had been beyond my reach, buried out of sight when I could have used it to calm my self-righteous rage over his affair. My whole identity was based on memories, the stories I told myself about who I was, and now I could see quite clearly that my memory was not an objective resource. It was not a library of facts where I could find the truth. I had deceived myself.

As I cleaned my house for the last time, walking through empty rooms, my questions bounced off the walls in my head until they were all I heard. Could the Juicer's presence in my life be explained by a hickey? Was their 1993 rendezvous revenge sex? Was the fern a gift to assuage his guilt for cheating on me? Did he think I cheated on him? Why hadn't I been honest with him about the hickey? How did I not see that he would have assumed it was so much more than that? How did I not see the damage I was doing by ignoring the incident? And why, why, why was I just remembering this now? How could I trust myself? How could I trust my own memory if something like this could happen? I was my own crisis of faith.

~ : ~

After the sale, I drove north through the Berkshires into the hills along the Housatonic River with no particular destination in mind. I was unmoored and invisible, a nameless asteroid hurtling through space. My future was imaginary. I was numb. Moon curled up behind me and went to sleep on the sheepskins I'd thrown in the back of the car. His metal food dishes clinked, syncopating the vibrations of the road. The car smelled like home. That was enough for him. I could see I needed to become more like my dog.

A few hundred miles later we stopped at a lodge on the edge of a mountain lake. Really, it was some guy's apartment above the garage of a dilapidated hotel in a dead town where the jobs had disappeared with globalization, and hardscrabble folks drank beer in plastic chairs on a gravel beach — the perfect destination for me and Moon. The guy had taken a temporary job in another state and the hotel put his apartment up for rent on Airbnb, cleverly promoting it as a carriage house with all the charm that sobriquet implies. He left behind a full closet of winter clothes, bits of dried food in the kitchen sink, and the ghastly smell of artificial fragrances. The balcony had a scenic view of the lake, but I couldn't sit. My farm chore energy surged and blew my circuitry.

I cleaned the kitchen sink. I didn't call the hotel desk and complain about the crispy spinach in the drain. I wanted to clean it myself. I needed to be busy. My nose was killing me. I went from room to room with a big trash bag and collected everything that smelled. Under the sink I snatched a gaggle of air fresheners, brightly colored plastic bottles of chemical cleaners, antibacterials and cans of insecticide. In the living room I gathered up his scented tissues, scented candles, and frightening little creatures plugged into the electrical outlets emitting sickening perfume. In the bathroom I confiscated his deodorant soap, raspberry red shampoo and a bowl of fake potpourri. Then I put the reeking trash bag outside behind the garage and opened every window and door to welcome in the lake air.

His furniture was in a circle around the television. I rearranged the table and chairs to face the view of the lake. Then the lamps needed to be relocated, and then the pictures on the walls didn't make sense. I drove into town and found a hardware store and bought some picture hangers and new light bulbs. I put a curio table in the bathroom with a tiny lamp I had repaired after I found it behind the cookie jar on top of the refrigerator.

In the bedroom I hung a sconce on the wall with a new light bulb so bright I could pick the lint off the rug, which was very satisfying until I got down on my hands and knees with my face close enough to smell the fibers. A perfect color scheme could not compensate for that funk. So the rug went into the closet with his red bed sheets and other linens ruined by modern chemistry.

Cleaning his apartment soothed my anxiety. My mind zoomed in on the task at hand, my fears receded into the background, and establishing order became the focus of all my attention. I had a sense of being in control. Organizing his stuff was an emotional arms race between my nightmares and my dreams. It stopped me from screaming at the walls. Removing the offending odors gave my dreams an edge. I could smell progress. My lost soul was seeking a familiar place to sit. Yes, I was invading his privacy. But I had to. His smelly apartment was my path to sanity.

I made the bed with my own sheets and blanket, and Moon and I crashed for the night. But on the second day I was gripped by the same drive to fix things and move stuff around. I couldn't hold still. I didn't want to think. I went from room to room looking for projects. I wiped down the refrigerator and the cabinet under the kitchen sink. Then I reorganized the dishes and utensil drawers and seasoned the cast iron frying pans. I went to the grocer and bought some white vinegar to run through the coffee maker, and while I was there, I bought new kitchen towels and matching potholders.

His collection of plastic magnets on the fridge door went into the Easter basket under the microwave. His Merlin figurines gathered in a coven around his hurricane lamp beside the flatscreen. I threw away the nasty Budweiser doormat and replaced it with the one that had been at the farm, the last thing I snatched before I left. Then I tied together his broken hummingbird wind chimes, put the red gauze curtains in the closet, and unplugged all the digital alarm clocks, radios and the TV. I unplugged the telephone, too, but the hotel desk asked me to plug it back in because it was the main line to the property. Last, I removed all the extra plastic chairs on the balcony. I didn't want empty chairs to remind me who was missing.

Night on the lake was luminous. Loons laced sunset to sunrise cooing oboes in the dark. In the morning pick-up trucks gored the highway, and the occasional gust of diesel floated in my window. Four young men on motorcycles pulled out of the hotel parking lot with deafening aplomb, speeding fearlessly into the day. An old man started a lawn mower and began to manicure the grounds with a fastidiousness I wished the owners would apply to the accommodations. Fresh cut grass flared my nostrils and floated me into reverie. Every lawn in my history came back to visit me with a love for home. I spent a few days just sitting on that balcony looking out at the lake, remembering.

Sleeping in the guy's bedroom, I dreamed that I had been away on a trip and when I came home, I discovered that Chet had not fed our baby while I was away. He said it never occurred to him. He was busy. So there was our baby in the cradle in our bedroom starving. I was panicked, but Chet was cavalier, as though the baby just wasn't his problem. As the baby shriveled into a rag doll, my heart broke. I filled the sink to cover her with water and rehydrate her. I rubbed her back and put drops of water on her tongue. But the water was too cold. We didn't have hot water. And Chet wouldn't help me. I tried to convince him it was important, but he was pointedly disinterested in reviving our baby. I begged him. *Please help get the hot water back*, I cried. But he was too busy. So I warmed the water in my mouth and brought my baby back from death's door. A tiny life forgotten, left for dead when she was still alive, alone in her bed in the corner of our room, so near, but so far from Chet. I woke up feeling sad, and the first thing I realized was that the baby was my marriage.

In my guest review on Airbnb the owners of the hotel said that I was "very self-sufficient." It was not a rave. They didn't mention how cool the place looked after I cleaned everything and rearranged the furniture. I thought about leaving the place the way I found it, but I couldn't do that. I turned a crappy little apartment into a darling carriage house, and I had an emotional attachment to the joy it gave me. I put my energy into creating a lovely space for myself and the space became a boomerang for my serenity. Finally, I could sit. I could meditate. The vibrations of the Cosmos could rip through the room without raising a cloud of dust or tripping over an extension cord. I couldn't dismantle that. It was a small scrap of accomplishment. I needed to remember it. My Airbnb guest review was the Sacrificial Lamb. Religious fervor has its price. For me leaving that carriage house more beautiful than I found it was proselytizing; the equivalent of leaving Gideon's Bible on the nightstand, a symbol of hope that others might find their way into The Light.

~ : ~

I packed up the car and meandered through the Northeast Kingdom for a few days just trying to stay on highways where I could see water. So far, my road trip was a grand tour of Limbo. In the mountains, rivers pooled into lakes that fed streams that became rivers again. I looked for trails where Moon and I could disappear into the wilderness. We went wading and sat on rocks watching fish glint in dappled light. The familiar scent of pristine woodlands filled my lungs. I put my hands on the moss. Nature was busy doing her thing, swarming, swimming, sailing. I had no thing.

Without the farm there was no clock. I didn't have to plan ahead or pace myself. Without livestock and a house filled with possessions the days grew longer. There was more space between minutes. After Chet and my mom died, my dad had said, "You're going to have more freedom than you've ever known. It will be interesting to see what you do with it."

Selling the farm, paying off all my debts, and shedding my possessions, for the first time I felt the freedom. With zero debt I felt physically lighter. The pressure in my head disappeared. I felt an inner calm that was almost childlike. I wasn't worried about anything. My nightmares went away. Debt had been a part of my life for so long I had not reflected on the absence of it. I had not considered the possibility of zero debt. Having zero debt was my one kernel of satisfaction in the mire of loss.

Driving along narrow highways between skyscraping trees, my thoughts reeled through my life and all that had happened to me. I mourned the loss of the farm and ranted about Chet's affair, questioned my choices and put my memories under a microscope. That fern haunted me. It didn't so much change my feelings about Chet as it changed my feelings about myself. For so long my self-image had been colored by my belief that Chet's infidelity was a violation of our sacred promise. The farm was my nunnery, a hide-away that allowed me to keep my secrets and marinate in resentment. But my secrets were no different in their destructive character than Chet's. They festered until they were lanced by a houseplant and I was forced to confront my own sexual history. My entire life was under review for sins of omission.

Before I met Chet, I had had a number of sexual encounters with married men, and I never thought about them being wrong. Their marriage was not my concern. As my mother would have said, I was just trying on hats. I never thought about being the aggrieved wife someday. I never expected to get married. When I met Chet, my history was washed away by love, by his acceptance of me as a person, by my dreams for our future together. Reconnecting with my own promiscuity made me sick. I was an idiot. The arc of karma is long, but it bends toward payback.

~ : ~

I missed my giant bathtub at the farm, so I went on a quest to find the loveliest bathtub in the wilderness. Driving around Moosehead Lake, there she was, the Victorian estate of a wealthy industrialist turned into a B&B. The proprietor maintained a meticulous orgasm of stuff, plush oriental rugs, William Morris wallpaper, gilt frames of aristocratic flora and fauna, and most importantly, he loved dogs. After a tour of the gardens, I dined on leftover pizza in my room, and Moon went to sleep.

The bathtub was deep enough to drown in, and the bath towels were veritable saddle blankets. The sublime soak relaxed my muscles and helped my bones rearrange themselves after days of sitting behind the steering wheel. Wrapped in Egyptian cotton sheets, I settled into the pillow-top mattress for a night of sweet sleep, pleased to be indulging myself. But just as my subconscious unfurled, I was awakened by Moon pacing. After a cranky reprimand I closed my eyes and he paced some more. Then I was really, really cranky and he paced frantically. Finally, I dragged myself out of bed, dressed, and we made the noisy trek down the polished oak staircase to the parlor and across the hand-tied knots of Asian slave children to the front door.

In the glow of etched glass porch lamps on the rolling lawn, I saw my worst nightmare traveling with a big dog. Moon had diarrhea, severe diarrhea, so much diarrhea, squirting, sputtering, spraying from under his cropped tail. I had been transitioning him from kibble to a diet of raw chicken wings to clean his teeth. He had been on a raw meat diet his entire life until the months before I sold the farm when things got complicated and feeding him kibble was easier. Hours in the car with his face next to mine gave me a whiff of his bad breath and a close-up view of his brown canines. I thought raw chicken bones were the cure. Rural grocery stores didn't allow me to purchase just a few chicken wings at a time, so we were traveling with an entire flock packed in melting ice.

Evidently, I was feeding him those raw chicken wings faster than his digestive system could adapt to his new diet. I so appreciated his consideration for our immaculate surroundings, his civilized restraint, and his airtight sphincter. It could have been a mess beyond all messes in our lux boudoir, and that kind of cleaning does not provide me life purpose and therapeutic comfort. The mere thought of the potential for disaster sent adrenaline tingling through me and I couldn't sleep. It was a lovely place, but perhaps a little too fancy for us. So I loaded the car and we got back on the road, and Moon went back to his kibble diet.

My own digestive system was suffering quite the opposite of Moon's and I knew I needed a big dose of fiber. In a busy border town, I was elated to find a homey diner with plastic tablecloths and fake plants. I ordered the homemade coleslaw and the homemade chili. But their slaw was sweet as jam and their chili was salty as a box of salt. My taste buds shut their ears to the begging in my lower intestines, and I couldn't eat. I paid my bill and got some ice cream at a minimart.

On a desolate highway between timber mills, where the smell of cut trees was pungent as diesel, I found an automated motel and called a number on the locked office door. Over the phone I punched in my credit card info to get the keypad code that would unlock the heavy metal door to my room. The place was deserted, but the room was antiseptic white, and the wi-fi was lickety-split. For two days I drank powdered coffee on an empty stomach until my intestines gleamed as if polished by cabbage and beans.

On the farm I had been living a kitchen-centered life. I hadn't thought about what eating would be like without my own kitchen. I hadn't thought about what my diet would be like without growing my own vegetables and cooking my own food. Standing in line at a bait-and-tackle minimart, waiting to buy a microwaved breakfast sandwich from a wrinkled old man in a dirty baseball cap, who had just sold the fisherman in front of me two dozen night crawlers, which he counted out of a white bucket on the floor with the same hands that touched my sandwich, I remembered the taste of my eggs, the aroma of melting butter, and the crunch of whole grain toast. The egg in the minimart sandwich probably came from a chicken that suffered, but I needed the protein, and something to soak up my coffee. This food was not for pleasure, it was fuel, a requirement of the process, worm dust included.

~ : ~

After weeks zigzagging between the Atlantic and the Adirondacks, autumn drew me back to the Berkshires. I visited friends and went to check in on my goats, Wendell and Berry. They were living in a small shed with their own paddock, fat from eating the Ritz crackers their caretaker fed them from his pockets. He was a retired farmer who missed his own animals, and he was amused by the goats pushing their noses against him, sniffing for treats.

I was glad to see them and felt both happy and sad when they recognized me. It was a brief visit to a place that did not belong to me. I knew when I got there that I was going to walk away from them again. They called to me again. I couldn't take them with me again. I made the choice to leave my goats behind again. I shouldn't have gone to visit them because I couldn't take responsibility for them. I wanted to know that they were okay, but I wasn't going to be the one to care for them. I wasn't going to be the one to decide their fate. They were farm animals. I told myself they were in good hands, and they weren't my goats anymore. I hoped their karma was better than mine.

When I drove away from the goats I went straight to the farm. Before we could even see the place, Moon went nuts, jumping around the back of the car, delirious with joy at returning home. His joy made my heart ache. He was desperate to get out of the car and mark his territory. That's when I realized he would be hard to control. I would have to keep him on a leash in a place that had always been his run. There was no way to explain our situation to him. This place still smelled like home.

My gardens were withering, the pastures were empty, the chicken coop was veiled by weeds, and the barn filled with another farmer's hay. Looking at what had been my farm made me feel physically ill. I was experiencing death again. My grief relapsed and my insides sank into a cold pit. I couldn't stay there, couldn't walk around, couldn't tempt myself with the feeling of return. I had no place to return to. This was not my home. I wouldn't be able to manage Moon if I let him out of the car. I could never make him understand that this place did not belong to us anymore. I couldn't make myself understand that. My logical mind knew what was real, but my arms wanted to hold my dead baby.

Returning to the farm fucked me up. To be sane, I had to go. For the first time I was unsure about my plan to have another house in the Berkshires. Being near the farm was too much of a reminder of all that I had lost. I needed to be someplace else. But where?

For a month I disappeared into a tiny cabin in the woods where I could shift my focus from driving to writing and get some exercise in my friend Laurel's garden. I had begun writing a memoir and I needed to document the changes in my thinking since I sold the farm. I could feel my point of view evolving, but I wasn't sure where it would land. I was a work in progress.

As soon as I arrived at Laurel's property, she took off for a week on a trip and I had her house and the cabin all to myself. Again, my farm chore energy surged, and I needed to be busy, to do something that felt meaningful, something that produced results, some task that would give me a sense of satisfaction when it was completed. I needed to clean. When I could have been writing, I cleaned.

Without asking permission, I went deep into Laurel's pantry and front closet, emptied out everything into the kitchen and the living room. Then I wiped down the surfaces, vacuumed and dusted, and put everything back in new order. Food on the food shelves, cleaning stuff with cleaning stuff, paper goods with paper goods, paint cans lined up on the floor, bicycle tools with bicycle stuff, coats hung by season, hats on the shelf, boots underneath. I had all the time in the world, time to be as meticulous as a stylist for a magazine photo shoot. I was staging Laurel's pantry to make it perfect looking. Perfect on the outside was my specialty. I needed order to feel in control of my life, even if it was fake order, somebody else's order, order on the outside to mask the chaos on the inside.

Too much living space triggered my fear of the unseen. My torment was the thought of what was happening that I couldn't see. I needed to see everything all the time. I sat and stared into Laurel's pantry. The order there soothed me. It gave me hope that my life would be tidy again. The simplicity of living in the cabin calmed me. It was a primitive room with no running water, no bathroom, no kitchen, and no electricity except from a long orange extension cord running to Laurel's house. Once the bed was made, there was nothing left to do. I peed in an old enamel pot and hauled water in a jug. Then I had to go to the house to clean.

Each day I wiped up every crumb in the kitchen, pruned her house plants, and vacuumed up the dust bunnies. The landscape around the house became my art project. I was happy to have my hands in the dirt again. I excavated boulders, built a rock garden, and planted herbs and lupine. Moon and I explored the forest and slept well in the crisp night air. The simplicity was meditative, but the season was changing, and nights were getting frosty.

~ : ~

Chaos is imaginary
a pattern we fail to recognize
Pressed against the glass demanding order
as our wake spreads across the sea
revealing our intentions

Each step you take is the path you make
Choose

Your oar disappears beneath the surface

all God's creation awaits
the imperceptible pressure of a thumb
against the long wood
You swirl the Cosmos
    rearranging molecules from here to Mars
You become
    somewhere it rains differently
    a tear evaporates
    a glass is filled
Your oar rises
    and even the sun waits for your next move

~ : ~

I found another temporary arrangement with another friend, and in October, Moon and I moved to the Hamptons, a wealthy suburban community on Long Island in New York, where my friend owned a vacation house that would be empty for the winter. There I unpacked the car and took up residence with a view of the water, a hot tub, a swimming pool, and white wall-to-wall carpeting. I was glad to be there and hoped it would be a serene place to write. I was continuing work on my memoir about the farm and staying in one place for a while would allow me to knuckle down and finish the first draft.

The house was a showcase of stuff decorated in neutral tones with flowing linen curtains, a formal dining room, and five bathrooms. There were two living rooms, one with beige brocade couches overlooking the garden, and another with beige linen couches overlooking the TV. Against this pale palette dog pee stains from a very little dog scalloped every room, the walls, the couches, the curtains, the chair legs and the woodwork, jagged little sepia arches about six inches above the floor.

Moon was confused by this new set of rules in these new surroundings. His first instinct was to cover the little dog's pee with a larger arch of his own. I could see it on his face. "What do you mean, I can't pee here? Everybody else does." It was very hard to be stern in a house that obviously had a long history of competitive peeing. So I set about the task of finding every dog pee stain and removing it.

For the first time since leaving the farm, my clothes hung in a closet, and I had a desk where I could sit with my morning coffee and write as long as I liked. When my creative brain flatlined, I explored the shore and got to know the ocean. It was a new ecosystem for me. Moon ran for miles on the winter beach while I investigated the plants, and watched fishing boats, seals, crabs and sandpipers. The infinite horizon drew me in, and I found myself going to the beach during storms to witness how the waves clashed against the clouds and hear Nature roar.

Time is slower when the darkness lingers on the land. Alone and anxious in my borrowed mansion, I paced from room to room to be sure nothing had changed since I last looked. Then when I couldn't stand doing nothing anymore, I reorganized the closets, washed lipstick smudges off crystal goblets, took the linens off every bed, laundered them and remade the beds, filled the salt and pepper shakers with salt and pepper, arranged vases with fresh flowers, and lined up seashells on the windowsills. Cleaning and writing dovetailed. While I was fussing over the perfect arrangement of things, organizing stuff that didn't belong to me, washing things that were already clean, I was reorganizing myself, sorting my ideas into piles, looking for damaged feelings and missing logic, picking out the nicest traits and crucifying behavior I didn't like.

Eventually the dog pee stains encroached on my writing time. I read websites and magazine articles about stain removal, shopped for chemical potions and mixed home remedies, spent afternoons on my hands and knees, observing the carpet with scientific rigor, making notes to myself, trying to understand how chemicals interacted with each other and the sun. There was no end to it. The carpeting was already 20 years old. Sometimes the potions worked, but sometimes the stains disappeared for a while and then came back. Often successfully cleaning one patch made the area around it look dirty. I wanted a perfectly clean white carpet, but the house had a history I couldn't erase. Still, I couldn't stop myself from trying.

In the Hamptons, I saw myself in a petri dish. I had choices. I didn't have to clean anything. The place had a property manager, a housekeeping service, a lawn care service, a gardener, and a swimming pool service. But I couldn't stop myself from doing chores. Once when the housekeeper caught me vacuuming, he almost cried. "Don't worry," I said. "I'll leave something dirty for you." He smiled weakly. It was obvious I was lying. I needed to clean.

~ : ~

In spring Moon and I moved in with friends in New York City. It was an experiment. For a while I thought I might want to live there again. We went for walks along the Hudson River and watched helicopters zoom like dragonflies above the water. All around us the land disappeared under bricks and mortar, except for postage stamp parks where farmers gathered weekly to sell their harvest, as if to remind us that Nature was out there, even if we couldn't see her. When I was young, I had loved this city, the anonymity and the freedom. But after 18 years on the farm, I struggled to adapt to the jarring machine noise, the tarry smell of diesel, the absence of the horizon, and the boxed-in sun.

Moon struggled, too. His mind was boggled by so many smells, and his ears were rubbed raw by foreign sounds; sounds that weren't animals or people but seemed to signal danger by their sudden shrillness. He couldn't relax and there was no place where he could relieve his anxiety with a good run. The dog parks in our neighborhood were so small he could only pace and sniff.

It was challenging for me to write in someone else's apartment surrounded by their stuff, distracted by their conversations. Moon barked at footsteps in the hall, doors slammed, children squealed in the courtyard, visitors came and went. I had arrived with a sense of momentum from writing in the Hamptons, but without that solitude my momentum soon fizzled. I wasn't getting anything done, and all I wanted to do was clean. But cleaning in a house that other people called home raised the issue of boundaries. I couldn't clean the things I wanted to clean. I had fantasies of painting the place and moving the furniture around. When I was there alone, I vacuumed and dusted, and reorganized a couple closets. But it was weird. I embarrassed myself by keeping the kitchen too clean. I don't know why I wasn't embarrassed by my car.

Driving through the Northeast watershed for months and going to the beach on Long Island, Moon had managed to get wet and grungy almost every day. But I didn't think twice about his dampness against the sheepskins in the back of my car. When their skins were stiff and dry, I had sent the hides of my two black sheep, Tea and Pinto, to a wool processor to be finished into shearling sheepskins. Moon and I spent many hours curled up on those cuddlesome skins, reading and watching snow fall. Our last night on the farm we slept on them on the floor in the empty living room, and the day we drove away I threw them in the back of the car for Moon's bed.

Thousands of miles of warm dampness fed jillions of biota colonizing those cuddlesome wool continents. The body odor of animals smelled like home to me. It was the bouquet of my ambition. Parked on the street in New York City, baking in the summer sun, my car roasted wet dog and old sheep into an aroma so thick you could slice it. Still, I didn't notice until I gave a friend a ride.

"Oh, my god," he winced and put down his window. "What's that smell?"

"Probably dog," I said, closing his window. "I'll turn on the air conditioner."

"That is definitely not dog. It's more like… I don't know what it's like…" He put down his window again and turned his face outside. "I don't think I can ride in here with the windows closed."

"Really? Is it that bad?"

"You can't smell that?" His eyes were watering.

"Smell what?"

"It smells like something died in here."

"Oh. Hmm… I can't smell anything. Must be wet dog."

"I have a dog." He put his hand over his nose. "It's definitely not dog."

"Maybe it's my sheep."

"Sheep?" He turned to look over his shoulder at Moon sleeping on the sheepskins.

"Those skins were my sheep."

"Your sheep?"

"I killed them and skinned them."

He winced. "You killed your sheep?"

"Yeah. They're really comfortable. Probably not as nice as the ones they sell at Ikea."

"No," he said. "Probably not."

It was a humbling exchange, but I had to laugh. Even my nose had a blind spot.

~ : ~

Eight years after Chet died, every man I saw had a checkbox beside his face. Would I, or wouldn't I? Under the right circumstances, I might. I probably could. I probably would. If he loved me. If he at least seemed like he might love me. I told myself parables of waiting for love, poignant tales of delayed gratification. I dreamed, I flirted, I bought some high heels and flashed some cleavage, I hid the sharp pointy parts of my personality and tried to be feminine and demure, I spoke softly and carried a big stick, desperate to be part of a couple again, to disappear into another person's life, to make their mission my mission, their world my world. I wanted a man to distract me from myself.

When I finally found a guy and contemplated the possibility of a new relationship with someone my own age, I could see the journey was fraught with peril. The clock was ticking and there was no time for incrementalism. Couplehood served a practical purpose. It was a safety net. Caregiving was expected. Chronic illness was part of the deal. When we tried to share living space, our boundaries and expectations repelled. Old habits died hard or didn't die at all. Forgetting was tainted by fear of dementia. I learned that sex, intimacy, sleeping together, and actually sleeping, were each discrete functions. Cohabitation was a bumpy ride, not the easy flow of youthful synergy. It was a process of negotiation and compromise. Concessions were measured risks. Romance is a drug. Some of us are addicted. Some of us are allergic.

Once again, I cleaned. I rationalized it as a way of expressing my affection, but he took it as an implied criticism. I felt like I was doing something useful because to me, his house was filthy. He felt like I was wasting my time because dirt doesn't matter. He didn't see the mouse shit in the linen closet, and I was too embarrassed to tell him about it. When he realized how I had washed all the tablecloths and napkins folded them and reorganized the sheets by bed size, he said the linen closet was a work of art. But I think that may have been the moment when he crossed me off his list. He wasn't interested in a woman who would rather do laundry than go shopping at Bloomingdale's.

Chaos fed his sense of adventure. He needed spontaneity to underscore his freedom. Advance planning was against the rules. I struggled with that. He liked to eat at random hours and fall asleep in his chair watching TV. I was still cooking and eating three meals a day. The sound of television reminded me of hospital waiting rooms and my mother's nursing home. The more he watched TV, the more I needed to cook and clean. One night while I was eating dinner without him at his kitchen table, he walked through the room and blurted out a Ralph Waldo Emerson quote about consistency being the hobgoblin of a little mind. I was living like a cow, eating dinner at the same time every day. He equated my farmishness with being dumb, and I didn't feel like arguing about it.

At 63, I craved the rush of love. I wanted the feeling of being cherished. My libido was dancing pirouettes waiting for permission to strip. My fears and logic were crushed by my desire for physical intimacy. I was willing to take ridiculous risks and make untold sacrifices. Nothing could be worse than what I had already been through. Now I see how lucky I was that he finally gave me the boot. My pattern of behavior was like dance steps painted on the floor. I was going in circles repeating myself, the very definition of nuts. There was no man for me. Except the dead guy. And the longer he was gone, the better he looked.

I was still lost when the one-year anniversary of selling the farm, July 2017, came and went with a gong, without a vision for who I wanted to be, where I wanted to go, or what I wanted to do, other than write, and to write I had to be alone, and being alone still felt bad to me. By myself I was a woman with one oar in the water, the other turned to ashes. I couldn't be alone without cleaning. Except when I was on the road driving with Moon in the back of the car, entertaining myself, indulging my curiosity. That felt great. I loved driving alone, wandering the planet, exploring. When I was driving, I didn't feel trapped or lost, my mind was limitless, and I forgot all about cleaning.

There. That was it. That was my epiphany. I needed to get back on the road.

~ : ~

Before I left New York City I had another revelation that swept over me, changing my story. Chatting with my friend Martha while I was cutting her hair, I told her about the memoir I had been writing. When I got to the part about the 1993 letter, and how it crushed me to know that Chet's affair had been going on since then, she interrupted me and said, "You know, just because *The Piano* came out in 1993 doesn't mean she saw it in 1993. In 2008 she could have rented it on Netflix or gotten it at the library."

Oh, my god. How stupid am I? How fucking stupid.

That letter had held me prisoner from when I found it in 2012 to this moment in 2017. Talking with Martha was the first time I had ever discussed the details of it with anyone. The film was my only way of dating the letter. I chose to see the date of the film as evidence of a long-term affair because Chet clearly intended to hide the letter where I found it, in that stack of sheet music.

I was already angry at him and the letter fanned the flames. An old love letter hidden in haste fit with my memory of the grappa bottle hidden in the bungalow, and the other grappa bottle hidden in his office at the college. His motive was established. It was a snap judgment and I didn't question it because it reinforced a story I already believed. But the letter itself wasn't dated. I never found the envelope, and I had never had a long thoughtful conversation with anyone about it until talking to Martha five years later. Once again, I had set a trap for myself by hiding my embarrassment about my marriage. Once again, I was sheltering a toxic secret to protect my perfect life from scrutiny.

I wished I could go back into my stuff and compare all the photos of the Juicer to see if the photo she had sent with the 1993 letter looked significantly younger than the other photos of her that she had sent with the 2008 get-well cards. But I had thrown away all the photos of her when I trashed all the other back-up material for my memoir. That was my big emotional purge before I sold the farm. Sometime around

June 2016, I threw away the calendars, receipts, letters, photographs, get-well cards, sympathy cards, medicine bottles, doctor reports and notes that archived these events. This is not science. This is memory. I erased the evidence precisely so a revelation such as this one would not have me stopping my life and excavating boxes desperate for answers. There are no answers.

21. Regeneration

In September 2017, I was on the road with Moon heading toward Seattle, carrying all the same stuff I had with me a year earlier when I sold the farm. But it was a completely different experience from that road trip. I was looking forward, not running away. No panic attack, no manic cleaning, no misery. I was gifting myself an open-ended adventure because — why not? Since I left the farm, I'd been grappling with installing myself in a permanent home. As soon as I gave up on permanence, I felt better.

Passing through the Great Lakes I planned to stay at a motel in a tourist town, but by the time I got there all the dog-friendly motel rooms were taken, so I went to the nearest 24-hour Walmart. I knew about the American nomads I would find there — people who live in their campers, trucks and cars — but I never expected to be one of them.

Stretched beside Moon in the back of my car, I could see an older couple through the window of their camper watching TV. A uniformed driver disappeared into the back of his cargo van. Most of the cars around me were older models, rusty and dented. No one was sleeping in a BMW in the Walmart parking lot. Employees smoked cigarettes on the sidewalk. Music tinkled in the distance. It was quiet. I crawled under my blanket and witnessed myself prostrate before the retail giant I had spent years deploring, thankful for a safe place to sleep.

That night I reupholstered my soapbox with humility. Crazy Wife Farm had been my religion. On the farm I had commandments about the right way to live, what to eat, how to raise my animals, how to use the land, what materials were acceptable, where to shop. I was a believer and I thought everyone who didn't believe what I believed was going to hell. So now, finding refuge at Walmart, I felt hypocritical.

My idealism was its own kind of prejudice. I'm a privileged, middle class white woman. I have the luxury of choices. I never had to choose between rural poverty and industrial agriculture or a big box store. We all choose our own economic survival. On my transcontinental joy ride, I was burning up fossil fuels, checking my apps for another dog-friendly motel in a strip mall, where I could get points on my credit card, coffee roasted by a global corporation, and a breakfast sandwich with protein from a factory farm. I had choices, and I chose comfort and convenience, just like everybody else.

~ : ~

Driving across the upper Midwest through a sea of yellow wheat, the days didn't matter. I had no calendar. I wasn't trying to accomplish anything. I didn't have a deadline or a destination or a dream to chase. All my life I had been in a hurry to get somewhere. I was in a hurry to find a man to be my partner. I was in a hurry to make money and live like a rich person. I was in a hurry to be a farmer and understand my relationship with Nature. I was in a hurry to crack the code on life. On the road I wasn't in a hurry. I meandered, allowing my curiosity to lead.

My intuition was my navigator as I followed a river bend, turned off the main road toward a church steeple, parked at a bakery with a homemade sign. Exploring the lives of other people I saw myself in contrast. My identity was taking shape again.

Walking in the wilderness, I felt my separateness, my individuality, my life force. My molecules were in communion with everything around me and yet I was disconnected as a tumbleweed, a soaring solitary bird against the blue, as alone as a person could be. That aloneness felt expansive. I was free, detached from my past, without a future. All my next moves would be a choice. That was exhilarating. My mind cleared of resentment for my losses and I saw that being alone was not a punishment. Alone time was my time.

The lush green of the Pacific Northwest opened my mind to a new realm of possibilities. A rainforest of ancient conifers drizzled dew from limbs of velvet moss, and I could feel my connection to trees again, my roots. The magnetism was still there. I was in the flow. Wild water bathed my senses and I felt calm. Renewed.

I went to Seattle first, but it was too dense, too much like the cities of my past. I wanted to feel the edge of change, not the aftermath. I intended to live a slow life, and I needed to see more sky. Portland was an easy place to stop and write. I thought I would rent an Airbnb place for a few months and hang out with my girlfriends, three women I had known for decades who happened to be living in the Pacific Northwest.

The Airbnb places were expensive, and as it turned out, renting a small apartment was affordable. So although I wasn't committed to staying anywhere for any length of time, I decided to rent a studio apartment in a building that wouldn't hold me to a long-term lease. I took a compass with me when I went to look at places to be sure I would be able to see the sun from my windows, and in an old warehouse district I found a simple room on the sixth floor where I could watch the circadian sky, and have my own kitchen again. In October 2017, the day I signed the lease I saw three rainbows. That seemed like a good omen. Nature was welcoming me to the Pacific Northwest.

It was the first time in my life I had ever set up housekeeping alone in my own place, no roommates, no boyfriend, no husband. That was a profound revelation for me. I was 63 years old and just learning how to live my life alone, single in the city, without a partner, or family, or the safety net of community. In my apartment I could feel myself just being myself. Without the farm as my cloak, I could see my silhouette. My identity was taking shape again. Aside from my three friends in the area, no one in Portland knew me, no one expected anything from me. my history was invisible, I wasn't a farmer or a wife or a widow or a loud mouthed activist. I had the complete freedom to reinvent myself

~ : ~

Portland is a bookish town. My curiosity is piqued by a city where there are more tattoos than neckties. That familiar East Coast culture of entitled white men in suit jackets and button-down shirts, striding boldly down the sidewalk, pushing on the world with a mighty sense of financial righteousness, that urban tribe was my tribe before I started farming. I find it conspicuously absent here.

A city of skin seems to have displaced the suits with a mural of ink totems exposed to the elements in every kind of weather. Flora and fauna, axioms and epitaphs, symbols of Nature past, present, and future are memorialized in the derma of bartenders and cab drivers, nurses and mechanics, schoolteachers and insurance agents. Their ink makes a public record of our kinship to the biome and each other. A new tribalism is emerging, a collective celebration of individualism and the brave acceptance of self. My thinking is ruptured by these naked ideas.

People here seem chatty. Check-out clerks at the grocery store, restaurant servers and baristas say "Hello, how's your day going so far?" It's such a simple question, but it exposes an ethos of kindness. In New York or Boston, that sort of uninvited familiarity would have struck me as an affront, made me suspicious, caused me to side eye the talking stranger. But in Portland talking to strangers feels neighborly, like people expect to know each other here, like there is a consciousness that floats among us. The culture of politeness co-creates a sense of community, and that makes me feel safer here.

~ : ~

As soon as I moved into my new apartment, stuff in store windows began calling out to me, pushing me to shop. I was still a stuff junkie. Shopping was risky. I decided to just camp for a while. I got a couple plastic chairs, a table and an airbed, and I used the kitchen utensils and bed linens I had packed in the car the day I left the farm. In Portland, my life was a clean slate and I didn't want to mess it up by repeating the mistakes of my past. The more space I owned, the more likely I was to rationalize cleaning instead of writing. I didn't want rooms I needed to check on to be sure nothing had changed. I wasn't going to be ambushed by another nest of secrets. I wanted everything out where I could see it. Living small helps me manage my anxiety.

Before I left the farm, I had rented a storage pod and filled it with my favorite stuff, the stuff I thought I would need in my new place in the Berkshires. I was being practical. Eventually I was going to have to settle down again. So amidst the storm of my diaspora I gathered the essential provisions for a kitchen, a bedroom, a bathroom, a living room, an office, a garden, and my wardrobe, and put them in the pod. It didn't seem like a lot at the time, compared to what I was giving up. In July 2016 I felt like I was losing everything, and the thought of my favorite possessions in that pod gave me comfort. No matter how far I traveled, my stuff would always be there waiting to welcome me home. But in Portland, my new minimalism forbade the encroachment of my old stuff.

The antique dealers and pickers in the Berkshires who had purchased my belongings in the years before I left the farm were glad to help me sell the stuff in my storage pod. All of it. I didn't attend the sale. It felt too much like attending a funeral. I gave them permission to open every box and make my decisions for me. When the sale was over, they shipped me 21 boxes of paper — my books, photos, journals and files — my archive.

Among the scraps of my past I found a handwritten note from Chet that said, "Bil, I love you. That's all." He left that note for me under a magnet on the refrigerator when we lived in Boston. Now that note comforts me.

He was the love of my life, and I don't think anything is going to change that, not time or distance or age. Through all the pain and trauma, my love for him holds strong. He comes to me in dreams and sometimes when I wake, I feel as though I was just talking to him a minute ago. Laughing, arguing — yes, we argue in my dreams, about the tractor or the fence or the cows. He is alive in the range lands of my subconscious, roaming in my chemistry, nibbling through the walls of my reality, reminding me of who I once was, and who I can be.

A gold cigar box of mementos sits on my bookshelf, the kind of thing I imagine grabbing if the place was on fire and I had only seconds to snatch what I could take with me. In it are my favorite photographs of Chet and me, our marriage announcement, invitations to our parties, notes and letters we sent to each other, pieces of paper that will decompose and be forgotten. A few framed photos of us hang on my walls. I can look at them now without dredging up anger. I forgive him. I forgive myself.

Nature wants us to have sex. I chose a virile male as my partner and he was promiscuous. So was I. Our monogamy was not instinctive. It was a loyalty test, and we failed the test. But our love survived. That's a contradiction I need to embrace.

~ : ~

My apartment was an ocean of freedom with me drifting alone on a boogie board between horizons, an expansive feeling, but also alarming. My calendar was empty for the rest of my life. I saw that I could just disappear and fade away, and few would notice. My intention was to write, but I had never had a writing practice the way a musician practices music or a consultant consults or a farmer farms. Writing was something that gushed out of me when my emotions were flailing, a place to put all that undirected energy. Writing was my release, not my work. Chet had told me if I wanted to be a writer, I had to practice. But I wasn't even sure what that meant, other than the obvious. A writer writes.

On advice from Virginia Woolf, I now had a room of my own and I was organizing my finances so I could live on a small stipend from the sale of the farm. It was a gamble. I could have reinvested that money in real estate or the stock market. But I chose to invest in myself.

When I started my memoir, I thought I was writing about Crazy Wife Farm. But working with a professional editor and gathering feedback from beta readers, I learned that my memoir was really about me — me personally. I needed someone to tell me that. I didn't see it. I wanted to write about the farm, not my feelings. I was way more interested in talking about goat horns than my mental health. In the first few drafts, I completely skipped over my lockbox and the embalmed pain hidden in the back of my mind. I didn't want to resurrect those dead emotions. I was still too embarrassed to talk about it.

Then a pattern of behavior emerged. I saw how over and over again I had avoided dealing with the mess in my head by cleaning up and organizing the messes around me. My emotions were buried under layers of coping mechanisms. My memories were a treadmill warped by repetition. Images had embedded in my thoughts like shrapnel. Pieces of me were missing. Reflecting on myself in the emptiness of my little room, I saw how my lockbox postponed the agony of the moment by storing it for a later date. But it didn't heal my injuries. My wounds were pickled in fear. One day I flashed back to that cave, where the psychic had seen me on my knees scrubbing in the dark, and I realized I was scrubbing my reality, trying to create a perfect picture.

By the end of 2018, it was coming up on the tenth anniversary of Chet's death. I was already raw with reminiscence, unprepared for the return of that familiar ache. But my bones seemed to know what time it was, and I was defenseless. I didn't want to feel that pain again. I wanted to be done with it. I wanted to outgrow it. I thought my feelings were something I could remove, like the stain in a rug. Scrub it long enough and it will go away. But alone in my apartment ten years after Chet's death, I slid into murky sadness and I felt awful in a very familiar way. That surprised me. I was disappointed in myself. I felt like I had failed to cure myself. What was wrong with me? I had travelled 3,000 miles from the farm thinking I was escaping those feelings, leaving them behind with his ashes and the windows that framed the pictures I wanted to forget. But Chet's death had stowed away inside me, and when the clock struck death, I was immersed in grief again.

That's when I ran out of gas writing this book. I was exhausted. If I was going to continue developing my craft as a writer, I needed some other outlet for my creativity, because this memoir shit sucked. For a while I did some journaling and social commentary, but without readers I was just jabbering into the void. It took a few months for me to concoct a purpose for my work. Then in January 2019, I launched a blog published every Wednesday. It was a way to reach out, and a promise to myself to stay focused on my writing practice for one year.

~ : ~

Blog post 4/24/2019 — When I was a teenager, inspired by Twiggy and Cher, my friends and I rolled up our skirts to make them shorter and put on make-up in the restroom at school where our mothers couldn't see us. Lined up in front of those sinks and mirrors, we ratted our hair into bouffants, padded our bras with our socks, critiqued our changing bodies, and gossiped.

Boy crazy was a phrase we used to describe a girl judged to be delirious with the desire to be part of a couple. All the cool girls had boyfriends. The coolest girls broke up with one boyfriend to start up with a better one. Girls were measured by their boyfriend's status and success. That's how it's always been.

Now I'm 65, and it's a rush to witness all those body changes all over again — shape, skin, face, hormones, hair. And I still follow the latest fashions, even if I don't wear them. But one thing is quite different in my late life metamorphosis. I'm not boy crazy. Since puberty I was either looking for a man or I had one. But being part of a couple doesn't interest me anymore. It's no longer a driving force in my life. That's a big change for me.

For 32 years of marriage my life was organized around another person. It took me years after my husband died to learn to live alone. There was no dress rehearsal for being single. Suddenly my co-pilot was gone, and I was flying solo. Then once I got comfortable with my circumstances, I had to face other people thinking that I wasn't whole if I didn't have a husband, that I couldn't possibly be happy, that it was risky. You'd be surprised how many people think a woman's life purpose is to be the accompaniment to a man.

I'm not looking for a partner because for the first time in my life, I have the freedom to focus on myself. In this next phase I want to concentrate on my own talents and ingenuity. I want to explore new dreams. Elder women are a powerful force for change in the world. We have the will, the wisdom, and the resources to tilt humanity toward wellbeing. That excites me. I want to be part of that.

I have my moments of anxiety just like everybody else. But I push through them because I believe in my future. I don't want to be somebody else. I'm living with my dog in a one-woman nest, looking forward to a new set of achievements, and I'm thrilled by the possibilities. My life is finally all about me, and it feels like a gift.

~ : ~

In 2017, as I was starting my new life in Portland, the #MeToo movement sprang onto the main stage of current events. Every day I read the news online and listened to podcasts and NPR, and every day I heard more about #MeToo. Hearing other women talk about their experience of sexual assault triggered feelings I had compartmentalized long ago. Memories of being raped popped up in my mind because rape seemed to be in the news every day. The constant discussion of other women's trauma caused me to relive my own trauma. I didn't enjoy it, I resented it, I wanted to put those feelings away and never look at them again. But as much as I resented the intrusion of #MeToo, I also appreciated it. I was learning that my experience of sexual predators and sexual assault was something many women shared. I saw that what happened to me wasn't my fault. I was starting a new life as a new person in a new place by going deep into my past and reconsidering who I was a half century earlier.

#MeToo opened a discussion of gender, the gender experience, how I lived in a very gendered world, and I knew instinctively that was true. Portland is a river of gender fluidity, on the bleeding edge of gender rights and nonbinary self-expression. I began to feel as though some cosmic tow rope had pulled me into this city to face my own issues with gender. Odd, because I was technically a senior citizen, and gender norms were less and less relevant in my life. Or so I thought. In Portland I learned that my gender is core to my identity from cradle to grave.

I read a magazine article about an isolated tribe of hunter-gatherers who are living today the same way humans lived 10,000 years ago — no government, no religion, no marriage, no monogamy. Women in the tribe are equal to men and couples pair up with no expectation of permanence, and no punishment for infidelity. Men and women have sex based on desire. Children are parented by the whole tribe, and everyone has the same rights. Lifelong commitment to anything but the tribe is unthinkable. Living naked in the bush, chasing down their food with sharp sticks, they can't afford to be idealistic.

My own personal anthropology had so many rules layered onto the simple life of those primitive people. I was envious of the egalitarian freedom of the women. I wondered if they ever broke into chick fights over a particularly delicious man. Did sex ever lead them to feel a sense of ownership of their partner? Did they experience love separate from sex? I thought about how I was raised, and I wondered how much of my feelings of betrayal and my sense of personal failure was cultural conditioning.

I was designed from birth to be a breeder. From the perspective of my family, my church, and my community, breeding was the highest and best use of a woman. I was trained to care for my offspring. I was given dolls to practice mothering. I attended a public high school where females were forbidden to wear pants and short skirts. Cleavage was not allowed. Exposure of a female's body parts indicated she was too easy to breed. If a woman was easy, a man could not be certain she carried his seed. Good girls were not easy.

Before Chet and I got married our families were ashamed because we were living in sin. When I moved into the Luna House in 1976 my grandmother wrote me a long letter about the Ten Commandments, my virtue, and the misery of Hell. I was a tainted woman. She said society would shun me because I was used. The first time we visited Chet's family in Ohio, his sister said, "Billie, if you give away the milk, he's never going to buy the cow."

When we first got together, we didn't believe in marriage. After we had confused our families by splitting up for a year in 1984, we saw marriage as a symbolic gesture that our relationship was permanent. But we had always believed in monogamy. There was never any question that we would reserve sexual intimacy exclusively for each other. Now I see how monogamy is a fanciful ideal, by definition a system out of balance, a lack of diversity, a monopoly. There was no monogamy on Crazy Wife Farm. Males are designed for promiscuity. A penis is designed to disrupt monopoly. Males are made to ejaculate without obligation. On the farm I saw males of every species disrupt monopoly every day.

Yet Chet was mine. He was occupied territory. I had a sense of ownership about him, and the Juicer was trespassing. Sex may be the opiate of the masses, but love is a claim on the soul, and monogamy was our first rule of love, a promise like a pie crust, made to be broken. But monogamy is not a law of Nature. In Nature diversity rules. The animals who are best at sex dominate the gene pool. Sex is power. We kill for sex. We risk food, shelter, wealth and security for sex. We give up social acceptance, the bonds of family and the stairway to heaven for sex. Sex drives us mad with desire. Sex masquerades as love. Illicit sex cheats us out of a predictable future. Sex is high risk behavior. We endure chaos for sex. We go to jail for sex. Kingdoms are lost and the course of nations diverted because a penis is placed in a particular hole. Sex is basic animal behavior. Even in this modern world, we are still animals.

~ : ~

Sitting alone in my apartment in Portland, immersed in memories of my own sexual history, and reflecting on how sexual intercourse had been the central act in two of the worst things that had ever happened to me — being raped and being cheated on — I wished for a different world, one where animal behavior was less significant, one where my self-image could be disentangled from my gender, one where the simple placement of a man's penis would not be so disruptive to my mental health.

The man who raped me was an animal. He was my doctor. After the abortion I was in physical pain. When he offered to give me a ride home from Harlem to Brooklyn Heights, I said yes because my gut hurt, and he made me feel cared for. But it made him feel like I was easy. When he asked if I wanted some company, I said yes, and he came up to my apartment with me. He was my doctor. He was supposed to be my caregiver. I trusted him. I was in a daze after a barbaric physical procedure, and I wasn't thinking clearly. I did want some company. I was alone in the world and I wanted to be comforted.

When the door closed behind him, and he put his arms around me and hugged me, I hugged him back. I was desperate for a hug. But that was a signal to him that I was easy. He took me down on the bed and

I said to him, "What are you doing? You just told me not to put anything up there for a month," and he said, "Don't worry, I'm clean." And then he pounded himself into me until he came, while I bled on the sheets and went blank, disappeared into the hollows of my mind, tripped out on my bad luck, and my lockbox was born.

He kissed me goodbye when he left, like I was his secret girlfriend, like he just stole a cookie from the cookie jar. I was in shock. Then he said, "If my mother and my sisters knew I had sex with a shiksa, they would kill me." In his mind, he hadn't raped me. In my mind, I had just been brutalized by a monster. But he had just fucked a woman who was easy. That's how men think.

For a very long time after that day, killing myself seemed like a way to be in control of my life. That's the one guaranteed thing about suicide, it's absolute control. Men were predators and I was prey. I should have known better than to bring a strange man up to my apartment, even if he was my doctor. Men are rapists. That was the social paradigm that prevailed in my mind until I moved into the Luna House and fell in love with Chet. Our love was my lifeboat.

I was raped 45 years ago, and the memory still shapes my outlook on life. Now I am an elder unlikely to be the target of an assault. But going to a medical facility and being treated by male doctors is still a trigger for me. It has taken me all this time to be able to say that. Other women lit my willingness to share my story. Millions of us have had the experience of being assaulted by a man, just because we are women. Learning that I was not unique gave me a context for my rage and a way of channeling it into a place more productive than blame. I write my rage. It's another kind of cleaning.

~ : ~

Blog post 6/12/2019 — When I was younger the whole world felt like a meat rack. And then one day, I wasn't on the menu. It's an adjustment. As a young woman, I lived in fear of malign intentions and sexual assault. Now I'm neither prey nor predator. It feels good. But I have to say some outlandish things to get noticed. Or I would simply disappear.

One of the reasons women over 60 become less visible in society is the hormone rush men don't get when they look at us. I'm not being snide. It's science. When men see women they wish to have sex with, they get a certain kind of feeling that they don't get when they look at their mother, or their grandmother. Civilization is organized around giving men that certain feeling because men rule the world.

Yes, Virginia, the world is organized around the male sex drive. Otherwise, why would we have stilettos? Seriously, look at how societies make rules to protect and isolate women from men. Wouldn't it be easier to just add a little estrogen to the water supply? I mean, if we can fluoridate our water to protect our teeth, why not add a little estrogen to dilute the oversupply of testosterone that's killing us?

Of course, men are not to blame. Nature evolved us this way. A penis is designed to be the diversity machine. A man's member can create hundreds of children without accountability or obligation. A uterus can host only one pregnancy a year. So, for a million years a woman has been a man's portable uterus. It made perfect sense at the time. Try throwing a spear while you're breastfeeding.

What's got everybody confused is today a woman doesn't need a penis to get food or children. She can buy sperm retail and throw a digital spear with one click to get food. Technology has made upper body strength unnecessary. No wonder men are having an identity crisis. What's the role of men if women don't need them? To add salt to their wounds, women live longer than men. I could live another 30 years, three decades during which my uterus will lay dormant in my abdomen, while my brain journeys where no man has gone before. Having a dormant uterus is not a blow to my ego. Try saying that about a penis.

If the meat rack is a model for civilization that maximizes the utility of men, I'm hoping for a shift to a new model that's less about competition and more about caregiving, a shift from quantity to quality of life. There's a reason babies are incubated in a uterus and not a scrotum. A uterus is a more protected, more nurturing, less risky place. So put this on your bumper sticker: THINK LIKE A UTERUS. Because a world that's better for the most vulnerable among us is better for all of us.

~ : ~

How naïve I was to think I would be part of a couple forever. I should have been planning to be a widow, but I didn't see it coming. Even though my grandmothers were widows, it wasn't part of my consciousness. No one tells little girls they're destined to be alone in this world. The facts of life should be extended to include the birds and the bees, and the bats.

My paternal grandmother lived to be 99, and my maternal grandmother lived to be 103. Their husbands died decades before them and as widows they learned to live their lives alone. In their last years they talked about feeling purposeless. Their active minds were bored by the limited capacity of their bodies to pursue their interests. They had no meaningful work once their husbands were dead, and their children and grandchildren were grown and gone. Society had no use for them. They talked about wanting to die. They knew their nursing home was short-term storage for their unnecessary lives. I saw how the nursing homes where my mother lived were compost heaps for useless humans. Technology has given us longevity without purpose. Old people are just another waste stream.

When we were young Chet and I planned to get old together, like planning a vacation. We expected to be in complete control. We didn't think of each other as caregivers. That word was not part of our vision for ourselves. We didn't consider our relationship an investment. We were lovers, not bankers. We didn't confront the difference between sex and intimacy. For us there was no difference. We had a sense of ownership about each other, a sense of entitlement, access, openness, complete freedom with our bodies. Sleeping together was fulfillment, a habit and a priority. The arrangement evolved incrementally. It wasn't a contract. It was instinct.

We thought when the time came, we would commit couples' suicide like Sophie and Nathan in *Sophie's Choice*. But not with a dark cloud over us. We fantasized a celebration of credit card charges for a luxurious hotel room, an epicurean meal, unlimited champagne, our favorite music, and a pile of heroin sprinkled over dessert. We thought our deaths would be our rocket to the moon. Dying together would be the ultimate consummation of our union.

Cancer obliterated that notion of the future. Union fell away with Chet's diagnosis. In a few sentences in a doctor's office we were on separate tracks, leading separate lives. He was going to be sick and I was going to be his caregiver. He was going to die, and I was going to live. I wish our society had normalized death and encouraged our preparations for it, but even the doctors couldn't talk about it.

When I became a wife, I should have expected to care for a dying husband. Most men die before their wives. I wasn't given the right dolls. A doll is a template. A Widow Doll could have taught me how to live the end of life the way Barbie taught me how to be a breeder. My Widow Doll would say "Good-bye" in 20 languages, and come with accessories like a coffin, a funeral pyre, mummy gauze, and a shark for burials at sea. If every kid played with a Widow Doll, death would be obvious. We'd spend a lot less money on healthcare, dying would be a better party, billions of us would celebrate Day of the Dead, virtual cemeteries would be the new social media, and maybe being a widow would lose its hideous stigma.

Now I hope to be as fortunate as Chet was, to come to my end conscious of the experience with the intention of finding peace. But Chet had me to organize the party. I was there to facilitate his vision. Who will be there for me? I want what Chet got — the music, the poetry, the candles, the flowers, and loved ones to hold my hand.

If I'm hit by a bus or blown up in a terrorist attack, I'll settle for the most expeditious disposal of my remains. But if I slide into chronic illness and fail to thrive, before I disappear in the fog of medication, I want to plan my death. I believe it's my right to choose my time to go. But I don't want my final act to be suicide. Suicide is loaded with the negative connotations of tragedy and hopelessness. I don't want my death to be a tragedy.

Euthanasia is what we do to animals that must die. I don't want to be euthanized. I want a new word for planning a joyful end to my life. I am thinking it's methanasia. Not you-thanasia, me-thanasia. I'm planning my methanasia in case I'm not lucky enough to die in my sleep. I don't want my death to be a crime. I want it to be a celebration. The government has no right to interfere with my methanasia. In fact, it's in the government's economic interest to let me go.

I want my death to create possibilities for new life on Earth. It's my honor, my oath, and my duty to recycle myself. Cremate me or compost me. Let Nature fold me in her arms. Dust to dust is the journey I seek. I want to share the beauty I've known with the lives that come after me. If death is birth in reverse, when my time comes, I want to lean into it.

I believe in the power of the Universe, the beneficence of Nature, and the sacredness of planet Earth. I believe my life here is a gift, my work here is my joy, and my death is an opening between this life and the next. I believe in life I will be loved as I have loved others, and in death I will be remembered as I have remembered others. And in those memories, I will live forever.

These ideas give me comfort and lead me to find the joy in my experience. I didn't realize the lessons life was teaching me until I took the time to reflect. Well, maybe I didn't take the time — time took me. Time is distance, and distance is perspective, and there is no rushing Earth on her journey around the sun. If I have any wisdom at all, it's the gift of time.

~ : ~

Blog post 6/19/2019 — Have you ever had one of those nights when you just couldn't sleep? Last night my mind was like a wild horse racing through every minute of the day, every person, every conversation, every problem, every burp and fart. Just running, running, running — running to nowhere. Should I get a cheaper apartment? Where will I park when I go to the eye doctor? Is my car too big? Should I get a smaller car? Why are my eyes always so bloodshot?

In bed in the dark, every ache and pain is cancer. Of course, I have cancer. Everybody has cancer. Why should I be any different? The headache behind my eye is a brain tumor. The red patch on my leg is skin cancer. The twinge of nerves in my hand is hand cancer. My skin tags are an invading army of itty-bitty tumors that will soon devour my hidden parts. Just please let them stay hidden. I hate skin tags. One day I'll just be an empty sack of clothes. Cancer will have eaten all of me and my skin tags will be homeless.

In the middle of the night, I could die of almost anything. I stare at the ceiling and imagine how my friends would find me dead in bed a couple days from now. Then I think about changing my t-shirt and putting on some nice underwear. I just bought these new bed sheets. Why wreck them just because I'm having a bad night? Maybe I should take down the shower curtain and sleep on that. Just in case the Grim Reaper stops by my apartment tonight and leaves a mess. I sleep better when I'm feeling prepared. Although I don't know how well I would sleep on my shower curtain. Maybe I should get a new mattress pad. You know, the kind that's waterproof, for children and old people, and people like me who suddenly die in bed.

Some nights are just like that. There weren't enough hours in the day to process my life story, and it spills over into the dark when my dreams should be power washing my brain. But some nights my mind is just too busy to dream. I catalogue my wishes, inspect my regrets, and think about how things could have been different, on and on like a running horse in a wide open space, so beautiful, so energetic, and so pointless. Running for the sake of running, toward the horizon, until the horse is too small to see, and I finally fall asleep.

Then I wake up. My skin tags have not amassed in one big clump on my face. My tumors are gone. That headache must have been, you know, just a headache. My eyes can see just fine. And I did not rip down my shower curtain to prepare for the Grim Reaper, who must have skipped over me, because here I am. Cool. I think it's going to be a good day.

~ : ~

On the inside I'm the same person I've always been, but on the outside, sometimes guys in the elevator call me ma'am. I know they're just being polite, and I appreciate that. The first thing people recognize about me, after my skin color, is my age. Elderhood changes what they expect.

I looked for a bar where I could feel welcome and meet my neighbors. I've always enjoyed the random conversation of a bar scene, connecting with new faces, and having a sense of belonging to a crowd. But now most of my neighbors are a generation or two younger than me. I often sit by myself at a bar, enjoying a festive beverage, reading on my phone. Once a young woman sat beside me and said, "Oh, aren't you cute." I didn't know how to respond. I felt like someone's toy poodle.

By history's lights I should be dead or tucked away invisible. Women got the right to vote in 1920. My grandmother was born in 1907 without the right of suffrage. It hasn't been that long. The world is just getting used to women challenging the status quo, leading and taking power, living independently, sitting alone at a bar, drinking a rye Manhattan, reading among a crowd that steers clear of grandma over there.

I'm not blaming anyone for my anachronism. The slow pace of women's evolution from mommy to master gave our species an edge. Humans were designed by Nature for one gender to be the killer and the other to be the birther. But technology is equalizing gender. Men have turned our world into a first-person shooter game. Peak male, peak greed, peak stress. It's not sustainable. Neutralizing gender could help restore the balance between competition and caregiving. I don't think the patriarchy ends in a matriarchy. I think the utility of gender has expired.

I live in a world without men except for the few surviving husbands still around. In most of the places where elder women gather, elder men have disappeared by divorce, disability, disinterest or death. In their absence we seem to recognize that the pain and sadness of losing a life partner is a passing phase. Elder women bloom in the wake of loss as they rediscover themselves, their abilities and their interests. A late life renaissance awakens our resilient minds to new possibilities. Not that we don't love men. We do. But by the time we get to elderhood, most of the men are gone. And as we learn to live without them, we become immersed in the world of women, and the characteristic behaviors of men stand in stark relief. We miss the love we had. But we don't miss the dominance of the other gender.

~ : ~

Blog post 8/21/2019 — This morning I woke and stretched against my pillows, looked up at my arms and saw my grandmother's skin. I remember when I was a girl looking at the papery tissue of her arms and the deep grooves in her hands, and thinking she needed to use more hand cream. Of course, now I know that hand cream isn't going to stop my skin from becoming parchment. Parchment is my destiny. But a plan could help me feel okay about that.

I have had the urge lately to make a plan, a big important master plan that will be my to-do list for the next decade, a yardstick against which I'll measure myself and keep my life on track. Having a plan would make me feel better about not knowing what I'm doing because it would look like I do know what I'm doing, and whenever I doubt myself, all I have to do is look at the plan. See? No doubt. There's a plan. I definitely know what I'm doing.

When I'm feeling uncertain about my future, I open Excel and start making spreadsheets, high tech grids I deploy to manage all the important issues in my life. I'm not putting my faith in some goop that comes in a fancy jar with slick advertising. I'm putting my faith in a software program that sorts information into little boxes, in a vast hive of boxes that can be converted into a pie chart. Organizing myself into rows and columns makes me feel in control. We all have our tricks for coping.

Age is climbing up on me like kudzu, and I feel like I need a plan for what to do with it. In my 20s I had a plan to manage rock bands in the music business and become rich and famous. That didn't work. In my 30s I had a plan to conquer a desk job and claw my way to the top. Did okay with that. In my 40s I had a plan to develop a software company and own it. Almost did that. In my 50s I had a plan to be a farmer and make a living from my farm. Complete disaster. Although I loved it. Now I'm in my 60s, single in the city, drifting through my days, yacking up the alphabet, using Facebook as a megaphone. And a little voice inside me keeps asking, what's the plan?

I have to remind myself that having a plan never gave me control over my life. But it would make me feel good to have my future plotted on a grid from now until I'm 90. Little boxes of text would give me comfort that I'm going to be okay. Then the sun shines in my window and the day spreads out before me as virgin territory, and I ask myself — Shall I crack open a spreadsheet and angst over my long game, or should I just go out and buy some hand cream?

~ : ~

Ten years after her death I have new compassion for my mother. I see more clearly our differences and similarities. My instinct has always been to be low maintenance because I grew up with a woman who was very high maintenance, and I saw how she alienated people. Her emotions were unruly beasts, wild and troublesome, pin pricks of discomfort and embarrassment. She never had the self-awareness to be more circumscribed. Among the mild mannered she was the boss cow. Among the bulls, like my father, she was out of control, unmanageable and unacceptable.

She was 71 when she showed up in the Berkshires, just six years older than I am now. She had lived as a single woman for 25 years, yearning to be a part of the family that rejected her. That rejection wasn't unreasonable. She was extremely disruptive with her demands and her always empty bank account. She had the bad habit of destabilizing us, a way of tipping any situation into calamity. Her bedlam was a mudslide that sucked me in because I loved her. I felt sorry for her, but I didn't want to be near her. That was the conundrum she brought with her to the Berkshires.

Now I relate to her in a way I never have before. I can feel her broken heart inside my own. I had no sympathy for her when I was a teenager, tangled as I was in my own web of loss with my parents' divorce. I couldn't have known then what it was like for her to lose everything she loved in the ruin of her marriage, the loss of her husband, the public humiliation of infidelity, the dissolution of our family home, and the departure of her children to new lives. One day she was integral to something ideal, something she believed in, a higher order that had been a lifelong goal, and the next day she was an outcast, adrift, unmoored, unloved and alone. Now I see the stones in her path, and it chills me to witness their alignment with my own. As much as I tried not to be like her... Well, here I am.

I look down at my hands and I see her hands, the same tea spots on my skin, the same wrinkles around my mouth, the same boobs and belly. I have become my mother. And yet, I know my consciousness is different. I believe I have a relationship with myself that she did not have with herself. I doubt she ever inquired of herself as I am now. I'm asking myself what kind of relationship I want to have with myself. Who do I want to be on the inside? What is the conversation I hold with myself? Who am I talking to and how do I feel about her? Because I don't simply want to be sane. I want to be satisfied, self-satisfied. I want to learn to love the life I have. I want to enjoy my time. I want to age fearlessly. These are my demands. This is my rebirth.

~ : ~

Blog post 9/4/2019 — I'm pretty sure I have resting bitch face. It's a real thing. It even has a Wikipedia page. But I've never felt bad about it. Since I was a teenager, people have been telling me to stop frowning and smile. My mother said, If you don't stop frowning, your face will stay like that forever. She was right. I furrow my eyebrows when I think. Now my wrinkles are like railroad tracks across my forehead. And I wouldn't trade them for a minute. They are the real me.

When I'm sitting in silence on a park bench or a barstool, and someone tells me to smile, I feel like they're telling me to hide my state of mind, as though I have an obligation to be happy and they're entitled to see me grin. I'm convinced I attract this remark because I'm female. All females are on display all the time. The whole idea of resting bitch face is proof. Even when we're at rest, we're subject to criticism for how we look.

Of course, there's a cure for resting bitch face. Millions of women are buying Botox, spending billions of dollars on treatments. I saw a TV commercial that showed 20-something women worried about their face lines, lines that weren't old enough to qualify as wrinkles, but were portrayed as a source of shame. According to the commercial, after Botox these young women were miraculously more confident in themselves, a remedy years of psychotherapy might fail to achieve.

I read a news story about a 35ish woman in Texas who burglarized a salon with an electric saw to steal her wrinkle treatments. On Instagram I see many women with that telltale bubble face, shining smooth foreheads and plump lips. They all look the same, perfect as plastic dolls. I went to the bakery and the young woman who served my quiche had one of those inflated faces. Her lips and her eyebrows were the only thing that moved when she spoke, the rest of her face was a mask frozen in place. Soon a girl's menstruation party will include gift certificates for Botox along with her first tampons. You're never too young to fear aging.

These lifelong Botox babes will be pioneering cosmetic treatments that haven't been invented yet. No one knows how decades of neurotoxins will change a woman's face muscles, her skin and her brain. One theory is that after 20 or 30 years of injections her face nerves will die, resulting in permanent paralysis. Her unused face muscles will atrophy, droop and sag in a phenomenon known as avalanche syndrome, where her flaccid tissue slides down on itself until her eyebrows become sideburns and her lips flap like café curtains, unable to enunciate half the alphabet. It's a high price to pay for beauty. More than I can afford. So, I think I'll just stick with the woke woman face I already have. Frowning keeps my face muscles in shape to speak my mind.

~ : ~

After I had signed the purchase and sale agreement to sell the farm, my Boston crew came to the farm one last time to help me pack and label the boxes that would be loaded into my storage pod. They weren't just packing up my history, they were putting their own memories in storage. For eight years they had been coming to the farm when the seasons changed to help me prepare for new weather and keep the farm in working order. They shared my sense of loss, and as they packed my stuff, they chose labels for the boxes that meant something to them.

One box was labeled "VIOLET'S BONES" in big black letters. The dealer might have sold them if he had opened the box. But he did not. My sale was strange enough for him given that it appeared to be an estate sale for a deceased person, but I was not deceased. To his customers it looked like an old lady had died with no family to dispose of her stuff. No one was there to filter out the super personal. My bras and underwear and socks and nightgowns were in those boxes. As was my great-grandmother's little glass jewelry box, returned by the estate sale shopper who purchased it when she discovered it was filled with baby teeth, perhaps a little too much of another family's juju for her taste.

When my cow Violet had died, I put her bones in the sun to whiten and dry. Then I hung her skull with its elegant horns on a nail above the woodstove in my living room. That was the last time I took a close-up look at her. My eyes were different then. I didn't see the translucent sheets of tissue clinging to the surface of her forehead, or the long hairs smeared between her horns, or the top of her esophagus where the end of her tongue had been, or her nasal passages leading from her nose to her sinuses, all preserved crisp as rice paper origami by the years of heat from my woodstove rising and drying her. When she arrived, bubble wrapped in a box at my little apartment in Portland, it had been a long time since I beheld viscera, and Violet struck me in a way a cow had not struck me before. She was icky.

On the farm icky was cool. But in my city life, icky is not my style. I found myself compelled to embrace this artifact of my history, but I didn't want old cow guts hanging on my wall. I had killed and cut up a dozen cows on the farm, but in the city, I cut up plastic trash bags and covered my table to ensure I could clean Violet's skull without a single errant biota getting on my nice clean floor. Then I took a toothbrush and a bottle of hydrogen peroxide and scrubbed her to a pristine alabaster glow.

As I cleaned Violet, I thought about my history with cows, how much I loved them, and how much work it was to keep them, the smell of hay in the barn and the meditative rhythm of mowing pastures, their plump tongues and wet breath, the sound of chewing and the moo of mothers calling calves. Violet's symbolism was undeniable. She was the cow that followed me to Portland, my ambassador from Crazy Wife Farm. Now she hangs over my desk, elevated to the status of Sacred Cow, dried flowers decorating her bullet hole bindi and a string of lights around her face. She enshrines my life as a farmer. Every once in a while, our third eyes meet, and she winks at me.

Sometimes I remember an object that must have been in my storage pod, a painted vase or a vacation souvenir, and I miss it. Those objects were markers on the path that got me to this moment, buoys floating on the surface, signaling the presence of things unseen beneath. I lost a map of myself when I let go of my possessions. But giving up that map is what allowed me to rediscover myself.

It's possible I'm happy in the most trite sense of the word. I think the last time I felt this enthusiastic about my life was in 2005, when I got my first cows. I have new dreams and I'm living forward, hungry for new experiences. To keep from drifting into a negative state of mind, I try to practice good mental hygiene. I sit and meditate. I walk Moon beside wild water. I will myself to stop wanting what I do not have. I seek ways of being that don't feed my anger. It takes initiative to be happy. Trite isn't as easy as it sounds. I want to feel happy, so I'm working on it.

With perfect hindsight, I see now that it was the burden of perfection that crushed me into believing I was a failure. My inner judge told me that I alone was responsible for all the pain in my life, as though perfection is ever possible, as though there is a life without pain, as though failures are not the steppingstones to success. A new person manifested in me when I smashed my lockbox and finally accepted the reality I had hidden there as core to my identity. To be whole I must integrate myself. Pain, grief and anger are part of who I am. Crying helps me think. Thinking helps me see. Aging gives me perspective. I am whole now, shimmering in self-reflection, learning to keep it real.

On a sunny afternoon Moon and I wade into the river. He plays with sticks while I'm deep in thought. Behind us crows gallivant in the woods, cracking up the silence with their raspy caws. Then a hawk breaks through the canopy, cutting an effortless spiral through an invisible vortex. The crows are after her, darting, nipping at her wings until the hawk is too high, beyond the realm of crows, and the gang returns home to the trees. All but one.

A lone crow climbs toward her target. Higher and higher the hawk ascends, a tiny black cross against the sky. Then the angry crow reaches her and two tiny black crosses dance above the land. The hawk floats. The crow lunges. The hawk floats. The crow lunges. Then a very near miss and the crow's point is made. She drops her head, turns her eyes toward Earth, wings against her body, an ebony torpedo plummeting as the hawk continues to rise. She is after all a crow. The arrow of time points her homeward. Her wings open and she disappears into the deep green, her fall interrupted by grace.

At 66, a new me blooms in the richness of my experience. I have survived these trials to take pleasure in life again, and I'm feeling blessed.

Acknowledgements

Many people have supported me, shared their resources and given me guidance to write this book. I owe them my thanks.

Thank you to my first readers Hester Velmans and Holly Morse, who helped me see the possibilities, and my early readers who gave me the encouragement to continue writing: Anne MacDonald, Maria Nation, Karen Karp, Lisa Goren, Claudia Crane, Catherine Reynolds, Sam Lee, Laury Epstein, Chris Mehl, Laura Young, Jim Young, Laurel Greenberg, Sam Ellis, Annette Fitzpatrick, Beth Harrington and Karla DeVito.

Thank you to Jennifer Browdy for months of coaching me through the memoir genre with profound insights and strategic improvements. Robby Benson generously gave me a master class in the craft of storytelling. Carmen Durfey gave me one big idea that changed the whole book. Hildred Billings gave me sharp feedback and my title. Ben Hillman's critical eye caught a glitch I missed. Thank you all.

Thank you to Jason Houston for unconditional support of my projects and sharing his extraordinary talents with me.

I could not have done this writing without the people who got me through my everyday life. Thank you to my parents Bob and Peggy Best, my neighbors at the farm, Beth and Wayne Schoonmaker, and my friends who sat with me for hours in their kitchens, Julie Scott and Jim Hall, Maria Nation and Roberto Flores, Anne MacDonald, Karla DeVito and Robby Benson, Annette and Kevin Fitzpatrick, and Beth Harrington and Andy Lockhart.

Thank you to my Boston crew, the Young family, Jim Young, Aaron Young, Bridget Young, Victor Johnson, Riley Johnson, Laura Young and Chris Mehl. Also Laurel Greenberg, Martha Bourne, and my dear friend Sam Lee who did not live long enough to see me finish this work.

Thank you to all of my friends and supporters, especially the many women I have met on Facebook. Your enthusiasm for my writing gives me strength.

And thank you to Chet for helping me find my power as a woman and a writer. He would have loved this book.

Discussion Questions

Thank you for reading my book. Please review it where you purchased it or wherever you read book reviews. Reviewing books is a way to share your point of view and support authors and booksellers. I appreciate your support.

If you are part of a reading group, I hope you find the following discussion questions helpful. My own experience in book clubs has shaped my thinking and I hope these questions will provoke a healthy dialogue.

If you have a reading group that meets for discussion, I would be glad to join you via technology like Skype or Zoom, if possible. Contact me by email at books@widowspeakpublishing.com to inquire about a discussion date.

DISCUSSION QUESTIONS

1. What was your favorite part of the story and how did it make you feel?

2. Do you agree with the choices Billie made or do you think she should have behaved differently?

3. What advice would you have given Billie about how to handle the Juicer?

4. Billie was very concerned about appearances, so she hid the truth. Did you feel yourself judging the people in this story?

5. How would you define midlife crisis? Do you think everyone has some sort of midlife crisis as they cope with aging from their 40s to their 60s?

6. Billie's anger at Chet's affair evolves over the course of the story. How do our feelings about monogamy, marriage and being part of a couple change as we age?

7. Billie's response to her failed marriage was to hide it. Do women handle failure in marriage differently than men?

8. Billie was unprepared to become a widow and live her life alone. How could women prepare for the possibility of living their lives alone?

9. What is the most significant change in Billie's thinking from the beginning of the story in her 40s to the end of the story in her 60s?

10. Billie had a plan for her career in her 40s, but she did not have a plan for what to do with herself after 60. How can we be encouraged to develop a vision for how we would like to age?

11. Billie was forced to downsize and ended up liking the freedom of minimalism. As we age how can we prepare in advance for a changing lifestyle, downsizing or starting over?

12. It took years for Billie to appreciate the independence of aging alone. What are some of the risks and benefits of staying single and alone in our 60s and beyond?

13. The way Chet chose to die and planned his death was radical and inspiring. How can men and women be encouraged to plan their death like a wedding?

14. At the end of the story Billie experiences a personal renaissance. What is the most enjoyable thing about the process of aging?

15. Billie shocked herself with the forgotten memory of coming home from work with a hickey on her neck. Have you had the experience of a long forgotten memory returning to you?

16. In her 60s, Billie looks at herself and sees her mother. When you look at yourself do you see your mother?

17. What are some ways Billie could have processed her anxiety other than cleaning?

18. Will you behave differently in your own life based on what you have read in this book?

About the Author

Billie Best is a wellness blogger at billiebest.com and author of two books, a memoir and a collection of essays and short stories. Her avid fans love her honest and funny advice on life beyond 60. She is a role model for fearless aging. After a long East Coast career in marketing and technology, and several years as a farmer, Billie resides in Oregon with her boyfriend and her dog.

Follow her blog and sign up for her newsletter at billiebest.com.

Facebook.com/billiebest

Made in the USA
Las Vegas, NV
10 August 2023